D1126428

The
Christian
Mom's

ANSWER BOOK

The Christian Mom's

ANSWER BOOK

Mike Yorkey & Sandra P. Aldrich

Chariot Victor Publishing
A Division of Cook Communications

Chariot Victor Publishing
Cook Communications, Colorado Springs, Colorado 80918
Cook Communications, Paris, Ontario,
Kingsway Communications, Eastbourne, England

Cover Design: Bill Gray
Cover Photo: The Stock Market
Interior Layout: Pat Miller

The Library of Congress Cataloging-in-Publication Data
The Christian mom's answer book/[edited by] Mike Yorkey & Sandra P. Aldrich
p.cm.
ISBN 1-56476-728-0
1. Mothers--Religious life. 2. Wives--Religious life.
3. Parenting--Religious aspects--Christianity. I. Yorkey, Mike. II. Aldrich, Sandra Picklesimer.

BV4529.C46 1999	98-31599
248.8'431--dc21	CIP

1 2 3 4 5 6 7 8 9 10 Printing/Year 03 02 01 00 99

CONTENTS

3—MOMS AND THEIR KIDS

4—MOMS AND THEIR TEENS

5—MOMS AND THEIR HOMES

6—MOMS AND THEIR GOD

9—MOMS AND TOUGH TIMES

DEDICATION

To my sister Greta C. Picklesimer who installed
her computer in our parents' home so I could
finish this book during a recent family emergency.

—Sandra P. Aldrich

To my wife, Nicole, who's been a great mom
to our two children, Andrea and Patrick.

—Mike Yorkey

FOREWORD

Every child needs a loving mother.

Some social architects would have you believe that the preceding statement is an archaic concept as we near a new millennium, but the timeless love and nurturing that flow from mother to child will never go out of fashion. Who can measure how much a mother's hug means to a crying child? What price tag can we put on a mother who loves and raises a child from infancy to adulthood, while instilling biblical principles that promote not only personal faith but civil responsibility?

The significance of a mother's love and understanding can never be discounted. That's why I support efforts such as *The Christian Mom's Answer Book*. Oh, this book won't answer every problem today's mothers face, but readers will find plenty of home-strengthening advice within its pages. The easy-read format is perfect for busy moms whose idea of a treat is snatching fifteen minutes for themselves. You can dive into a chapter, learn a few things, and then get back to your family. Or you can keep the book next to your nightstand and wind down at bedtime with a few minutes of enjoyable reading. May you see through these pages that you are not alone. And may you rejoice in the privilege of encouraging and imparting godly wisdom to the next generation.

Beverly LaHaye
Chairman and Founder of Concerned Women for America
Author of *Understanding Your Child's Temperament*
and *The Spirit-Controlled Woman*

INTRODUCTION

Dear Moms,

As an "older woman" in the church, I (Sandra Aldrich) take seriously the Titus 2:4 direction that I am to teach the younger women to love their husbands and children. I've learned much in my half-century on this earth (far more about some topics than I ever wanted to know), and if I can keep another busy mother from making some of my mistakes, then I want to do exactly that. Let the situations in these pages encourage you in your important role and offer even more ways to handle the challenges around you.

Mike Yorkey's name is on the cover of this book along with mine. Mike and I go way back to our years together on *Focus on the Family* magazine, when I was the senior editor and Mike, as editor, was my boss.

Mike really understands the challenges of motherhood. In fact, when I—a widow—agreed to join the Focus on the Family staff in August 1990, my children and I were living in New York, but the ministry was still based in the Los Angeles area. Mike, bless him, fought for me to move two-thirds of the way across the country to Colorado Springs, where Focus on the Family was poised to move in August 1991. Mike did this because he knew it was important that I not move my teens twice in two years.

That year of "telecommuting" from my Colorado Springs home proved to be a great season of motherhood for me, and it was all because Mike dared to consider the work the Lord had given me, instead of demanding what the usual work environment called for.

Mike has written two other question-and-answer books: *The Christian Family Answer Book* and *The Christian Dad's Answer Book*. But when Chariot Victor asked him to do something for mothers, he replied, "But I'm not a mom!" Then he added, "I'd love to work with Sandra again." So here we are—a young husband and father and a middle-aged mother—together encouraging moms.

We've included in the text great authors with whom we've worked in the past, but not all of this information will be what you need just now. Skip those portions or pass them along to a hurting friend. But always remember that we believe mothers, in this fast-paced electronic society, still have the most important jobs in the world.

So read this book with your head held high, and know that this veteran mother is giving you a hearty Kentucky hug across the miles.

Sandra Picklesimer Aldrich

1

Moms and Their Husbands

1

It's Always Courting Time

· ·

■ **I've been married three years, and I'm finally learning that a good relationship doesn't just happen. In other words, I have to work at it, right?**

In marriage, little things make big differences. For example, there's a dramatic difference when your husband refers to you as a "vision" instead of a "sight." There's also just a day's difference in time, but light years of difference, between your beloved telling you that you are like the first day of spring compared to the last day of a long winter.

On the serious side, let's say you go on a diet-and-exercise program to lose forty pounds. Over a period of ten months, you'd have to lose around two ounces a day to meet your goal. People who are successful at whatever they do reach their objectives by a series of little things they do every day.

Some of these "little" things will make a dramatic difference almost immediately, while others will take time. A lot depends on the condition of your marriage at the moment and whether you take the steps grudgingly because you've got "nothing to lose" or whether you take them with a loving, expectant attitude. But please hear this: Regardless of your attitude when you start the procedures, the process of doing them will ultimately produce results.

■ **What are some of those little things I can be doing?**

The "Golden Rule" clearly says you should do unto your mate as you want your mate to do unto you. Please notice the instructions say we are to initiate the action. There really are many instances when husbands and wives need to "spoil" each other. Wives, you can bake him a cake or prepare a special dish you know he enjoys.

Whether you and the kids enjoy it isn't important; you prepare that dish just because you love him. If you send him off to work with a cold lunch, be sure to include a warm note. Just let him know you'll be looking forward to seeing him when he gets home in the evening. Not a big deal, but it can make a great difference.

You can remind your husband that a little thing like calling you during a coffee break is no big deal either, but over a period of time, little things do make a big difference. A simple little thing, even like regularly opening the car door for you, can tell you that he thinks you're special.

Now, obviously, you're physically capable of opening it, but he should personally feel good when he's privileged to do such a simple little thing like opening that door for you. It serves as a constant reminder that you are important, and he wants to be constantly aware of taking the action steps that say, "I love you."

Look for those things that can ease your husband's path and make your own life and marriage happier. If you and your husband are both working outside the home, then dealing with the children, preparing the evening meal, and doing the laundry do *not* fit under the category of "women's work." These tasks are family responsibilities and *opportunities.*

If the family includes a husband and a wife and a couple of children, that means four people created the work. If four people created disorder in the home, but only one is doing the work, an impossible burden is placed on that one. You function as a team. It's that simple.

When your husband does *anything* that makes your trip through life a little easier, a sincere "thank you" is important and appreciated. If you expect your husband to do something because it's his "job," the odds are long that it will be done reluctantly, poorly, or not at all. If you express appreciation, results are far better. Those little thank-yous are indications of *class*.

■ **My mother told me many times that we might not all be rich and smart, but we can all be kind and courteous. Is that what you mean?**

The sixteenth-century French writer De Sales was right: "Nothing is so strong as gentleness; nothing so gentle as real strength."

The next thing you have to know is when to apologize. Many times husbands and wives act considerably less than mature (would you believe childishly and selfishly?) when they hit a snag in their relationship, and stubborn pride (hardheaded arrogance might be more accurate) erects a serious roadblock in the marriage.

■ **Give me an example.**

Let's say the husband says, "If she showed more affection, I'd come home earlier." Meanwhile the wife says, "If he came home earlier, I'd show more affection."

Remember, when disagreements take place, who makes the move to make up isn't important. The one who makes the move demonstrates the greater maturity and love, as well as the greater concern that the marriage not only will survive, but thrive in an atmosphere of love and understanding. And when you are wrong, the most important words in your vocabulary are "I'm sorry, Honey. Will you forgive me?"

■ **I received an unusual present from my husband for our anniversary. When he arrived home from the office one Friday, very tired from a hard day, he said, "Honey, we need to run one errand before I take you out for dinner this evening." Then we drove this circuitous route, and we finally ended up at one of the nicest hotels in Dallas, where my husband had arranged a special weekend of relaxation together. That's one anniversary I'll never forget!**

You're a fortunate wife. But let's say you can't afford something so extravagant. Similar options may include fixing your spouse his favorite meal or letting him take you to that incredible restaurant you've always wanted to visit. None of these approaches fits the budgets of all families, but here's an affordable challenge.

Some evening, when the kids are asleep and it's a good time to talk, discuss how you can get a break from your child-rearing responsibilities. If you get on the same wavelength, he should offer you complete freedom for a day. He can get up early with the kids, prepare their breakfast, and take care of their every need. Meanwhile, you could visit friends, shop a little, have lunch out, catch a movie, walk in the park, or "live it up" in general.

In the meantime, Dad is back home looking after the kids and gaining a new appreciation for what your days are like. This approach helps both husband and wife gain a new respect and admiration for each other. The kids win too because they get to know their dad much better when he spends time with them doing the things you normally do.

With careful budgeting and planning, most couples can squirrel away money for a heavy date or short weekend trip during which you can devote 100 percent of your time and attention to each other.

Even an unhurried stroll will open the door of thoughtful conversation, and you'll be amazed at how much a regular thirty-minute walk will do for the marriage. From time to time, you need to turn off the TV and devote your time and attention to each other. This assures your husband that he is important to you, especially if you look each other in the eye as you talk.

■ **I've found that when our marriage goes south, it's because we stop laughing. It must be this hurry, hurry, rush, rush, do it now, instant everything world with all the distractions we face.**

Surely one of the most effective tools at our disposal to keep romance alive is a sense of humor. Husbands and wives have got to do things together that will help them laugh.

■ **My husband *always* forgets our anniversary, unless I do some serious "reminding" for a week leading up to our special day. He doesn't think it's a big deal, but I sure do. How can I get him to see things my way?**

We all like to feel important and be remembered on our birthdays, anniversaries, Valentine's Day, Christmas, and other special holidays. If you're the recipient of a gift you are less than enthusiastic about, don't forget that behind the gift is a thought, and the person who had that thought is your mate. Your husband chose the gift to please you. So, if he gave you the wrong kind of perfume for your birthday, use it anyway. Don't leave it on the shelf till next year so you can pitch it out during spring-cleaning.

If he gave you a sweater, and you don't particularly enjoy wearing sweaters, go ahead and wear it occasionally anyway. That's just a gracious way of saying, "Thank you for loving me and thinking of me when you bought this gift."

When your husband makes a mistake and buys a gift you don't want, please don't do what this one lady did. She publicly berated her husband for buying her a dress that was the wrong size and color. She told him in no uncertain terms he should know she wore a smaller size and that green was not her color. What she effectively did was discourage him from ever again attempting to buy her anything.

Please understand that whether the gift is a ten-carat diamond, a cruise around the world, or a two-dollar bauble, it isn't the gift itself but the thought behind the gift that really counts. As the medieval character Sir Lancelot said, "The gift without the giver is bare."

> **A LITTLE FORMULA FOR A HAPPY MARRIAGE**
>
> Take one cup of love, two cups of loyalty, three cups of forgiveness, four quarts of faith, and one barrel of laughter.
>
> Take love and loyalty and mix them thoroughly with faith; blend with tenderness, kindness, and understanding. Add friendship and hope. Sprinkle abundantly with laughter. Bake it with sunshine.
>
> Wrap it regularly with lots of hugs. Serve generous helpings daily.

■ **I can't help but think that this courtship-after-marriage stuff takes a lot of time.**

You're right, but the return on this time investment is enormous. Not only are the ongoing rewards exciting, but it takes considerably less time to maintain a loving relationship than it does to repair a broken one.

This material is adapted from Courtship After Marriage *(Thomas Nelson) by Zig Ziglar. Copyright 1991. Used by permission.*

2

Lonely Husbands, Lonely Wives

. . . .

■ **What's the number-one problem confronting married couples today?**

This answer may surprise you, but it's isolation, according to Dennis Rainey, national director of Family Ministry for Campus Crusade for Christ. Husbands excluding wives and wives excluding husbands is exactly what happens when loneliness and isolation infect a marriage.

When you're excluded, you have a feeling of distance. You experience a lack of closeness and little real intimacy. You can share a bed, eat at the same dinner table, watch the same TV, share the same checking account, and parent the same children—but you can still be alone.

You may have sex, but you don't have love; you may talk, but you don't communicate. You may live together, but you don't share life with one another.

■ **That surprises me, but if it's true, then I'm sure an alarming number of people in good marriages are unaware of this problem.**

If you're still not convinced, then check out this bold statement: *Your marriage naturally moves toward a state of isolation.* Unless you lovingly and energetically nurture your marriage, you will begin to drift away from your mate.

■ What happens when my husband and I begin to drift apart?

One of the foundational Homebuilders Principles of Dennis Rainey's seminars is this: *If you do not tackle your problems together with God's help, you will fall apart.*

Lloyd Shadrach has helped Dennis in his ministry to families, and he is sensitive to the lessons God has for him. One time, Lloyd took a walk after a fierce thunderstorm rumbled through Little Rock, Arkansas. As he walked down a road lined with massive, towering oak trees, he had to step over dead limbs that had been blown down. Decaying branches—once lodged amid the greenery above—now littered the landscape below.

"It was as though God was giving me a personal object lesson of what 'storms' can do in our lives," said Lloyd. "In the middle of the storm when the wind is gusting, the lightning is popping, and the storm clouds are getting darker, it's difficult to believe our troubles are purposeful. But God may allow a storm in our lives to clear out the deadwood so new growth can occur. Isn't it interesting how fresh the air feels after a storm is over? Sort of unused."

In the same way, God wants us to trust Him in the midst of storms. He wants married couples to grow together and not fall apart.

But then:

▶ A child drowns in a swimming pool. The mother blames herself, then abruptly turns on her husband.

▶ A husband loses a job. The subsequent financial troubles cause a wife to stop believing in him. Their disappointment in each other causes them to retreat from meeting one another's needs.

▶ An unplanned pregnancy and increased pressures at work provoke a husband to question his commitment to the marriage.

What most couples don't realize is that trials represent an opportunity for them to sink their roots deeper and to gain stability in their relationship.

■ So you're saying that most couples fail to anticipate trials and problems?

If they do, it's because of their human nature, which prompts people to think none of those things will happen to them. When troubles do hit, many couples simply don't know how to respond. The trauma brought by the problem is not the real issue. The real issue is the response the couple makes to that trauma.

According to studies conducted by Dr. Mavis Heatherington, 70 percent of marriages in which a child dies or is born deformed end in divorce within five years. Why does this happen? Because the couples simply did not have a strategy for living that goes beyond romance. They didn't know how to hold their relationship together and even make it stronger during that desperate period of suffering and pain.

■ Is there a strategy couples should have?

Part of the strategy for facing troubles is to realize that God allows difficulties in our lives for many reasons. While He does not *cause* difficulties, He does allow them. Malcolm Muggeridge once wrote: "Contrary to what might be expected, I look back on experiences that at the time seemed especially desolating and painful with particular satisfaction. Indeed, I can say with complete truthfulness that everything that I have learned in my seventy-five years in this world, everything that has truly enhanced and enlightened my experience, has been through affliction and not through happiness."

■ How does this relate to marriage?

Consider this word picture: The Green Berets train over and over and then over and over again. They repeat some exercises until they are sick of them, but their instructors know what they are doing. They want them to be so prepared and finely trained that when trials and difficulties come on the battlefield, they will do things by reflex action.

That's a great illustration of how Christians should face marriage together. We should be so well trained in God's plan that our reaction to crises and difficulties will be an automatic reflex, not a panicky fumbling around. If we wait until a crisis hits and then turn to the Scriptures, we won't be prepared—and we'll be more susceptible to the Enemy.

■ What's the best way to handle trouble then?

If there's a simple principle for handling problems, it's contained in these five words: "Give thanks in all circumstances" (1 Thes. 5:18).

This isn't a simplistic excuse to put your head in the sand and ignore reality. On the contrary, it's the key to dealing with the storms life can bring your way—and that includes the little things as well as the big upheavals and challenges.

Giving thanks in all things expresses faith. Those five little words express our belief that *God knows what He is doing*. And that He can be trusted.

This material is adapted from Lonely Husbands, Lonely Wives *by Dennis Rainey. Copyright 1990 by Word Publishing.*

3

Working Through Marital Conflict

■ It wasn't a happy evening. From the moment my husband walked through the door, I was in an irritable mood. It was a combination of things: the kids had finally gotten to me, a friend said something unkind, and I wasn't feeling well. I didn't care how my husband's day went, and I knew it was just a matter of time before I blew up and turned my wrath on him.

When we had finished eating and cleaning up the kitchen, my husband got up and went to the living room, where he sat down to read the newspaper. That's when it started.

"You're not going to read that paper, are you?" I asked.

"Well, yes. Why shouldn't I?"

"If you have time to read the paper, then you have time to bathe the kids and put them to bed."

"Mary, I've had a tough day, and I have to leave for a church board meeting in forty-five minutes. Let me relax for a while."

Though I had suspected this would happen, I still wasn't ready for it. I could feel myself getting defensive, and my response was less than understanding. We argued until he left for the meeting. When he returned home, the atmosphere

was sullen and silent.

Then we lay in bed, one foot apart yet hundreds of miles from each other emotionally, both bodies as stiff as Egyptian mummies. Neither one dared to move an arm or leg lest it accidentally touch the other and be interpreted as a desire to talk it out, or—horror of horrors—*apologize!* We were in for another long night of conflict, and that's what happened.

Our relationship is on hold. What happens next?

Ah, the road to resolution is often bumpy. Of course, there are as many ways to react to conflict as there are personality types.

Some people simply **withdraw.** They think the best way to solve a problem is to run from it. But that doesn't solve anything. It just builds a wall between them, as happened in your case.

Other people **fight to win.** They won't quit until they've proved that they're right and their opponent is wrong. But that just drives their mates further away, as your husband can unhappily attest.

A third response is to **yield.** The person who always yields may think she is right, but it's not worth the hassle to prove it, so she just gives in and tries to forget the whole thing. But that builds resentment, which is sure to come out in one way or another.

A fourth method is to **compromise**—each one giving a little and trying to meet in the middle. Sometimes that is the only way, but it does carry with it the danger that neither mate will feel he has been completely understood or that his needs have been met.

■ **So why is there so much conflict in marriage? Can't two reasonably intelligent and mature adults live together in peace?**

Yes, they can. But there will always be differences of opinion; no two normal people will always agree on everything. They can work through those inevitable disagreements and resolve their conflicts.

■ **How is that?**

The best way to resolve conflict is to seek a solution that will satisfy the needs of both of you. To reach this desirable goal, you should begin by striving to turn your conflicts into *love fights*— exchanges that not only resolve the conflict, but actually *increase* your love for one another.

Then consider following these principles in the process of a love fight:

▶ **Adopt a learner's posture.** Both spouses will win if they can learn and grow through the experience. Couples need to establish this goal from the very beginning.

Once you realize there is tension between you, the most important thing is not to make your husband understand your point of view or to win the argument. Instead, the important thing is to learn something valuable that will help you become the person God wants you to be.

If you really want to resolve a conflict, you need to reach out and begin to work toward strengthening your relationship—even if that means being vulnerable and making some changes in *your* life.

If neither one of you has the natural inclination to do that, it will also help to pray: "Lord, help me to have a teachable spirit. Relieve me of my defensiveness, self-righteousness, and anger, and help me learn something that will cause me to grow." If you can maintain that attitude, you'll be well on the way to resolving conflict.

▶ **Listen with your hearts.** Some wives will tell their husbands how unreasonable they are acting, correct their inaccuracies, refute their logic, pick at details, and explain why they spoke and acted as they did. But an inspired proverb says, "He who listens to a life-giving rebuke will be at home among the wise" (Prov. 15:31).

Whatever you say, your goal should be to listen—without arguing, without answering back, without justifying your actions, without trying to get him to acknowledge your needs. Your only comments at this point should be to agree or to seek further clarification.

■ What if something he says is untrue or unfair?

Then you should simply say, "What I hear you saying is . . ." and then share your impression of what he said and ask him if you're understanding him correctly.

■ If I follow these principles, what should I gain?

There are two things you should want from your husband: one is unconditional love, and the second is understanding. You want him to understand not only the meaning of the words you are saying, but what you really mean—the hidden meaning. You want him to try to feel with you—you want to feel his support even when he does not agree with you. You want to be considered valuable to him.

But if you want him to understand you, you have to make yourself understandable. You must be willing to answer questions, to share your mind honestly, to avoid becoming defensive, to make yourself vulnerable, and to listen and think before you speak. And you must be willing to look at things from his viewpoint.

■ I have a tough time keeping my emotions under control. When I am falsely accused or misjudged, I get angry on the inside and reflect that anger in some way.

Anger will never help you to resolve a conflict or help you grow: "For man's anger does not bring about the righteous life that God desires" (James 1:20). Ephesians 4:31 says that God wants us to put our anger away from us.

How do we overcome anger? *Not* by bottling it up. If we do that, it inevitably surfaces in one form or another. Neither should we direct that anger toward ourselves—that is one of the major causes of depression.

The healthiest way to dispel anger is to admit it audibly ("I'm feeling angry right now"); identify the reason for the anger ("I feel angry when you speak sharply to me like that"); forgive the other person for failing to meet your expectations; and finally, kindly express your needs and desires to your husband. If you can do this, a resolution is just around the corner.

■ In my heart of hearts, I feel I must accept some of the

blame, although I'm not sure why. Any thoughts?

If you are serious about strengthening a relationship, you must ask yourself what *you* have done to agitate the conflict. If your husband feels hurt, unappreciated, criticized, or rejected, then you must examine your attitudes, words, and actions. What have you done to contribute to those feelings? Even if your actions were unintentional, the tone of your voice or the expression on your face may have fueled the feelings, and you must be willing to acknowledge that.

But another key concept in all this is to keep short accounts. Your husband's job might require a lot of travel, and good-byes are an increasing part of your relationship. If there were times when you parted without resolving a conflict, what would happen if that were your last good-bye?

Suppose something happened to him before you were reunited. Could you live with yourself? It would be extremely difficult. That's why it's important to keep short accounts and to resolve your conflicts quickly and completely in a manner that keeps your love for one another growing stronger.

■ **If I were to choose the one area that has caused us more problems than any other, it would be the area of communication. I blurt out almost everything that comes into my mind, regardless of how it might affect Jim. If I was angry about something, I seldom kept it a secret. Jim never had to guess what I was feeling. I told him in no uncertain terms, sometimes in loud, angry, insulting, and belittling tones.**
Anything wrong with that approach? It's worked for us.

Honest communication does not mean that we must blurt out everything that comes into our minds. Some things are unmistakably hurtful and are better left unsaid. But it does mean that we begin to develop a greater transparency about our thoughts and feelings.

■ **So how much should I tell?**

One good rule is to share whatever affects your attitudes or actions toward your husband. If he is feeling the effects of your temper or mood, then he has a right to know what is on your mind. If you are irritated with Jim because he didn't compliment your dinner, then he has a right to know. And you have an obligation to tell him about it in a kind, calm manner—without laying the blame on him.

Honestly admitting what is on your mind will help you grow emotionally and spiritually. As you do so, the pages of your mind will open wider, contributing to a greater intimacy between you and your husband.

As you continue to share your souls and then eagerly listen to each other, you will be drawn closer together in an exciting and mutually satisfying bond of intimacy. And that's the foundation you need to overcome marital conflicts, because they *will* happen.

This chapter is adapted from writings by Mary Strauss and her late husband, David. Mrs. Strauss now lives in Escondido, California.

4

My Husband Just Won't Change

. . . .

■ **How many times have I gone to my pastor carrying a list of grievances about my husband? It's not that I don't love him—I do—but it's hard coping with a husband who will not change or is incapable of changing. Sometimes it gets to the point where I wonder if I can still live with him, but I know divorce can't be allowed in my vocabulary. I need some help, because this is a real spiritual battle.**

Before we get into some typical specifics, let's get some things out of the way. Your husband is "hardwired" to be the sort of person he is. Hopefully, you knew what this man was like when you married him. If there were things you didn't like about him, but you thought you could get him to change after you were wed, you thought wrong. Barring spiritual intervention, people don't change that much—especially under pressure from a mate. For "better or for worse"—if this was part of your marriage vows—the person you married is the person you'd better learn to live with.

■ **You mentioned that my husband is "hardwired" a certain way. Is that why he can't change?**

The reasons people resist change are many—genetics, force of habit, circumstances, payoff, comfort zone, you name it.

■ Sounds hopeless to me. So how do I get my husband to change?

Begin by abandoning the idea that you are going to bring about the change. If your husband is going to change something, he's going to do so for any of a variety of reasons—divine intervention, a felt need to change, a big enough payoff, or avoidance of pain.

Speaking of pain, here's a rule you can take to the bank: People change when the pain of remaining the same exceeds the pain of changing.

■ Can you give me an example?

Let's say a friend of yours who is known for his high-energy "Type A" behavior has a heart attack. He is rushed to the hospital, where he undergoes a triple bypass. The doctors warn him that a lack of exercise and high-fat diet could lead to the same event again.

He changes his behavior. He now walks half an hour a day on a treadmill, stays away from doughnuts and desserts, and behaves in a much less "hyper" manner. As a result, he's quite healthy. Fear can bring about change.

■ That's one of the things I'm talking about. My husband loads up on junk food every chance he gets. I make nice salads and offer him fruit, but he prefers his cheeses, his fatty meats, and his nachos.

Realize that it's natural for men to crave more protein than women need. They have greater muscle mass and a heavier bone structure to maintain. They need proportionately more protein and minerals. This is especially true if their jobs involve physical labor.

There are ways you can help here. First, don't buy fatty cuts of meat. Serve more chicken, turkey, and fish, but try to make it taste good. Men like foods that taste good. They don't often like to "graze" on salad greens. Sprouts may be good for you, but somehow they don't stick to a man's ribs. As your man begins to eat more healthfully, reward him with occasional small portions of his favorite junk foods. Don't cut him off altogether or he'll start "cheating" on you—stopping by Dunkin' Donuts on the way to work.

■ **I just can't get my husband to exercise. He's like a huge couch potato. He just slouches in front of the TV, watching football like a bump on a log.**

Men actually like to work out, but they prefer to do it with a training partner. Help your husband find a male buddy who is about his age and weight, and encourage them to play racquetball together, work out with weights, or step on the StairMaster machines.

Challenge him to work his way up a racquetball ladder. Show up at important games to cheer him on. Praise him for his progress.

■ **My husband is a workaholic. He's always at work. The kids are growing up, and he doesn't even know who they are. And when it comes to me or my needs, forget it. His work comes first. How can I change this?**

Men tend to derive their identities from the work they do. When men are introduced to each other, the first thing they try to establish is what the other person does for a living, and where they fit in the pecking order of life. Men "rate" each other according to their relative status in the working world.

If you challenge your husband about his work habits, he'll probably respond with, "Well, I'm doing it all for you and the kids. How else can we afford to live where we do?" The implication is, if he works fewer hours, there'll be fewer dollars to spend on everyone, or he won't be able to successfully climb the corporate ladder.

He's got a point. Today's corporate environments are quite Darwinian. The employees who survive and keep their jobs are those who are utterly dedicated to them—often at the expense of their family lives. Modern companies demand a lot of their employees, and frankly, their managers couldn't care less about what's happening in their workers' homes. They claim the first pound of flesh, not the last. It's not right, but it's the way it is.

You and the children may have to accept the idea that everyone has to sacrifice if you want Dad to bring home enough money to provide for everyone's wants and needs. On the other hand, if you'd rather have Dad home, then be willing to sacrifice some material prosperity. Chances are, you can't have it all.

■ **When my husband comes home from work, he often heads for the den and turns on the TV. That's when I want to talk to him about what happened during the day, but he turns a deaf ear. How can I get him to listen to me?**

Give him a chance to make the transition between work and home. Don't dump the day's crises on him the minute he walks in the door. Chances are, he's had a tough day and he needs a little time to "decompress." Give him some space. When he's ready, he'll listen.

When he walks in the door, make him feel welcome. Let him know you are happy to see him. At the same time, if possible, let him know he's walked into a sanctuary, not a zoo. He's home. This is his castle, not a place of torment. Believe it or not, some men go to work and work long hours of overtime, or take as many trips as possible, to escape the stress of their home environment. Many working women do the same.

Here's a living principle: People tend to move toward pleasure and away from pain. Are you and the kids a chronic source of pain for your husband? If so, don't expect him to be drawn to you. Some pain is necessary. Try to balance it with enough pleasure to make it worth bearing.

■ **That sounds like a cop-out. You're asking me to fake it. If I've had a hard day, and I've got problems with the kids, I need my husband's help. Why should I fawn all over him and make him feel like a king? He never does that for me.**

If you're talking about a true emergency, then it does need to be dealt with right away. Most things, however, are not emergencies. Give him a chance to make the adjustment, and he'll be more inclined to treat you reciprocally. Besides, what you do for your husband should be unconditional. It's not based upon what he does for you, or how he treats you. It's based upon the divine standard that each of us is called to live by, regardless of the outcome. We don't love our children, for example, because they behave perfectly—we love them because they are our children.

■ **Not long after we were married, I discovered that my husband likes to get physical with me. By that I mean he pushes me around and sometimes hits me. He also thinks it's OK to spank me when I "get out of line." I'm tired of taking this abuse. What can I do?**

No Christian husband has the right to "get physical" with his wife in the sense that you described. The command for husbands is to "love your wives even as Christ loved the church and gave Himself for it." You have two choices: either make him realize that this behavior is unacceptable, or leave him. You don't have to live with abuse. It is not a husband's right. Both of you are equally created in the image of God. You have the right to equal dignity on those grounds.

Husbands who abuse can and should get help. There are many highly effective counselors who specialize in this sort of behavior. Encourage your husband to see one of them. If you separate to avoid abuse, you can make that a condition of returning.

No husband should ever pose any kind of a threat to his wife, any more than the Lord is a threat to His own body, the church. Too many wives have felt that they must live with abuse as a way of expressing "submission" to their husbands. This is a false, and deleterious, notion.

An occasional flare of temper is understandable. It happens to all of us. Physical abuse is never acceptable, however, and when it becomes the rule, firm action must be taken. Abusive behavior must not be tolerated or it will become entrenched.

■ **I just don't understand the way my husband expresses his sexuality toward me. He wants me to do all kinds of perverse things to satisfy him. The other day he asked me to dress up like a French maid and then come to bed.**

Men and women, for the most part, express their sexuality differently. For men, visual stimulation is important. Many husbands wish to be seduced or "vamped" by their wives. They wish their mates to act out certain roles that turn them on sexually. Where is it written that a wife should not play along with these stimulating games? Sex between married people ought to be fun. God created sex, and He said that it was "very good" (Gen. 1:31).

There's nothing wrong with being creative about sex, so long as things do not become abusive. There are appropriate boundaries, but for the most part, the kinds of fantasy games husbands and wives play with each other are perfectly acceptable. Try to make your husband's sexual experiences with you as stimulating for both of you as possible. Use your imagination. He will, to use a biblical metaphor, be more inclined to "drink waters out of his own cistern."

A word of qualification: there is no justification in such sexual games between legally married heterosexual couples for adultery or bringing in third parties of either sex. Nor is the type of physical abuse that sometimes occurs in "kinky" sex acceptable. Scripture says, "No man ever yet hated his own flesh, but nourishes and cherishes it, just as the Lord does the church." It is unnatural to inflict pain on the object of one's love. In the preceding verse, Paul wrote, "In the same way, husbands ought to love their wives as their own bodies. He who loves his wife loves himself" (Eph. 5:28).

■ **When it comes to things I need to spend money on for myself and the children, my husband is always on an economy drive, but when he wants a new toy—a power tool, a gun, a vehicle—he always seems to be able to find the money for it. What can I do about this obvious inequity?**

Ideally, within a Christian value system, each family member puts the needs of other family members ahead of his or her own. Sometimes husbands are simply unaware of the needs of others.

Making him aware may be part of the answer. Bring him into the decision-making process. Show him what certain outdated or outgrown garments look like on the children. Show him household appliances that need replacing.

Ask him to either fix them or replace them—or let you replace them. Much of the problem here involves communication. Responsible husbands will often respond favorably once they are made aware of the problem.

This material is adapted from writings by Brian Knowles of Arcadia, California.

5

Building That All-important Self-esteem

- -

■ **I know my husband wishes I were more outgoing, but I'm shy by nature and feel uncomfortable joining the conversation when we're out with other couples. The other wives in our group always have something intelligent or witty to say, and there I sit like a bump on a log. Why am I like this?**

Your situation sounds similar to a story Dennis Rainey and his wife, Barbara, tell when they speak to couples. They describe a smart, pretty young woman who was chosen as one of the Top Twenty Freshmen Women by her university, but who harbored deep feelings of insecurity. As a child, this young lady received love and encouragement from her parents, who had provided her with the example of a stable marriage. There was little stress for her. Life seemed perfect . . . until junior high.

While her friends reached puberty quickly and began to develop physically, she did not. Her chest remained flat and her legs skinny, and her hips developed no contours. Throughout the first six years of school, she had felt confident, sure of herself, popular. But as a seventh-grader who was slow to develop, she began to question her worth. This self-doubt was further fueled by her best friend, who one day asked, "Are you sure you're a girl?"

Those words hit like a lightning bolt from a dark cloud. Fear that she would never develop began to whisper in her inner spirit. Her personality changed. She became quiet, reserved, shy. Constantly comparing herself with others, she always came up short in her own eyes. She felt unpopular, unattractive, and awkward, without personal value, and alone. And no one knew of her fears.

Finally, she began to blossom. In fact, she became very pretty, yet inwardly she had developed a negative view of herself. Throughout high school she saw herself as inferior, and she thought everyone else saw her that way too.

■ **You've just described my early teen years, especially about comparing myself with others and coming up short. Only I was overweight, and even though I've slimmed down some, I still feel chunky. . . . But what happened to the young woman the Raineys talk about?**

Determined to forge a new self-identity, she decided to go to an out-of-state college, where she could start fresh. She succeeded. Honor after honor came her way. She earned good grades, participated in numerous campus activities, and became very popular.

Behind this newly found niche of success, however, was an insecure individual. She became an outstanding performer, yet no one, not even she, realized that at the heart of her performance was a little girl who was afraid to be known. The accomplishments gave her confidence a boost, but she still needed the acceptance of someone who really knew her. She needed to be accepted for who she was apart from her achievements.

One year after her college graduation, she fell in love with a young man who appeared to have it all together. He was the extroverted, confident person she was not. Their whirlwind romance found them married after only four months of dating.

She later found out that, although he was secure, he had needs too. He was impulsive, brash, and overzealous. And behind his air of bravado and pride, he was hiding some insecurities of his own.

■ **I have a feeling things had to come to a head sooner or later. What happened?**

After only a month of marriage, both began to realize much more was going on inside each other than they had bargained for. One night, after an evening out with some friends, they stayed up talking about how inferior she felt in public settings. Her questions about her worth stunned him. He couldn't believe that this beautiful woman, his wife, could possibly feel that way about herself. He had absolute confidence in her.

After several of these late evening "chats," he finally realized his wife really did have some serious self-doubts. In fact, her withdrawn behavior at social gatherings began to irritate him. He silently questioned, *Why does she retreat into her protective shell of silence, when I feel so comfortable with people? Why can't she be like me?*

■ **That's what my husband has hinted at! Did they survive? Are they still married?**

Yes, they did survive. And not only are they still married these twenty-five years later, they use that story to encourage other couples struggling with some of those same issues. Who's the couple? Dennis and Barbara Rainey, themselves.

As they tell their audiences today, they had some critical choices to make back then. Would Dennis accept Barbara fully and love her during her times of self-doubt? And would Dennis be vulnerable and risk being known by a young woman who might reject him? The choices were tough. In retrospect, they believe those days were among the most crucial in their marriage. In those initial months, the foundations of acceptance and the patterns of response were laid.

As their fears and insecurities surfaced, they also discovered the critical importance of a healthy, positive self-concept to a marriage. They further began to recognize the magnitude of the responsibility they each carried in building up or tearing down the other's self-esteem. And they began to see that their own self-image either crippled or completed their marriage relationship.

■ **OK, that's an area where my husband and I both could use some help. We don't encourage each other; in fact, we're more prone to tear each other down. So why aren't we better at building each other's self-esteem?**

You're not alone in wondering that. The Raineys are often asked that very question. As they searched for an answer, they studied the conditions in our world that they believe are largely responsible for the present epidemic of poor self-esteem. They're convinced that a mate's evaluation of his or her self-worth is affected by four current social trends.

First of all, we live in a culture of self-fulfillment, and we seem focused on finding individual identity. The result is that we are a restless, self-indulgent society whose members often use each other to gain the acceptance they feel they deserve. Thus, we feel used and not genuinely needed, valued, or appreciated.

When performance and possessions become the ultimate measurement of worth and value, society then applauds people for what they have *done* and what they have *acquired* without applauding who they *are*. In a culture that says self-esteem is to be built on self-achievement, we generally don't cultivate the relationships that would foster feelings of lasting significance. As a result, we are driven in the wrong direction by a wrong standard of value.

■ **You're right. I often think that I haven't done any of the interesting things the other women my Bible study have. I'll have to think about that for a while. What other social trends did the Raineys find?**

That our society is rocked by divorce, which has created internal fissures and fractures in the child's identity that he or she carries into adulthood. A Chinese proverb says, "In the broken nest there are no whole eggs." Broken homes generally do not produce whole people.

It's not that those who come from broken homes are not valuable. They are, but much like an earthquake, a divorce is followed by years of emotional aftershocks, especially in the children. The tremors of fear, anger, and guilt all rumble away, internally eroding a young person's self-image. He may have no idea for years how this broken relationship has created internal fissures and fractures in this identity.

Children are affected not only by legal divorce but by emotional divorce as well. Emotional divorce occurs when a husband and wife decide just to "live together," settling for a mediocre marriage. Even Christian marriages, it seems, are contaminated with dangerously low, nominal commitments. As a result, the children suffer—deeply.

■ **Ouch. Now you're hitting too close to home. My parents divorced when I was ten, and my husband's parents chose to stay together for "the sake of the children." We're both carrying a lot of emotional baggage. What else did the Raineys discover that affects our self-esteem?**

How's this: Fading dignity in marriage. In today's society, the traditional marriage relationship is under attack and suspicion. Because marriage has been robbed of the honor intended as indicated by Scripture, husbands and wives often feel they must look elsewhere for the personal fulfillment and encouragement that build self-esteem.

But marriage hasn't failed—people have. Since the perception of marriage as a consecrated estate often has been tarnished, married couples may feel insignificant, as though they are trapped in a dying institution. The individual self-esteems of both you and your husband are bruised by these antagonistic ideologies.

■ **I guess both my husband and I are dealing with some issues that go a lot deeper than just his wanting me to be a better conversationalist. Is there any hope for us?**

Of course, there's hope. Failures, past and present, can be overcome. That is one of the encouragements for us as Christians. There is always the potential for change. God has not left us without hope or power, drifting aimlessly. The Scriptures offer a powerful promise: "For nothing will be impossible with God."

That's exactly what the Raineys experienced in their marriage— growth and hope. You and your husband can experience that too. Take a look at "Building Blocks of Self-esteem" on page 48 and start putting those principles into practice. You'll soon see that marriage provides one of the best possible relationships in which two people can build the self-image of each other.

This material is adapted from The New Building Your Mate's Self-Esteem *by Dennis and Barbara Rainey (Thomas Nelson, 1995).*

BUILDING BLOCKS OF SELF-ESTEEM

1. Accepting Unconditionally. Total acceptance is the most important foundation in building your husband's self-esteem. Without it, your marriage rests on the shifting sand of emotions.

2. Putting the Past in Perspective. Contribute a positive, hopeful perspective to your husband's imperfect past.

3. Planting Positive Words. Your words have the power to contaminate a positive self-image or to heal the spreading malignancy of a negative one.

4. Constructing in Difficult Times. Weather the storms of life by turning toward one another and building into each other rather than rejecting each other.

5. Giving the Freedom to Fail. Release your husband from the prison of performance with the golden key labeled "the freedom to fail."

6. Pleasing Your Husband. By focusing on pleasing him, you communicate that he is valued, cherished, and loved.

7. Doing What Is Right. Your genuine applause for right choices will motivate your mate toward an obedient lifestyle.

8. Helping Your Husband Develop Friends. By encouraging your mate to develop close friendships, you enable others to affirm his value and significance.

9. Keeping Life Manageable. Completing the construction of your husband's self-image requires making tough decisions, knowing your values, thinking prayerfully, and keeping life simple.

10. Discovering Dignity Through Destiny. True significance is found as we invest in a cause that will outlive us.

6

What Wives Wish Their Husbands Knew About Leadership

. . . .

■ **My husband provides well for our family's material needs, but our spiritual and emotional needs are impoverished. I've talked with other mothers, and we believe that it's no coincidence that we're living in a time dominated by headlines about failed leadership in government, business, and the church, but my biggest concern is the lack of male leadership in the home.**

Another frustrated spouse told me that her husband spends more time with his hobbies than their children. His work requires him to be around people, so he believes he deserves to be left alone at home, she said. Other women worry about their husbands' lack of involvement in church or spiritual activities. I know this is a big problem, but what advice do you have for me?

Beverly LaHaye, president of Concerned Women for America (the nation's largest organization for women, by the way), has heard from thousands of mothers like you. She notes that in 1 Timothy 3:5, while talking about the qualifications of leader, the Apostle Paul writes, "If anyone does not know how to manage his own family, how can he take care of God's church?" Clearly, leadership begins in the home. If we have strong, godly men leading our families, we'll have a stronger church and a stronger society.

"I've observed that more women participate in Bible study classes than men and experience a deeper spiritual growth," said Mrs. LaHaye. "Since expectations for husbands are built from the Word, they are disturbed when the husband falls short as the family's spiritual head."

You, as a wife and mother, shouldn't expect perfection, of course, but you do need a husband whose personal life is in proper relationship with the Lord, who is forgiven for past sins and recognizes that he can't be the spiritual leader to a wife and family without the Holy Spirit's help.

A godly man will concentrate on building up his spouse. He will pray for and with her and encourage her spiritual growth. He will focus his love on her alone. True commitment necessitates fleeing from sexual immorality in his thought life, reading material, glances, and actions. There will never be unfaithfulness if the husband turns away from the first lustful thought or glance, if he determines before God he will live a faithful, moral life with desires only for his wife.

Being a faithful, loving partner influences the results of parenting. When children know their parents love each other, they need little explanation about the character of God's love, and it helps prepare them for future adult love.

■ Is my plight common or is it rare?

Not all husbands fall short of this biblical model. Many take seriously their role as spiritual leader for the family. Unfortunately, a growing number do not. Spiritual training for too many children of Christian couples is bounced between the mother and Sunday School. But Ephesians 6:4 clearly tells fathers to bring up children "in the training and instruction of the Lord."

The Lord can work around a father's lack, of course. Many single moms have to be in charge of their children's spiritual training. And spiritually mature young people have come out of homes where there was no father. Beverly LaHaye's husband, Tim, is an example. His father died when Tim was young, and his mother had a profound spiritual impact on his life. He has spent more than fifty years as a godly husband, minister, and author. (Tim is coauthor of the *Left Behind* novel series about the end times.) Still, he recognizes the need for balanced responsibility and was a strong model for Beverly and the children.

■ **I've sensed that sometimes I have to pick up the slack when my husband just will not do anything to build up the family spiritually. How can I impress on him the fact that fathers are called to lead the family in spiritual instruction?**

Recent studies show that dads who spend time alone with their children more than twice a week—giving baths, preparing meals, helping with basic care—rear children who become compassionate adults. A dad's involvement helps the child develop higher self-esteem, better grades, and more sociability.

Perhaps you should start by asking your husband to give you more of a hand with the kids. Once he gets involved, there's a strong possibility that he will develop a stronger emotional bond with the children—and this may lead to a growing desire to see to their spiritual instruction as well. It's natural for you to long for your husband to have more spiritual involvement with the children, who seek a role model.

Ideally, dads should start with their children while they are young to capture their respect and admiration. As mentioned before, it requires spending time with them—from building with blocks to batting balls around the yard to going fishing and camping to learning to drive. During these times, questions and conversation will develop that let a dad build spiritual character into his children.

■ **My kids are hitting the middle school years. Is it too late to begin?**

One of Beverly's favorite stories is about a father she once met. He was an active businessman and Christian leader, but he carved his schedule around daily contact with his three sons. Beverly and Tim were guests when they observed this family in action. That evening, the father explained that he made a determined effort to have individual prayer with his sons. That's when he excused himself and escorted each son to his own bedroom to pray together. When he returned, he told the LaHayes that when he was away from home at bedtime, he would call and pray with each one by phone. On those few occasions when it was impossible to make contact with the boys, each son knew that wherever Dad was, he was praying for them at that time of night.

Once the father was traveling in Europe for two weeks, and the time difference plus expense made phone calls too difficult. This creative dad made a cassette tape for each boy to have by his bedside, and every night each could hear Dad praying for him.

The availability and presence of a godly man in the lives of his wife and children has far-reaching effects, extending to society as a whole. By loving his wife as Christ loves the church, spending quality time with his children and providing spiritual guidance, a father's influence will continue into successive generations. Psalm 112:1-2 is a promise for all time: "Blessed is the man who fears the Lord. . . . His children will be mighty in the land; the generation of the upright will be blessed."

A man willing to follow the admonition in Deuteronomy 6:5 to "Love the Lord your God with all your heart and with all your soul and with all your strength" will be the spiritual leader of his home, will love his wife as his own body, and will be a role model to his children. What a pillar of strength this man will be to his family!

Perhaps your husband can read this chapter and be reminded of the spiritual leadership he needs to give to his greatest possession— his family.

This material is adapted from writings by Beverly LaHaye, which originally appeared in Christian Herald *magazine. Her latest book is* Understanding Your Child's Temperament *(Harvest House).*

A Promise
Worth Keeping

. . . .

Editor's note: Who hasn't heard of Promise Keepers? The ministry, with former University of Colorado football coach Bill McCartney at the helm, became the religious and social phenomenon for the 1990s. Millions of men attended huge stadium events that sparked tremendous changes in their lives—and their families. The platform speakers at Promise Keeper events encouraged men to embrace the "seven promises of a Promise Keeper," which included their roles as husbands, fathers, and leaders in the community. Perhaps you as a wife and mother have been greatly impacted by having a "Promise Keeper husband."

In the fall of 1997, Promise Keepers undertook its biggest event ever: the "Stand in the Gap" rally held in Washington, D.C. Two days after the event in our nation's capitol, the following column appeared in USA Today *by William R. Mattox, Jr., an award-winning writer who serves on* USA Today's *board of contributors. As you will see, the way he tied in the "Stand in the Gap" rally and the still-fresh death of Princess Diana is provocative and intriguing.*

Promise Keepers Not About "Woman Haters"

by William R. Mattox Jr.

As hundreds of men made their to Washington for the recent "sacred assembly" sponsored by the Christian men's group Promise Keepers, I kept thinking about the "sacred assembly" held not long ago in London's Westminster Abbey to mourn the death of Princess Diana. And I kept wondering: What if Prince Charles had been a Promise Keeper?

What if Prince Charles had kept the promises he made at the wedding of the century back in 1981? What if he had honored his vows to have and to hold? To love and cherish? To forsake all others? Would Diana have divorced him? Would she had been tooling around Paris late at night with another man? Would her life have ended so tragically?

I raise these questions not as a way of blaming Charles for the car crash in Paris, nor to suggest that he was somehow solely responsible for the breakdown of his marriage with Diana.

But I have to believe Diana's life would have turned out much differently if Prince Charles had been faithful to the vows he made to her. I have to believe Diana's life would have been much happier if Prince Charles had chosen to love his wife instead of Camilla Parker-Bowles. And I have to believe that there would be a little less cynicism about the quest for "true love" depicted in Hollywood productions like *The Princess Bride* if Prince Charles had acted a bit more like Prince Charming.

"Diana brought to life, on the grandest scale, the archtype of the princess inscribed on every girl's heart," wrote Marjorie Williams in *Vanity Fair*. "A female colleague who was then in the Air Force remembers her fellow military intelligence trainees, fresh from the rigors of basic training, sitting at a predawn vigil in their barracks to watch the royal wedding, their eyes glazed with yearning."

Of course, Prince Charles is not the first man ever to let a woman down. "Men Behaving Badly" wasn't just the name of a television show—it was an all-too-accurate explanation for why America is in cultural decline.

Which is why the Washington "Stand in the Gap" Promise Keepers gathering was held. The event, which attracted at least

700,000 men, was most unusual by Washington standards. Rather than being a time for airing grievances that government is supposed to fix, the Promise Keepers' "sacred assembly" was a time for men to gather together and acknowledge their need to commit themselves to being better husbands and fathers, to being better men.

That, one would think, should be music to women's ears. Yet, strangely, Promise Keepers was under attack from feminist organizations like the National Organization for Women. NOW seemed to regard PK as a grown-up version of the "He-Man Woman Haters Club" that Spanky and his gang organized in the *Little Rascals*. According to NOW's Rosemary Dempsey, Promise Keepers promotes a "misogynistic message" that says "men must take back control of the family, be the head, the boss."

To be sure, Promise Keepers does call upon men to lead their families, but the leadership model it offers is not that of a domineering "lord of the manor." It is, instead, a model of "servant-leadership" patterned after the foot-washer from Galilee who said He came "not to be served, but to serve" (Mark 10:45).

Perhaps this explains why a recent study by University of Kentucky sociologist Gary Hansen found that the men most apt to help their wives with household chores are orthodox Christians who believe the Bible is God's Word and the answer to all important human problems.

David Blankenhorn of the Institute for American Values finds it curious that feminist groups object so strenuously to PK's mission. "The more I listen to Promise Keepers' message—that men should be faithful to their wives and involved in their children's lives and willing to express emotion and quick to admit mistakes—the more I hear echoes of those frustrated housewives who gave 1960s feminism so much of its animating spirit," he said.

Other observers draw similar conclusions. "Men haven't joined Promise Keepers out of some secret desire to learn how to subjugate their wives or girlfriends," wrote CBS News analyst Laura Ingraham. "They want to be better husbands and fathers."

Similarly, syndicated columnist Kathleen Parker wrote, "If half a million white guys commit each year to work for racial harmony, to spend more time with their kids, to pray instead of striking out, to work on an imperfect marriage rather than seeking solace on

Sunset Boulevard, who's worse off? Maybe I'm missing something, but this sounds like progress to me."

Apparently, the wives of many PK men agree.

After her husband attended a Promise Keepers event several years ago, Lori Day of Springfield, Missouri wrote a letter asking, "Where is my husband? He didn't come back from the Promise Keepers conference in Dallas. A man came back who looked like my husband, but he didn't act like my husband. I don't want my old husband to return—I love my new husband's actions and attitudes. I wish every wife could have a Promise Keeper man."

Similarly, Alethea Bickell of Wichita, Kansas reported, "Before he went to Promise Keepers, I had filed for divorce. It was that bad. But something dramatic occurred. I sent a frog (to Promise Keepers) and got back a prince."

There is a certain irony in Alethea Bickell's statement. For we usually think of princes and princesses living happily ever after in some enchanting castle or majestic palace, not in a split-level in Wichita.

But if there is any lesson to be learned from the tragic life of Princess Diana, it is that all of the rubies and crowns and horse-drawn carriages do not make one a princess. The love of a prince does.

Let's hope Promise Keepers gives us more princes.

2

Moms and Their Families

Finding a Family Heritage

. . . .

■ **Our three-year-old daughter, Codi Jo, loves to look at photo albums with pictures of her aunts, uncles, and cousins. Although we live several states away from many of our relatives and see them infrequently, she knows all of them by name. What more should I be doing to instill in my daughter a love and appreciation for our extended family?**

As a mom, it often falls on your shoulders to pass on to your children a knowledge of your family roots, and you do that through telling stories. Do it at the dinner table, or turn off the TV and tell your children what life was like growing up. Or maybe you can pass along family stories that you heard as a youngster. Did your great-great-grandfather move to California in the 1880s to build a new life? Were your parents immigrants? Were any cousins killed in World War II or Vietnam?

Be sure to include spiritual stories, since it's important that your children understand their Christian legacy. A memorable episode in Joanne Sloan's life was her grandfather's baptism; it seemed that everyone in east Texas witnessed seventy-year-old "Daddy Tuck's" dunking in the Sabine River. By telling stories like that again and again, you will validate them as milestones in your spiritual family history.

As the psalmist said, "Tell of all his wonderful acts" (Ps. 105:2). Talk about life-changing experiences in your relatives' lives—conversion experiences, answered prayers, miracles, and mission efforts.

■ **The other night, the kids came home with a homework assignment (they go to a Christian school) to ask us to name two times when God did something remarkable for our family. I couldn't name one. Is this why telling spiritual family stories is important?**

Throughout Scripture, there runs an underlying concern that the younger generation will forget—or never hear in the first place—about the "mighty works of God." The most striking example occurred when Israel crossed the Jordan River to begin the invasion of Canaan.

■ **What happened?**

The Lord had Joshua stop everything and appoint twelve men to pile up a monument of stones on the bank. Why? "To serve as a sign among you. In the future, when your children ask you, 'What do these stones mean?' tell them that the flow of the Jordan was cut off before the ark of the covenant of the LORD" (Josh. 4:6-7).

God ordered them to create something visual for the sole purpose of triggering questions from the kids.

Hey, Dad—what's that?

Those rocks? Ah, let me tell you about the day God did something incredible for us. . . .

■ **How can our family do something like this?**

By starting a notebook of "memorial stones"—occasions when God showed His love and care and power in a specific way. The longer you reminisce, the more things you'll recall that you really don't want to forget—things you want your children to know about, such as

- ▶ The time you got that job you desperately needed and prayed for.
- ▶ The time God healed someone in your family.
- ▶ The time an unexpected award or honor came along.
- ▶ The time God spared a family member's life.

■ **As for passing along my family heritage, what are some more ideas for doing that?**

- ▶ **Share mementos of the past.** It may mean trekking to the attic or unpacking boxes in the back of your closet, but it will be well worth the effort to show your children keepsakes that connect them to their family's past.

  Relics from the past can be a learning experience for your children. Joanne Sloan can remember as a child begging her mother to open up her cedar chest and show her once more the 1940s wedding gown and the pictures she took in Dallas during the war. The clothes, as well as the hairstyles and cars in the photographs, taught Joanne much about the times.
- ▶ **Visit significant places.** Take your youngsters to your childhood homes. If they are still standing, show them their grandparents' ancestral homes. Give your children a tour of any memorable childhood places—churches, parks, football fields, swimming holes. Take them to your old high school or college campus—including the building where you met your future husband one fall day!
- ▶ **Encourage them to talk to relatives.** A strong relationship will develop between generations as they listen to each other. Whether it's a great-aunt in a nursing home who has stories about the Great Depression or a great-grandfather who remembers his first ride in a car, relatives have much to offer children about the past. Alex Haley, author of the family saga *Roots*, knew the importance of having relatives pass on stories. "When an old person dies, it is like a library burning," said Haley.
- ▶ **Don't be afraid of your own past.** Some people don't want to learn about their family's past because they are

afraid of what they might discover. In fact, if we ask enough questions about our ancestors, most of us will probably find out about a cattle thief in the family, an illegitimate child, or other painful incidents.

We have to remember that we "all have sinned and fall short of the glory of God" (Rom. 3:23), but "if we confess our sins, he is faithful and just and will forgive us our sins and purify us from all unrighteousness" (1 John 1:9, NRSVB).

▶ **Benefits.** Children gain many benefits from learning about their heritage. Youngsters are provided with a link to the past, a sense of security that is so important in our mobile society.

Learning about their spiritual history should also motivate your children to excel in their Christian walk and challenge them to pass on their spiritual legacy to their own children.

NEED HELP WITH YOUR STORY?

Still not sure how to capture your memories? Heritage Publishing & Heirlooms can help turn family stories into a printed book.

"My parents are retired missionaries living in California," says Marcia Moellenberg, who owns Heritage Publishing with Gwen Stephenson. "I wanted my children to know them as real people. So I gathered family stories, asked my parents questions to fill in the missing parts, and then printed a fifty-page book about them."

Soon, as others heard about Marcia's work, she was asked to pen their stories, too. When you contact Heritage Publishing, the company will help you gather information, write, edit, and publish your family history. The fee is not cheap, but should be well worth it. For more information, contact Heritage Publishing & Heirlooms, 1414 Allison Drive, Loveland, CO 80538.

This material is adapted from writings by C. Joanne Sloan of Northport, Alabama and Dean and Grace Merrill of Colorado Springs, Colorado.

2

Please Pass the Manners

. . . .

■ **We were having spaghetti the other night when I realized that I'd been lax in teaching my three children (ages nine, six, and five) table manners. Twirling a few strands of angel hair onto my fork, I leaned over my plate, ready to take a bite. At the same time, I glanced over at my six-year-old son, Daniel, taking his first bite of pasta.**

Just one problem. Daniel had left at least fifty strands of pasta dangling from his mouth, and if that wasn't bad enough, he was grasping the overhanging strands in his fist, all the while inching the food up and into his mouth.

I started laughing, but my husband didn't think it was so funny. Do good manners matter? It's not as though having refined manners is the be all and end all of life's achievements.

Good manners do matter, though you don't see a whole lot of them out there these days. But keep in mind that children can't teach themselves table manners. Given free rein and a chow-laden table, most ravenous kids will grab and stuff with abandon, conscious of only one objective: to relieve the pang in their bellies.

Nevertheless, you still want your children to have good manners, not because you fancy them hobnobbing with society's elite, but because part of the privilege we have as Christians is to behave with dignity and self-respect. We are, after all, spiritual descendants of nobility, children of a King.

■ **That evening, I realized my children would probably never learn the niceties of fine dining without some outside help. Unfortunately, my husband has told me that I lack the, shall we say, *finesse* that comes with good breeding. Queen Elizabeth, I'm not. Where do I get started?**

You could prowl the public library aisles, checking out enormous, 50,000-page tomes on etiquette, but that isn't realistic. Reading a children's book or watching a video on table manners to brush up on the subject might be more up your alley.

Once you're conversant on etiquette—your friends in Bible study will faint from surprise—maybe your kids will learn a thing or two. "Did you know," you could announce one evening, pointing to a plate of steamed, fresh asparagus in the center of the table,

WHATEVER HAPPENED TO SAYING GRACE?

by Elaine Hardt

Every Thanksgiving, millions of families sit down and express thanks to Almighty God for their blessings and for their food. But what about the rest of the year? Are we forgetting to give thanks on a daily basis?

When our children were little, grace was a short, rote prayer: "God is great, God is good, and we thank Him for this food. Amen." The boys were so cute the way they lisped and folded their chubby hands so seriously.

To us as parents, saying grace was very important because it taught several things. To say grace as a family showed respect and verbalized appreciation to God for the food and those who prepared and served it. Saying grace reminded us that a miracle had taken place. A farmer's seeds had become edible food so we could have sustenance. God made all of this possible through the sunshine, rain, and soil by His mercy and grace.

If we don't take a moment to thank God for our daily bread, then we are missing an opportunity to teach children how fortunate we are to have enough food. If saying grace hasn't been a daily routine at your house, this is a good time to begin. Gratitude to God is always in good taste.

"that you're allowed to eat asparagus with your fingers?"

Your children will eye the unfamiliar vegetable suspiciously. Since you've been teaching them to refrain from voicing one's opinion about food one dislikes, they may struggle to stay silent. Then serve one stalk to each child, along with a dollop of ranch dressing for the palate. Have one of your adventurous sons be the first one to dip the asparagus tip into the dressing and take a nibble.

"It's good!" he will announce, scooping up more dressing with the rest of his stalk. "I want more!"

From there, you can press on. The children can learn that napkins go on laps. They can learn to chew with their mouths closed. They can ask to be excused, sometimes even politely. And your children can start remembering to thank Mom "for the nice dinner."

■ **What are some other things that I *have* to teach my kids? I think good etiquette is very important.**

Here are ten suggestions for teaching small children table manners:

1. Eat together. Don't feed the kids at 5:30 and then eat later with your husband when they're asleep. The more your children sit down at the dinner table with you and Dad, the sooner they'll learn what's expected of them.

2. Have a plan. Select one or two manners to work on at a time.

3. Set reasonable goals. All kids are different. What's manageable for one child may frustrate another. Be sensitive to your children's abilities. It may be necessary to delay teaching how to hold a fork or use a knife until they're a little older.

4. Be flexible. If your kids are burned out from a hard day, lighten up on the manners. There's always tomorrow.

5. Have fun. Children love to pretend. Set up an elegant table and invite the children to "tea." You could be the "butler" and serve them with panache. Let them dress up and act like princes and princesses.

6. Reward progress. If finances permit, plan an occasional meal out at a sit-down restaurant. This can be an incentive for your children to practice their manners.

7. Use the library. There are lots of children's books and even a few videos that teach or reinforce manners.

8. Use the calendar. Anticipate upcoming events, such as holidays or weddings. Find out, if possible, whether holiday meals will be buffet style or sit-down, formal or informal.

9. Be positive. Kids react negatively to *don't*, but are challenged by *do*. Instead of "Don't smack your lips," try "Do keep your lips together while chewing."

10. Explain why. Whenever possible, teach your children the "why" of manners. Sometimes, just knowing why makes all the difference.

CHILDREN CANNOT LIVE BY BREADSTICKS ALONE

by William R. Mattox, Jr.

More families today are eating out, taking out, or calling out for their evening meal than ever before. And unlike the Macarena, this doesn't appear to be some sort of passing fad.

Instead, grazing-on-the-go has become as American as (home-baked?) apple pie. While eating meals prepared outside the home is particularly prevalent among singles and childless couples, ordering out is becoming increasingly common among families with children—especially time-starved, two-earner households.

Take-out meals are becoming so common that some quick-service restaurants like Boston Market are now building their advertising campaigns around the idea that families can share more time together if they leave the cooking—and cleanup—to others.

Now, my take on family take-out dinner is this: There is nothing like a home-cooked meal. Never has been. Never will be. Even if Mom can't cook like Aunt Bea or Dad frequently chars the hamburgers, a home-cooked meal has a certain quality that no Boston Market can ever replace.

Sure, it takes time to prepare a meal for the family. And yes, you can almost count on Junior to spill his milk all over the kitchen floor at some point. But the best things in life aren't hassle-free. And as every test-taker knows, time invested in preparation isn't exactly time wasted.

In fact, the most important ingredient in a good ol' fashioned family meal is (if you'll pardon the corn) togetherness. While the average time devoted to family meals has declined slightly over the last generation, several recent studies

continued next page

suggest that as many as 75 percent of all families still eat dinner together several times a week.

Apparently, some households are actually taking Boston Market's advice and scrimping on the time they spend on meal preparation and cleanup so that they can still have time to share in rich dinnertime conversation together as a family. And lest there be any doubt, rich dinnertime conversation is a very good thing.

Student achievement, for instance, shows that children in families that regularly dine together do significantly better in school than children who are malnourished in the mealtime discussion department. Consistent mealtimes give parents regular opportunities to question their children about how they are doing in school.

Yet, when our mealtime conversations do not rise above reports like "Kevin Blanton-Holt stuck a grape up his nose in the cafeteria today," I still wouldn't trade our family dinner hour for anything. That's because I'll never forget the time when my wife asked our four-year-old son, David, to finish his vegetables so he could have ice cream for dessert.

"I can't, Mom," David groaned in response. "The healthy side of my stomach is full, but the dessert side is very empty."

He got his ice cream.

This material is adapted from writings by Elaine Minamide of Escondido, California. Elaine says she's working on which silverware to use with the kids. Elaine Hardt lives in Prescott Valley, Arizona. William R. Mattox, Jr. is a consulting editor at USA Today *and a consulting editor at the Family Research Council in Washington, D.C.*

3

Looking into the Adoption Option

. . . .

■ **"Just relax!" my friend Sara told me when I didn't get pregnant the first year we tried to start a family. I wished the problem were that simple. Uptight teenagers get pregnant in the backseat of cars. Yet dozens of well-meaning friends told me to relax! I relaxed through tests and exams. I relaxed through a series of infertility drugs. I was *not* relaxed when I opted for surgery—I was desperate. But none of the doctors had the medical magic my husband and I needed. The day came when we had to face reality. Nothing more could be done.**

You are grieving—for the children you'll never see born, for the all-too-quiet house, and for those first steps you'll never witness. You are grieving for the first lost tooth that will never go under a pillow and the first set of car keys you'll never hand over. You are grieving for an auburn-haired daughter with your husband's laughing eyes.

Ultimately, as it is for millions of couples, you will decide that the loss is too great, and when you do, you and your husband can pursue adoption. Your dream of a family is too deep.

Please know that you are swimming against the tide. Less than 7 percent of unwed teenagers place their babies for adoption. Around half abort, and the rest become single parents.

Those who choose to carry their babies to term often hear that adoption is "giving away their flesh and blood," rather than a self-sacrificing way to provide a good home for a child they love. If you do adopt, you will be among the 25,000 parents who beat the odds each year. Estimates of the number of prospective parents waiting to adopt range from 1 million to more than 2 million.

■ **Those are daunting statistics. So how can we beat the odds and adopt?**

Start at the top. Psalm 68:5-6 says it is *God* who is Father to the fatherless, and *He* places the solitary into families. The first step to successful adoption is prayer. The next step is to determine your adoption options.

■ **What are they? I hear there is a whole array of them.**

The first is **agency adoption,** in which the birth mother makes an adoption plan with an agency of her choice, entrusting it to handle the legalities and place her child in a loving home. Adoption agencies vary in size and services from small church-supported ministries to large organizations. These private agencies usually offer counseling for the birth mother as well as the adoptive parents, who may still need assistance in dealing with the grief of infertility.

In addition, agencies like the Edna Gladney Center in Fort Worth, Texas provide living accommodations and an on-site hospital for the birth mother. Gladney also offers middle and high schools on the grounds. For the birth mother who has completed high school, it has a career development center offering classes on a variety of subjects.

Adoption is also available through the department of children's services in each state. These state services are known as public agencies and are generally the least expensive way to adopt. Whether adopting through a public or private agency, prospective parents should understand that after birth, the baby will be placed in foster care until the waiting period for the birth mother to change her mind has passed. This protects the adoptive parents from the emotional trauma of bonding to a child they may not be able to adopt.

■ What if we don't fit an agency's profile?

Then you might consider another form of adoption known as **independent placement** (also known as private adoption). In this situation, the birth mother makes an adoption plan with a lawyer. She either chooses the adoptive parents herself, selecting them from profiles of prospective parents, or she allows the lawyer to choose the adoptive parents. Counseling services are not generally provided in independent placement, although the birth mother and adoptive parents are sometimes counseled by their minister or other local clergy. State laws allow independent placement in forty-four states.

■ Who pays for the attorney fees?

Although statutes vary, the adoptive parents generally must pay attorney's fees, court costs, and the birth mother's medical bills, and in some cases, part of the birth mother's living expenses until the child is born. Parents adopting through independent placement may still use foster care during the waiting period, as is done in agency adoption, or bring the baby directly home from the hospital. Most skip the foster care, believing that it is in the child's best interest, emotionally, not to be placed in a transitional home during the bonding period.

■ I've heard of "open" adoptions, in which the birth mother and adoptive parents get to know each other—and even stay in touch after the adoption. Can you tell me more about that option?

You have two ways to go: **unidentified vs. open adoption.** Whether adopting through an agency or independent placement, couples may go the traditional route or have an open adoption. The first is confidential, shielding the identities of birth mother and adoptive parents, while still exchanging necessary medical and vocational histories. The second lets the birth mother and adoptive parents openly know one another. They often meet before the birth of the child and continue a relationship afterward.

■ Are open adoptions a good idea?

Many adoption experts are wary of these relationships, and they should be prayerfully considered. The risk, of course, is that the child will be confused about who his or her mother is. Is his or her mom the adoptive parent or the birth mother? Ann Kiemel Anderson's book *Open Adoption: My Story of Love and Laughter,* may help anyone considering this type of adoption.

■ How does one start the adoption process?

Attorney Jack Petty, director of Bethany Adoption Services in Bethany, Oklahoma says, "First, contact all the local adoption agencies in your area to see if you fit their parent profile. Ask how many placements they've made, whether they require money up front, and if they have a prequalification application. Don't limit yourselves to the large state or national agencies. You may get more attention through local church-supported or small denominational agencies. I have a high level of trust for these agencies, though they are less known."

The next step is to find an attorney with experience in local and Interstate Compact adoption. The Interstate Compact on the Placement of Children (ICPC) states that no child can be sent across state lines without first getting approval from the Interstate Compact office in *both* states. "Ask for attorney recommendations from adoption agencies, your state's certified specialist in adoption, a local judge, the welfare office, or the state bar association," says Petty. "Another way is to go to the courthouse and find out which lawyer handles the most adoptions."

■ How long is the average waiting period?

You can expect to invest fifteen months to two years to adopt a child. Couples seeking to adopt are often almost afraid to talk about the process. They often keep their plans to themselves. Unfortunately, that is the worst thing to do.

■ Why is that?

That's because parents who want to adopt can strengthen their odds by networking and spreading the word they want to adopt. You should join parent support groups. People who have already adopted are the best resource adoptive parents can find.

Another successful strategy is gaining the support of physicians, pastors, and other professionals in your community. These people may be counseling a birth mother who has an adoption plan and is searching for a couple to parent the child.

■ We know a couple in our church who successfully made an international adoption. It was a lot of work, but they are one happy family now.

More and more couples are looking beyond our borders to adopt. Linda Hicks and her husband, Alan, adopted their Korean daughter through Dillon International in Tulsa, Oklahoma. "We didn't even apply for a domestic adoption," Linda recalls. "We knew from the beginning that we wanted to adopt internationally. I remember the day Alan and I first read about Caroline. We both had a set of papers with a picture on the last page. We were careful to turn each page at the same time so neither of us would see the picture first. When we were ready for the last page, we turned at the same instant—and burst into tears. Bonding with an adoptive child often takes time, but we bonded with Caroline the moment we saw that picture. We couldn't love her more deeply."

■ Doesn't international adoption mean that you have to fly to that country to pick up the child?

Sometimes. Kay Moore, from Jacksonville, Texas, flew to Honduras with a representative of the Texas Baptist Home for Children. In the Central American country she got her first look at Joshua, the infant she and her husband, David, hoped to adopt.

While the missionary who usually cared for Joshua was in the United States, Kay, unable to speak Spanish, stayed at the mission for six weeks and cared for Joshua. Six months later, David and Kay flew back to Honduras to finalize the adoption and bring Joshua home. Kay and David are among the many couples who adopt from countries requiring the parents to travel there.

"The plane trips were expensive," Kay admits, "but there is something about seeing your child's birthplace that gives you a deep respect for his roots." Later, the Moores traveled once again to Honduras to adopt their daughter, Jolisa.

But in other foreign adoptions, such as ones done through Holt International in Eugene, Oregon, the Holt representatives fly with the foreign child from India, for example. (See related story.)

■ My husband and I feel led to pursue a "special-needs" adoption. What can you tell us about this option?

While domestic and international adoptions of infants comprise a large part of the children adopted each year, an estimated 36,000 children of the 300,000 in foster care are ready to be adopted. Many of the waiting children are classified as "special needs"—sibling groups who need a home together, minorities, older children, or those with emotional or physical difficulties.

Looking through the photo books of children waiting to be adopted is a good way to get an idea of what would be involved in adopting a special-needs child. Many couples, having heard that "special needs" means severely disabled, dismiss this option too quickly. Some children merely had the misfortune of entering the system a year or two past the "cute" stage.

■ We've been trying to adopt for years, and we've just about lost hope. Is our dream of having a family over?

Robin Porter tried to get pregnant or adopt for seven years. "I was mourning for children so deeply I had to turn it over to God," says Robin. God did not leave her or her husband, Vic, comfortless. Instead He gave them a Scripture: "You have turned my wailing into dancing" (Ps. 30:11). Three months later, they adopted their son, Ryan. For twelve long years they prayed for a daughter, even though their prospects looked bleak.

One Sunday, the Lord gave an elderly woman a Scripture for

someone in the congregation. Wondering who the words were meant for, the woman stepped to the podium and read, "You have turned my wailing into dancing."

Vic and Robin knew God was moving on their behalf. The following week, a friend met a woman carrying a baby across a grocery store parking lot. She told Robin's friend that in two days the little girl would be turned over to the state and undoubtedly sentenced to years of foster care.

She called Vic and Robin and told them about her chance meet-

AN ADOPTION STORY TO REMEMBER

Andy and Becky Hammer, a Denver couple in their early thirties, had been married seven years, but they were childless. They had gone through the infertility process, and Becky was tired of doctors' offices and invasive procedures.

Then Andy and Becky heard Dr. Dobson's "Focus on the Family" broadcast with Tim and Christine Burke. Tim is a former major league pitcher who quit the game to spend more time with his family, and he and Christine had adopted three foreign children. Their story inspired Becky to call Focus on the Family and find out more about international adoption.

Focus gave her the phone number of Holt International, and the adoption process started. It took nearly a year for the paperwork to get done, but then they were told that they could adopt Abigail from Pune, India.

Abigail, just 18 months old, was put on a plane in Bombay with two Holt representatives. The plane was to fly her from Bombay to Denver with stops in Frankfurt and Washington, D.C.

Andy and Becky went to the airport September 15, 1995, never so excited in their lives. When the plane landed at Gate 42, one of the first persons to come out of the jetway was Dr. Dobson! He had boarded the plane in Washington, where someone had told him that Abigail was in the back of the plane. Dr. Dobson walked over to the expectant couple and said, "I've seen your baby. She's tired, but she's beautiful." Then he gave them a warm hug.

Then Dr. Dobson asked if he could stand by and watch Abigail come off the plane and into their arms. "Sure," Becky said, and when that incredible moment occurred, they were all wiping tears from their eyes.

Since then, the Hammers have decided to adopt again. They expect to receive a boy from the same Indian orphanage sometime after this book comes out. This time, however, they don't expect Dr. Dobson to walk off the plane first.

ing. Ten days later, they drove hundreds of miles to stand before a judge, who granted them custody of the child.

"We hadn't seen our daughter when we went to court," Robin remembers, "but the judge stared at me, bewildered. Then he said, 'I think you're in for a surprise.'

"When they put the baby in my arms I couldn't believe what I saw! She had my unusual coloring and my own red hair. Between her eyebrows was a birthmark that matched Vic's. I knew it was God's signature. When I looked up, everyone in the courtroom was crying, but I was laughing. My joy was more than complete. God found my baby in a parking lot! He can do *anything.*"

The adoption was finalized several months later. Only the Father of the fatherless could have orchestrated this homecoming. He truly does turn wailing into dancing.

This material is adapted from writings by Melanie Hemry of Edmond, Oklahoma.

ADOPTION RESOURCES

▶ *The Adoption Directory* is a comprehensive guide to state statutes on adoption. Check your local library or write Gale Research Inc., P.O. Box 441914, Detroit, MI 48244-9980, or call toll-free (800) 877-GALE. Cost of the directory is $55.

▶ The National Adoption Center
1218 Chestnut St.
Philadelphia, PA 19107
(215) 925-0200
Outside Pennsylvania call toll-free (800) TO-ADOPT
A telecommunication network connects agencies around the country, allowing prospective families and special-needs children to be registered and matched.

▶ Adoptive Families of America
3333 Highway 100 N.
Minneapolis, MN 55422
(612) 535-4829.
This national adoptive-parent organization, which publishes a bimonthly magazine *Ours*, has a 32-page packet of free information for prospective parents.

▶ The National Committee for Adoption
1930 Seventeenth St. N.W.
Washington, DC 20009
(202) 328-0120.
The committee publishes the Adoption Factbook, a summary of state adoption regulations, adoption statistics, current adoption issues, financial considerations, and adoption resources. Cost is $41.95.

▶ Bethany Christian Services
901 Eastern Ave. N.W.
Grand Rapids, MI 49503
(616) 459-6273.
Bethany Christian Services is the nation's leading private adoption agency.

▶ The American Academy of Adoption Attorneys
P.O. Box 33053
Washington, DC 20033
This national organization has members in 38 states. *continued next page*

▶ Academy of California Adoption Lawyers
926 Garden St.
Santa Barbara, CA 93101
(805) 962-0988

▶ Holt International Children's Services
P.O. Box 2880
Eugene, OR 97402
(541) 687-2202
This nonprofit organization strives to unite homeless children from foreign
countries with adoptive families in the U.S.

How Much Will an Adoption Cost?

It can cost thousands of dollars to adopt a child. The least expensive adoptions
are through public agencies—usually around $1,000. Charges for both private
agencies and independent placement range from $5,000 to $15,000. Those
fees cover pregnancy and adoption counseling, medical care, and legal bills.

Many private agencies charge less, relying on contributions to make up the
difference. Either way, make sure the agency or attorney can account for the
services rendered.

4

All for Family Nights

. . . .

■ **Between work and school, Little League and ballet lessons, the orthodontist and PTA, we're racing so many directions that meals are often like pit stops. If all we needed to refuel was our bodies, that might be OK. But to cross the finish line, I sense our family needs something more. What can recharge our relationships?**

Have you considered having a Family Night—an evening each week devoted to slowing down and spending time with those you hold dear?

■ **I like this idea. Where's a good place to begin?**

Get out your calendar. Pick the night of the week with the least ink. Now, write **Family Night** in big bold letters on that night and draw an arrow straight down the rest of the month. Show your children and get them excited. From now on, one night a week will be Family Only.

Once you've begun Family Nights, don't make other plans. Don't even answer the phone. The commitment to these nights will speak volumes to your children about your commitment to them. Forget the other invitations and opportunities. Years from now, none of you will remember the things that fell by the wayside, only the moments you shared. You may someday hear your grown-up children reminiscing, "Hey, remember when Mom thought she had us all beat in Monopoly, then Josh got all those hotels on Boardwalk and Park Place and won instead?"

■ **What type of activities go well for a Family Night?**

Save bowling and miniature golfing for those times when you can't think of anything to do. When planning a Family Night, remember the focus isn't on expensive activities, but on building relationships and family unity. Here is a list of ideas to get you started, but once you're off and running, you'll think of plenty more.

Fifteen Fabulously Fun Family Nights

1. Silhouettes. On a large roll of butcher paper, trace each family member's silhouette. Cut and decorate with crayons, markers, yarns, ribbon, etc. Discuss what you like about each other's appearance. Be specific: "I love the way Paige's hair curls right under her chin."

2. Songfest at the Sea (or the nearest body of water). Find a songbook of old Americana ("My Darling Clementine," "Sweet Betsy from Pike," "Shoo Fly") at the library. Take a light dinner (as simple as bread, cheese, and fruit) to the beach or lakeshore, then snuggle in blankets and sing by sunset or flashlight.

3. Charades. Children love charades. A large family can divide into teams, but even a family of three can adapt: each person writes down his or her song, movie, or book on a slip of paper and passes it to the second family member, who acts it out for the third. After all, it's not the competition, but the zaniness that makes charades fun.

4. Winter Picnic. When there's a blizzard outside or a huge rainstorm, cut a big yellow sun and hang on the wall. Spread a checkered tablecloth on the floor. Turn up the heat and let everyone wear shorts. Serve hot dogs or barbecued chicken, potato salad, and deviled eggs. Plan your summer vacation.

5. Summer Snow. This is for when it gets really hot. Rent a snow cone machine with flavored syrups. Notice how much cooler you feel after a snow cone. Make snowballs with the ice and have a snowball fight.

6. Juggle Mania. Find a book on juggling at the library or bookstore. Use tennis balls, oranges, or whatever strikes your fancy. Help each other learn to juggle. Talk about how our lives can feel like a juggling act. What happens when something drops?

7. Card Games. Play any games your children want. Decide in advance to lose. Delight in the thrill they get when they win.

8. Family Tree. Share any information you have about your ancestors with your children. Draw a family tree. As a family, write what you would want your own future descendants to know about you. What are your strongest family values?

9. Make a Motto. Ask everyone in advance to be thinking of a family motto, for example, "One for all and all for one." On Family Night discuss the possibilities, adopt one, and illustrate it on paper. A future Family Night could include making a banner of your motto.

10. Face Painting. Buy a set of face paints from a dance or theatrical supply house. Paint each other's faces. Create a drama using the characters you have become.

11. Memory Lane. Fill a large tray with family objects: toothpaste tube, baby bottle, small teddy bear, scissors, pen, watch, etc. Give everyone paper and pencil, then let them look for sixty seconds. Cover the tray and have everyone write as many objects as they can remember. Why did each family member remember certain things? What will you remember most about your family?

12. Acrostics. Gather all your art supplies: markers, glitter glue, and stickers. Print names on slips of paper, fold, mix up and draw. Each family member makes an acrostic for the name drawn, decorating as beautifully as possible. For example:

Spunky
Athletic
My brother
Up Early
Earnest
Loving

Present with a flourish. Applaud for each.

13. Family Academy Awards. Get out the camcorder for your own night at the Oscars.

Examples: "Best Performance in a Fit-to-Be-Tied Scene" to Dad when three-year-old Benjamin brought the garden hose (running) into the house. "Best Direction of a Chaotic Crowd" award to big brother Joshua during the last trip to the zoo. Special "Lifetime Achievement Award for Never Losing a Child Permanently" to Mom, who has a knack for finding anyone.

14. Seasonal Banners. As holidays approach, spend an evening making a family banner that can be stored and displayed year after year. For example, in November, buy a poster board turkey (at Target or Hallmark). Use glue and dried beans, unpopped popcorn, and wild rice to accentuate lines. The whole family can work on this at the same time, talking about what you are grateful for. When complete, glue turkey to piece of felt. Use contrasting felt to make the words "Thanksgiving in Our Hearts" and hang in dining room for Thanksgiving.

15. Moonlight Walk. Go for a walk in the moonlight. Whisper. Enjoy the nighttime beauty around you.

The closeness you feel after having fun together will buffer your family in the days ahead. Seal your time together with a prayer, thanking God for His grace in the week past and praying for more of the same in the week ahead. Then have something sweet and delicious before you say good night.

These days it seems we're all speeding down the superhighway of life. Keep the race in perspective and put your family first. Don't put off the rest stops—they'll get you back on the road refueled and more ready than ever for the next part of the journey!

■ **What if I want to add a spiritual perspective to do something together?**

You certainly can. In fact, you can use Family Nights to pass along values to your children. Jim Weidmann and Kurt Bruner, who both work at Focus on the Family, have come up with dozens of ways that Family Night craft ideas can be turned into opportunities to impress our beliefs and values in the lives of our children.

■ Sounds interesting. Can you give me an example?

They have a fun lesson called "When Your Tongue Does the Talking." The point of the lesson is that you can't take back the damage of your words.

To do this lesson, you'll need a tube of toothpaste for each child, paper plates, a $10 bill, and a Bible. Give each child a tube of toothpaste and a paper plate. Instruct them to empty their tubes onto the plates.

Let the kids have fun making swirls, towers, and other designs with the toothpaste. If you like, have a race to see who can empty his or her tube first.

Then place the $10 bill in the center of the table and say, "You have five minutes. The first person to put all his or her toothpaste back into the tube wins the $10. Go!"

■ Is my money safe?

Safer than if it were in Fort Knox. There's no way to get the toothpaste back into the tube. After the five minutes are up, throw away the tubes, toothpaste, and paper plates and wash any hands that need it. Then ask these questions:

1. Which was harder, squeezing the toothpaste out or putting it back in? Why?

2. How is this like words coming out of your mouth?

3. When have you wished you could take back words you'd already said? What happened when you couldn't?

Remind your children that when we use our words to hurt others, we can apologize, but we can never take back what we said. It's hard to forget when someone has said a mean thing. Then leave them with this little slogan: "Do it God's way, watch what you say."

This material is adapted from writings by Barbara Curtis, a prolific writer and author of Small Beginnings *(Broadman & Holman), and by Kurt Bruner and Jim Weidmann, authors of the* Heritage Builders Family Night Tool Chest *series (Chariot Victor Publishing).*

5

We're the Sandwich Generation

. . . .

■ **Last Christmas, I thought it would be a wonderful idea to spend the holiday with the folks out-of-state and arrive back home before New Year's. My dear husband liked the plan. I knew my mother and father would be thrilled about having all of us there for Christmas. There was only one problem: Our teenage daughters didn't want to go.**

"It's fun seeing our relatives," they protested, "but not now. We want to be *here* for Christmas!"

At my insistence, the girls had missed their high school homecoming game to attend their grandparents' fiftieth anniversary celebration. I was reluctant to push them to make another trip, so we didn't go. I guess I made the right decision, but why do I feel so bad?

Because you're feeling torn between your aging parents and your teenagers. It's not easy being responsible for two generations at once. Situations like this are familiar to most of us who have elderly parents and are still busy with the demands of child rearing. What do we do when Dad needs a ride to his doctor's appointment and Junior wants us at his game? How do we respond when our daughter at college asks us to come for parents' weekend but Mother expects a visit on her birthday? What happens when our parents and our kids have different opinions about appropriate dress or music?

■ You mean I'm not the only one facing this situation?

Far from it. These are the dilemmas of the "sandwich generation"—a term coined by Barry Robinson when he was communication counsel for the American Association of Retired Persons. The sandwich generation, he says, are people caught between two or more generations and carrying some responsibility for both. These are people like you who care about their older and younger relatives and don't want to hurt or ignore either.

Some families have no problem keeping things in perspective while they develop mutual understanding. Many adult children are somehow able to follow the fifth commandment (Ex. 20:12) to honor their parents and still keep from exasperating their children (Eph. 6:4). For most of us, however, there are times when we feel pulled by the conflicting needs and opinions of the older and younger generations.

■ Are others feeling guilty too?

Of course. That often comes with the territory, especially when we make a decision that is sure to leave somebody unhappy. "If you don't want to spend Easter with me, that's OK," a widowed mother told her grown son who was planning a long-promised trip to Disney World with his wife and children. Her comment caused such anguish that he almost canceled the vacation. In fact, he might as well have, since the trip was already spoiled for him.

It isn't surprising that sandwich pressures often create resentment and anger. Mix this with confusion about how to handle the demands from both sides, and you have a picture of the turmoil that churns within many middle-aged adults.

■ So what can I do?

Dr. Gary Collins, president of the American Association of Christian Counselors has several suggestions:

Pray. Prayer is first on his list of coping priorities. You might expect that comment from a Christian counselor, but it's a practical suggestion. After all, it's difficult to be angry with someone for whom you pray.

"Pray continually," Paul instructed in 1 Thessalonians 5:17, and then added "give thanks in all circumstances." God understands the sandwich generation, and He is able to give us the wisdom and patience to deal with the pressure.

■ **What else does Dr. Collins suggest?**

Remember the little things. He says that his parents began to experience a number of physical problems after having enjoyed unusually good health over the years. So he began to call more frequently to express concern and to see how they were getting along. "Your calls are better than any medicines," his dad said. The fact that we care is important—and will provide encouragement for our parents.

But on the other hand, caring does not mean taking responsibility away from either parents or children. Dr. Collins occasionally quotes Jill Smith's *Survival Handbook for Children of Aging Parents* in which she warns that our desires to be helpful cause many of us to start doing for older people what they are still able to do for themselves. "The real tragedy of trying to manage an older person's life is that . . . the older person is infantilized. The older person gets treated as a baby (which he is not) and damage is done to his self-esteem, which is the most destructive of all."

Jill Smith goes on to say that real caring involves giving needed help but not taking over and forcing family members to be unnecessarily dependent, which creates resentment and puts more pressure on the one caught between the generations. Try to keep that in mind when you feel pulled in two directions.

■ **What's the first thing to remember to keep from falling into the trap of treating my parents like children or ignoring my children's desires?**

Try not to make decisions without consulting the people

involved. This isn't always possible, especially when children are very young or elderly parents are not able to think clearly. Nevertheless, people in all generations like to feel needed, respected, loved, and useful. They want to know that their views and opinions count—even when you disagree.

Tension can often be lessened by offering a choice: "Mother, I've already promised Jon I'd go to his game that night, but I can take you to visit Margaret Saturday morning or Sunday afternoon. Which would be better for you?"

■ But what about those times when my parents and teens disagree?

Try to stimulate cooperation and understanding between the generations. Actually, teenagers and their grandparents have a lot in common. Both are experiencing physical changes. Both are adjusting to new roles in society. Both may have financial problems. And both have to deal with you! If they can learn to communicate with each other, home life is likely to be smoother.

You will sometimes have to explain to your daughters why their grandparents think as they do. You will also have times when you must try to help your parents understand the younger generation.

This isn't easy, especially since you don't want to pit one generation against the other. For example, if one of your daughters reacts to your parents' view about money, you can remind her not only that they're living on a fixed income but that the Depression years left an imprint upon today's spending habits.

Also, you don't have to comment on every issue that comes up. Remember, years ago, when you discovered that some of your children's behavior could be overlooked? Well, it's the same here: If you don't make an issue of everything, you are more likely to be heard when really important disagreements arise.

The same is true with your parents. You may communicate well and have an excellent relationship, but you have probably learned that some topics, such as politics, are best avoided. Instead of challenging statements with which you disagree, let them pass or try to steer the conversation in a different direction.

■ **Wow, I'm already learning to bite my tongue. Recently, one of our daughters decided it was fashionable to wear black lipstick and black fingernail polish. I chose to say nothing, hoping this was another stage that would pass. But when my dad saw her, he remarked, "Some parents just don't care how their girls look." In the interest of peace, I ignored the comment.**

Good for you. Obviously, you learned long ago that explosions or even lengthy explanations accomplish nothing. Besides, you undoubtedly have a deep respect for the resilience that has carried your parents through many challenges.

■ **What else do I need to add to my list?**

Determine, at times, to be firm. In some situations we must make a decision and stick with it. It isn't always possible to keep everyone happy, so we do the best we can and brace for the disapproval.

Dr. Collins has an example of this principle. He says that for most of his childhood, he lived in a three-generation home. He watched his parents care for his elderly grandfather, whose physical problems got worse as the years passed. Sometimes he and his sister longed to be alone with their parents, so occasional afternoons without the grandfather were scheduled. Even those rare outings produced conflict.

"You wait!" their normally even-tempered grandfather would proclaim with anger. "You, too, will be old some day and won't want to be left behind."

Of course, they felt guilty, even when leaving him with other relatives. But the parents didn't allow his comments to ruin those special hours for their children.

In the midst of your decision making, don't forget to make time for yourself. In our effort to keep peace in the family and avoid conflict, we can become twenty-four-hour-a-day servants to our parents and children. Before long, we feel compelled to sacrifice ourselves, our time, and our incomes to family demands. Of course, there are times in life when we must be "on call." But this isn't always necessary.

Round-the-clock duty can wear us down, and we can burn out

when we don't pull away for rest and rejuvenation. Each of us needs time to develop our own friendships, interests, and recreational activities. At first, we may feel guilty about taking time for ourselves, but periods away can lead to greater stamina and increased ability to handle the pressures when we return.

■ **I guess I'm making better progress than I thought. After all, I can understand why my parents would like us to come for the holidays, and I can understand, too, why my daughters don't want to go.**

You've grasped a major coping principle: Try to see the situation from the other's perspective. Granted, when children are self-centered, or elderly parents are opinionated or set in their ways, it is difficult to be patient. Most of us find it easier to *react* than to *reflect on* why our children or parents think as they do.

For example, we remember the grandparents who insisted their sixteen-year-old grandson not be allowed to work at a fast-food restaurant after school. They wanted him studying or playing sports. The teen's mother bit back harsh words even though she wanted to remind her parents she didn't appreciate their undermining her authority.

Instead, she promised to think about what they had said. She intended only to buy some time. But as she pondered her parents' reaction, she remembered her mother having said something about how fast the years go by. She realized her mother actually was lamenting the now-adult daughter's own teen years when she had worked to help them pay bills. That realization allowed her to talk to her parents, easing their guilt. Her reflection had helped her unlock a pressured situation and thus improve communication.

Of course, not all of our conflicts are so easily solved. Good relationships never come easily, but are the result of concern and hard work. The emotional bonds between teens, parents, and grandparents can present some of life's greatest joys as well as challenges.

All three generations *can* grow together—with God's help—as they move from one stage of life to another. It is not an impossible task.

This material is adapted from material by Dr. Gary R. Collins, president of the American Association of Christian Counselors.

6

Leading Your Elderly Parents to Christ

. . . .

■ **My parents are getting up in years, and I worry about their salvation. I know I should talk more about the Lord when I visit, but I get all tongue-tied and don't know what to say, so I avoid the subject. Part of the problem is that in the past, when I have tried to talk about my faith, they've rebuffed me. Sometimes it seems as though I can witness to everyone except my mother and father.**

Take heart; you aren't alone. The question of how to share the Gospel with unbelieving parents ranks as one of the most pressing for adult Christians.

Why is it so hard to tell the people who love us about the One who loves them even more? Because we are "the children." They have been our teachers, guides, and authorities. Maintaining respect for our parents while sharing the message of repentance and faith is like walking a tightrope; it requires practice, perseverance, and plenty of prayer.

■ **How do I begin?**

Since every parent-child relationship is unique, no single answer exists. The best approach is guided by the Holy Spirit. But the following are some ideas to get you started:

▶ **Live a consistent Christian life.** Your parents will be more inclined to listen if they see you practicing what you preach. Actions do speak louder than words.

▶ **Be alert to opportunities.** A young couple lost their five-week-old daughter to sudden infant death syndrome (SIDS). Throughout the ordeal, the bereaved young father comforted himself and his unbelieving parents with Scripture. After praying for their salvation for years, he reports they now attend church regularly and are very close to making a public confession of faith.

▶ **Offer practical help.** The Book of James says that true faith includes ministering to widows—and that would be especially true for one's own mother. Caring for a needy parent entails sacrifice. However, we may gain the opportunity to lead our elderly parent to Christ.

■ **What you're saying is a relief to me. I thought sharing my faith meant sitting down with my parents and opening the Bible.**

We trust that will come, in time. But for now, just keep loving them. In fact, ask the Lord to love your parents through you. Age often accentuates negative personality traits. Pray that God will help you focus on the *positives*. Make a mental list of your parent's good points and concentrate on them. If your parents are antagonistic toward your faith in Christ, remember this is *spiritual* warfare. Guard against bitterness and discouragement.

A pastor's wife was frustrated that her parents didn't understand her commitment to the Lord. "After every visit I'd find myself mentally rehashing our conversations, exaggerating their offenses, and imagining what I should have said."

Then she claimed the promise of Colossians 1:11 for encouragement: "Being strengthened with all power according to His glorious might so that you may have great endurance and patience."

■ **I can really identify with that pastor's wife; I replay our conversations too, and then get upset all over again. What reminder do you have for this problem?**

Combine tact and boldness. Sonnie became a Christian while in college. On her next visit home, she told her parents about her faith in Christ. She didn't get the response she wanted.

"My mother was speechless, and my father said, 'Some religion is OK, but don't get fanatical.' I continued sharing truths whenever I went home. I gave my mother a subscription to a daily Bible reading guide. She began reading the Word and renewed the subscription. She has slowly embraced the Gospel."

Under the shield of tact, it's tempting to procrastinate, waiting for a "better" opportunity to witness. Yet, if you hold back, you may be cushioning your parent's path to condemnation. One of Satan's favorite strategies is "Wait."

■ **That's a rough area for me too. I'm always telling myself that during the "next" visit, I'll get serious about their souls. But my dad's health is failing since he developed diabetes, and I don't know how much time he has left. Even though he knows I'm worried about where he stands with God, he dismisses my concern. What else should I be aware of before I talk to my parents?**

Consider their religious and intellectual background. Bob, a professional writer, cannot talk to his father about spiritual things. His father comes from a culture in which only an ordained minister has the authority on such matters. The idea of an ordinary person being knowledgeable about God is unthinkable to him.

Other parents may feel inadequate, thus resenting discussions that underscore their lack of knowledge. Kristi, a live-in companion to an elderly woman, says, "Many older people are unfamiliar with Bible stories and Scripture passages that are crystal clear to us. Some speak English as a second language and may never have learned to read very well. It's important to take time to explain what you're saying rather than just rattling off verses."

■ **OK, I'm taking notes. What else?**

Keep in touch. With families scattered about the country, this may not be easy. However, communication maintained through letters, calls, and visits is a good witness to your parents and a way to monitor their material and spiritual needs.

Encourage your children to write too. Grandchildren, like angels, can tread where others dare not. Let them witness whenever they have the opportunity. Children can be disarmingly direct when it comes to their faith. While you may be tempted to restrain them from saying too much to Grandmom and Grandpop, do this only if you know their statements will make things worse.

Pray for discernment and use Scripture as the occasion warrants. Remember, "the word of God is living and active. Sharper than any double-edged sword, it penetrates even to dividing soul and spirit . . . it judges the thoughts and attitudes of the heart" (Heb. 4:12).

Sonnie consistently witnessed to her parents for years before her father responded. "Soon after he arrived for a week's visit, he said he wanted to make sure that what he believed was true," she says. "He asked me to show him the truth from God's Word. We spent the next hour looking up Scripture and discussing the meaning. When I said we had covered the essentials, he replied, 'That's what I believe.' "

God is patient—a trait we need to exhibit as we wait for Him to work in our parents. Give the burden for their salvation to the only One who can do anything about it—Jesus Christ.

Perhaps as you are praying for your parents, He has already provided an answer—a godly neighbor, a friendly pastor, a Christian volunteer at the nursing home—to share His love and truth with your parents.

This chapter is adapted from writings by Elizabeth Erlandson of Lincoln, Nebraska.

ENCOURAGEMENT WHEN YOU THINK THEY WEREN'T SAVED

by Sandra P. Aldrich

Years ago, just before we left for the Wednesday night service, I received word that one of my cousins, whom I'll call Eddie, had committed suicide in Michigan. I drove to our church in an emotional fog, mulling over the few details—the drugs, the shotgun blast that didn't kill him right away, the collapse into his mother's arms.

I wondered where his dad had been. Probably drunk. . . . I felt the fury rising as I thought of Eddie's determination never to be like his dad. But then drugs began to dull the hurt in his life, and he was hooked. When he realized that he was mirroring his father, he'd pulled the gun out of the closet, determined that the family pattern would stop with him.

My greatest torment, though, was the destination of his soul. Our grandmother had repeatedly outlined the plan of salvation to him, pleading with him to turn to Jesus. But Eddie was too busy having what he called "a good time." Too busy, that is, until the afternoon when he had seen his dad in himself.

At church, I dropped my children, Jay and Holly, off at their classes, then slipped into a back pew. I tried to listen as Dr. Hess taught from the Book of Acts, but scenes of the eternal lake of fire kept darting across my mind.

Then Dr. Hess interrupted himself. "That reminds me of a story," he said, and he launched into an account of the crew of an 1880s whaling ship:

> Two of the sailors were Christians who shared their faith every chance they got. Most of the others would either ignore them or listen politely; a few even agreed to attend Bible studies with them. But one sailor cussed them repeatedly, daring them to mention God in his presence.
>
> One afternoon the angry sailor was coiling ropes on the deck just as the ship pitched dangerously, tossing him and the ropes overboard. His fellow crewmen scurried to pull the ropes up, wondering if he would still be in one piece.
>
> They'd seen this happen before; often the sailor tangled in the ropes would be cut in half.
>
> As they tugged on the ropes, hauling his body to the surface, they were amazed he was still intact. Even though they thought he had drowned, they rolled him onto a barrel to force the water out of his lungs.
>
> Suddenly, he spewed sea water, then coughed, fighting for breath. As his mates leaned over him, he finally spluttered, "I'm saved!" As they

continued next page

thumped more water from him, they agreed, saying they had thought he was dead when they first brought him up.

He shook his head. "No, I'm saved like those two," he said, and he pointed toward the two Christians.

Gradually, he stammered the story. "When I hit the water and felt the ropes tighten around me, I knew I was a goner," he said.

"And I knew that if those men were right, I was going to have to face God alone. Just before I blacked out, I said within myself, 'Jesus, I'm sorry. Please stand with me.' Now I'm saved like those guys."

Dr. Hess concluded, "He truly had been saved in those moments and went on to live a godly life. But if he had died in the ropes, the Christians would have thought he had gone to a Christless eternity. We are not to judge the destination of another's soul."

As he turned back to the Book of Acts, he said offhandedly, "I don't know why I told that."

But I knew. Maybe in Eddie's final moments, he had remembered our grandmother's pleas to reach out to Jesus. Maybe the Lord was wiping away tears of regret and repentance from Eddie's eyes at that very moment.

As soon as the service was over, I told Dr. Hess why I believed he had been compelled to tell the story, and I thanked him for being sensitive to the Holy Spirit. He was delighted. Perhaps he had needed some encouragment too.

3

. . . .

Moms and Their Kids

1

Hot Ideas for Summertime

. . . .

■ **School's been out for several weeks, and the novelty of summer has quickly worn off. As the temperature heads toward three digits, my impatience is rising too. I don't want to mark time until the school bell rings again. What are some ways I can have a memorable summer of fun and learning with children?**

First off, show them that housecleaning can be fun. Well, that might be a slight exaggeration. But don't call it "housework"—refer instead to "The Challenge of the Day." Have the kids predict how long it will take to clean a room and then set the timer. Put a peppy tape on the stereo and tackle the cleaning together. Lively Greek folk music will do the trick.

You'll find that the tasks are completed best if you work *with* them. Children are often overwhelmed when we send them into a room and say, "Clean it." It's far more effective to ask, "What do we need to do in here today?"

It helps to be a little zany too. One mom often escorted her sons into their room and announced, "Let's get going here. I'll start with the sheets." Then she tossed several coins under their beds, so once they started hauling toys and T-shirts out into the open, they discovered an immediate reason for continuing. Even on the days when she didn't toss coins, they cleaned under the bed—just in case she had hidden a nickel under a loose sock.

■ **How clever! But most of the time, I can do the housework better—and faster—without the kids. Should I give them other chores?**

No, don't. Efficiency is not the name of the game; helping your children learn responsibility is your goal. Explain why a certain job is important, and then demonstrate how you want it completed. Have the child try it while you're watching. Encourage by telling your child she is a "good little helper." That simple expression of appreciation will make her work all the harder.

It's OK to remind children that someday they'll need to know how to houseclean. Even ten-year-old boys are thinking, *When I have my own place, I can have my own things on the shelf and my own food in the refrigerator.* So when you clean, say such things as "I know this looks like something Mom should do, but you'll need to know this someday." Your kids will put that early training to good use.

■ **What about having some fun? I don't want my kids to remember summer as a time of drudgery and chores.**

Produce your own dramas! Help your children dig out old clothes and design costumes for a play about your family. Mom and Dad, this is for you too—makeup and all. Check the local thrift shops for unusual outfits to use in acting out a favorite Bible story. Use scrap material to turn a child into a tree or animal. You might ask family and neighbors to join your impromptu productions as well. Don't forget to take pictures for the album.

■ **What are some other fun things we can do?**

Introduce your preteens to the kitchen. When you turn the kids loose with your cookbook collection, some interesting ideas can evolve, especially as you let them create their own "restaurant" with place mats, centerpieces, and assorted props.

Can your kids ham it up? When it is their day to cook, have them draw pencil mustaches on their faces and speak in false French accents. Turn your kitchen table into "Pete's Cafe" or "Rob's Diner." As they get older, gradually give them practice in browning the meat or peeling the potatoes. And don't forget to teach them how to clean up.

■ What other activities do you recommend?

Just look around the garage. Do you have any old appliances or electronic equipment (toasters, mixers, tape players, or VCRs) gathering dust? If you do, let your youngsters take them apart (under your supervision, of course) and see what they're all about.

While you're at it, check out what's lying around the house with an eye for science. You can do a lot with magnets or a magnifying glass, sand, dirt, and pebbles. And don't think that sandboxes are only for toddlers. Kids can spend hours constructing cities and roads—with only sand, water, and twigs. Also, staking out a square foot of the backyard with popsicle sticks and observing bugs there gives an interesting view into a child's world.

■ I don't want my kids to totally lose their reading and studying skills. How best should we use our local library?

On hot afternoons, the local library provides a great place for the whole family to cool off—and read a bit. Biographies are especially good because they provide plots for homemade dramas and examples in dealing with challenges such as discouragement and temptation.

If your youngster isn't ready for independent reading, you can read a page for him or her, using your most entertaining and dramatic voice. Then let your child read the next page. Encourage the young reader to have fun. Fill in the mispronounced words without comment. Stop in the middle of the story and talk about how the book began, the setting, and the characters. Ask your children what they think might happen by the end. Then read on and see how the story concludes.

■ **Any suggestions for outreach—ways to serve others?**

Have a family meeting to choose a Christian service project you can do for the summer. Maybe you'll opt for a weekly visit to an elderly person in the neighborhood or volunteer to spruce up the church grounds.

■ **All these are great ideas, but I'm thinking,** *This takes time— I'm already too busy.*

Of course, making the most of summer takes a little planning, cooperation, and enthusiasm. But you'll be amazed at the creativity that blossoms under your guidance. It may help to remember there will never be another summer quite like the one coming up. Your kids will never be the same again. And many of these "teachable moments" will be lost forever. As you help your children discover their world, isn't that worth the effort?

HERE ARE SOME OTHER THINGS YOU CAN DO . . .

When it's summer, you have more time to do something special with your children—really make a memory. Try one of these surprises, or think up your own.

▶ Surprise your children with a trip to a waterpark, big municipal pool, nearby lake, or reservoir. Kids love water more than anything, especially when it's hot. You'll appreciate the break too.

▶ Serve animal pancakes to the kids for a special breakfast.

▶ Make stamps out of potato halves. Let them make postcards for their grandparents with their special "stamps."

▶ Buy finger paint and let the kids finger paint to their heart's content.

▶ If you're feeling more adventurous, buy balloons and let them make water balloons. If you really want to get wild and crazy, participate in a water balloon fight with them.

▶ Make a video with your children, complete with plot, actors and actresses, and lines to learn. It will be their very own production!

▶ Find that pet you've always talked about getting—cockateel bird, Yorkshire terrier, Persian cat, or slinky iguana. Be brave!

▶ Buy a hummingbird feeder and watch those cute little birds "roar" in for regular visits.

► Take the family to a ball game. Whether it's a big-league game at a downtown stadium or a rookie league game in the bush leagues, there's nothing like relaxing with the family at the old ball yard. Go even if you don't like baseball!

This material is adapted from writings by Elaine Hardt of Phoenix, Arizona.

2

Take the Reluctance Out of Reading

. . . .

■ **To a nonreader like me, this book consists merely of a few ounces of ink spread and dried judiciously throughout a pound of paper. What is the joy in sitting alone and motionless, hour after hour, staring at these pages?**

To those of us who love to read, however, these dabs of ink can transport us into worlds and times far beyond where we are sitting—delivering knowledge, joy, sorrow, laughter, and, most important, wisdom. To us, it is incomprehensible that some find it a chore to read.

■ **Well, count me as one of those moms who's never found it easy to read, and you can include my children in the mix. Since I'm raising up a family of reluctant readers, how are you going to motivate us to read?**

Sigmund Brouwer, founder of the Young Writer's Institute, has spoken to thousands of students in Christian and public schools across the United States and Canada. What he's learned is that it's next to impossible to motivate children—or adults like you—by arguing the importance of reading. Brouwer says the single best motivator is to show reluctant readers the *fun* of reading.

■ How does he do that?

The first step is by matching a story with the children's interests. For instance, Louisa May Alcott's *Little Women* is a wonderful book—but not very many active boys would think so. Time and again, school librarians have told Brouwer that most reluctant readers who are boys still go through sports magazines and sports books. Why not, for example, find exciting sports stories for these reluctant readers? Hunting stories for boys who like hunting? How about horse stories for girls who like horses?

The second step is to make sure the book has a reading level your child can comprehend. Yes, readers develop their vocabulary only by stretching themselves, but those are readers who already know reading is fun. To poorer readers, difficult vocabulary only reinforces their sense of inadequacy. Like many adults who avoid computers, struggling readers are afraid to feel stupid. The book will not be an enemy, however, if it is easily understood through a lower vocabulary level.

The third step, once you've found an appealing, easy-to-read book, is to introduce your reluctant reader to the story. Merely handing the book over to your child as a task, or even as a gift, is rarely enough. A proper introduction means involving your reluctant reader with the book.

The easiest and most effective way is to read the first few chapters aloud. By doing this, you are sharing a precious gift—your time. You are also role modeling the reading habit, and you are there to answer questions or initiate dialogue about the action or characters in the book.

■ We have teens in the house. Is it too late to get them reading a lot?

While reading aloud on a regular basis is considered the best way to develop a love of reading in younger children, don't be surprised when your teenaged reluctant reader responds as well. After all, along with the enjoyment of listening to a good story, your child implicitly understands that you care enough to share the learning task.

Find books that start quickly and promise excitement, humor, or mystery. Give your reluctant reader a taste and leave him or her hanging. Some parents and teachers effectively use a scattergun approach. Day by day, they'll introduce their reluctant readers to the beginning chapters of many different books, trusting that at least a few stories will "set the hook" and engage the child.

During your reading sessions, don't hesitate to stop and ask questions about the action or the characters. Just before the end of a segment, or halfway through exciting action, ask for predictions about the outcome. Both are great ways to increase a reluctant reader's involvement with the book.

Remember, few can resist a good story. Hook a reluctant reader with a particular book, and the power of that good story becomes an immediate incentive and reward to continue.

Unless poor eyesight or some other physical problem is the cause of a child's hesitation, most reluctant readers can be turned around. All it takes is for them to get through one book they've enjoyed. It will give them the confidence to tackle another. And another. With practice, their reading improves, and as their reading improves, so does their confidence. You will have helped create a positive cycle and provided them with one of the most important educational gifts a child can possess.

■ **What are some other tips that can help reluctant readers learn the pleasure of reading?**

1. Run through a three-point checklist.

▶ Read the dust jacket. If the subject is appealing, go to step two. If the book doesn't seem interesting, pass it by and look for another title.

▶ Read the first chapter. It's the author's job to make a book fun or interesting, not the reader's. If the author doesn't do a good job in the first ten pages, set the book aside. If, however, the book still looks interesting, go on to step three.

▶ Read any page in the middle of the book. Put up a thumb

or finger for every word not understood. If five words are reached on one page, set the book aside. The vocabulary is too difficult. Practice will make the book possible later, and like a good friend, it will wait for a return visit.

▶ If a book passes all three tests, you can promise your reluctant reader it will be as much fun as watching a movie in his or her head.

2. Allow nonserious reading choices.

We hope our children will learn from reading the Bible, commentaries, the classics, and instructional books. Yet, much as children are weaned from milk to solid foods, reluctant readers need lighter material first. Bill Myers' *Wally McDoogle* series, for example, is zany, fun reading with good inspirational messages. Even comic books, once you've screened them, are excellent ways to encourage reluctant readers to see that stories are more fun on paper than on television.

3. Stick with a series.

Titles in a series have consistent characters and consistent reading levels. Reluctant readers feel much more comfortable attempting another book when they know they can handle the vocabulary and when they are looking forward to meeting old friends from previous adventures.

4. Don't force a reader through a book.

Give your reluctant readers the option of setting a book aside if it doesn't hold their interest. This encourages selective and analytical reading. Their price for taking this option? A simple review stating why the book was not up to their standards.

5. Encourage alternatives to book reports.

For readers who struggle with reading, a standard report seems like punishment for getting through the book. As a home-schooling parent, you may want to try the following alternatives; if your child is schooled away from home, approach the teacher and suggest these options:

▶ Write and illustrate an advertisement to persuade someone to purchase the book.

▶ Choose or write a theme song for the book, explaining

what the song means and why it suits the book.

► Write a new ending for the book, stating why this ending is better.

► Create illustrations for the book, with a brief written explanation for each illustration.

► Write a question-and-answer interview article with one of the characters in the book.

This material is adapted from writings by Sigmund Brouwer, an author of thirty-three books. His latest titles include the Lightning on Ice *series for juveniles, mysteries set in the world of hockey.*

BUT WHAT IF I'M A RELUCTANT READER?

Not all parents love to read—especially aloud. If you're among this group, these ideas will help:

► **Choose a book you'll enjoy too.** Enthusiasm is the key to enjoyable storytelling. If you like the story, it will show without extra effort on your part.

► **Plan ahead.** Choose and read through the segment you want to share later. Not only will familiarity help prepare you, but you'll be ready for any questions your youngster may have.

► **Don't be afraid to try different voices for different characters.** You'll be surprised at how much fun this can be, and even older kids appreciate the "acting."

► **Trade places.** Let your child read a few pages back to you.

► **Monitor your child's response.** If you both decide the story isn't fun, stop and discuss why. Then choose another book together. This is a great opportunity to teach critical reading skills.

3

Teaching Children to Work

. . . .

■ **When I see neighbor kids slouching on the couch, wasting the day with TV, I know I want something better for my three kids. I want them to grow up to be productive citizens. How important is it to teach children to work?**

That question can be answered in one word: very.

A few years ago, a state rehabilitation center asked Seattle counselor Jean Lush to treat men who were classified as unemployable. These men were not derelicts, but nicely dressed and well-spoken.

After six months of seeing these men, she found one common factor: None had learned to work while he was young. Each had a different reason; some of their families had been well-to-do, others were slightly handicapped and never had been required to work. Some grew up with no one around to care *whether* they worked or not.

But a surprising number had good, kind mothers who wanted their home to be a cushioned retreat. Some mothers actually told them, "You'll have plenty of time to work when you're older. I want you to have a happy childhood."

■ **Gee, that's something I've said to my kids on past occasions.**

You have a lot of company, but little did those mothers in Seattle know what they were saying. A happy childhood where nothing is required? That's a paradox. Children who have no responsibilities tend to quarrel *more* than those who are busy. These attitudes roll over into their schoolwork too. Teachers say, "I can't motivate them because their parents don't require anything at home."

■ **But I make my children play the piano five times a week, and we have soccer and baseball in the spring and fall.**

Many parents think that when children have sports practice and music lessons, that's enough. But these pursuits are disciplines of a different kind that have little to do with basic responsibility to the family.

Part of what goes on in the home is the development of teamwork. For family life to function, everyone depends on the contribution of someone else. Household chores should be divided into two categories: routine contributions and extra jobs.

■ **What are routine jobs children should have?**

Making beds, dusting furniture, and emptying the trash should be part of the children's unpaid responsibilities. But the extras—those duties beyond their usual chores—should provide opportunities to earn additional money. The differences between the two divisions should be clearly defined within each family.

For instance, let's say you have a green thumb and love to grow vegetables. If you ask your children to pitch in for more than a half hour, some of that extra work should be rewarded.

Children need to be in charge of a little bit of money, so allowances are good ideas. But allowances must be independent of their chores, unless the child is absolutely lazy and never makes any contribution. (Then curtailing the allowance would be a good motivator for most children.)

■ **I get frustrated when I have to explain to my kids how to do a certain task over and over. It seems like I have to watch them**

like a hawk, which is as much work as doing the chore myself.

Nobody requires a mother to be a "super*mom*." But one hat mothers should wear is that of supervisor. We shouldn't expect to explain the job once, say "Do it," and have the task done. Even the best children don't work that way.

When you're with children, concentrate on hands-on instruction. Keep so close to your child that you can touch him or her. Children learn by conscious imitation and by unwitting imitation.

Instead of saying, "Go make your bed," do the task *with* your child. Get on one side of the bed and have your child on the other. Pull the sheet up and say, "Look, I've got wrinkles on my side," and make a sweeping movement with the hand, pushing out the creases. The child follows with the same smoothing motion.

■ **But I'm a single mom, so I don't have time to do this in the morning before I leave for work.**

Of course, a mom who works outside the home isn't going to do this as easily as a stay-at-home mom, but it can be done. The children of single mothers have to work with her because when she comes home her second job is waiting for her. Single moms can do a great job in this area, but they will usually have to use the weekends to catch up.

■ **My mother was a perfectionist. When my sisters and I did something wrong, she'd say, "There you go again. Just like Aunt Ida." We dreaded that statement. Being compared to Aunt Ida was a character assassination because she hated doing anything. What approach should my mother have used?**

She should have lifted you up, saying things like, "My, you kids are doing a great job. You know, I didn't work like this when I was a kid. I always wanted to sneak off and play in the tree house."

Keep up a steady prattle. "Look at you kids. I can't keep up with you. You're great workers." Really laying on the encouragement gives a sense of accomplishment.

As your kids learn the principles of work, you can always teach them that there's a *best* way to do it.

If you're teaching your son how to use a grass trimmer, say, "Hmmm, let me see the way you're holding that grass trimmer. You know, if you hold it this way, you'll be able to edge the lawn just right." Then watch your son tilt the grass trimmer just the same way.

It doesn't matter how fumbling or poor their work is, children must never be robbed of the feeling that they can do it. And the parent, as supervisor, must always find something to praise, even if it's only to say, "I love your willing spirit."

■ **I know all jobs aren't created equal. Some are downright onerous, such as taking out the trash. It's a constant battle in our home. What can I do?**

Not all jobs are fun. This is where the need for consistency comes in. If one of your child's daily chores is to take the trash out to the garbage bin, then you need to see that he or she gets it done.

■ **My child, however, knows all the clever excuses. His favorite is when he melodramatically puts his hands to his head and moans, "I don't feel good, Mommy."**

You must remain nonchalantly firm. Some children will drag their feet until finally the mom says, "Oh, forget it. I'll do it myself. It's quicker that way."

The minute a mother says that, she's lost the battle. Don't let that happen. Teaching children to do chores is part of your basic duty, even if it means slowing down and working with the child. The extra effort will pay off.

But don't expect precision from the child. Some children don't have the needed coordination to make a bed correctly. The parent must know what children are capable of at a certain age—and that will differ greatly.

■ **I have a nine-year-old boy who's capable of making his bed, but I just can't seem to lead this horse to water.**

Don't let him ignore his bed. Keep "inspecting" his room, making sure he hasn't kicked anything under the bed or stuffed toys in drawers and wardrobes.

It's important to require the best that a child is capable of because the minute he gets to school, the teachers will require it. They aren't going to make much allowance for sloppiness. And when a youngster grows up and takes his or her first job, quality control is going to be very important. Sloppiness is a hard habit to break.

This material is adapted from writings by the late Jean Lush.

4

When the Kids Are Home Alone

. . . .

■ **What should parents do when children are too old for a baby-sitter but too young to be on their own?**

Diane Jones asked herself that same question just before the first time she left her four children home by themselves. She instructed Sarah, twelve, Cary, nine, and Daniel, six, to be good while their infant brother, Spencer, took his nap. "I'll be back in twenty minutes," she said, as she rushed off to the local supermarket to buy milk and diapers.

But when she returned to her street, she drove up to every parent's nightmare: two fire trucks in the driveway, a paramedic ambulance on the front lawn, and two police cars at the curb!

The blood drained from her face. She struggled to catch her breath. How was she going to tell her husband she'd killed their children?

She hastily parked the car and jumped out. Hysterically, she ran toward the house, but a husky policeman grabbed her in a bear hug. She struggled against his clasped arms, straining for the porch.

At that moment, Diane's three oldest children came thundering out of the house, sobbing.

"What happened to the baby?" Diane wailed.

"Nothing," Sarah managed. "He's still asleep."

Bewildered, Diane looked from child to child and realized they were crying only because she was crying. The policeman directed her attention to a downed electrical wire near the driveway. He hadn't been trying to keep her from going to the house—just away from the dangerous wire that had fallen while she was gone. A neighbor had spotted it and called the electrical company; hence, all the emergency equipment.

With her knees still trembling, Diane escorted the three children back into the house. She didn't leave them home alone for a *long* time.

■ **That has to be every parent's nightmare—coming home to a street filled with fire trucks and paramedic units. We've all heard reports of a sudden fire that claimed innocent lives in minutes. Yet what parent hasn't found it more convenient to leave his or her young children home alone?**

Despite the dangers, leaving children home alone is a regular occurrence in millions of homes across the country. Some parents, as in Diane's case, have their children "baby-sit themselves" while they run a quick errand. Others feel their kids are old enough to be left unsupervised while they attend a PTO meeting or enjoy a "date night" dinner. But for many two-income and single-parent families, their children come home from school to an empty house, where they do homework, watch TV, or wait until their mother or father arrives from work.

A few parents are more brazen. In the early '90s, while Kevin McAllister (Macaulay Culkin) was foiling bad guys in the hit movie *Home Alone*, David and Sharon Schoo of St. Charles, Illinois were were vacationing in Acapulco, Mexico. Meanwhile, back in Illinois, authorities discovered that their two children, Nicole, ten, and Diana, four, had been left behind for *nine days* while their parents were working on their tans.

■ **I remember seeing on CNN those parents being hauled off to jail. Although the Schoos acted inappropriately—most**

would say stupidly—when can parents leave their children home alone?

Here are a few suggestions to make sure your children are safe at home when you're not there:

► **First, determine if your children are old enough.** Look at the maturity level of the child. Most parents feel children under the age of ten are too young to be left for more than fifteen to twenty minutes—and only during the daytime. For evening hours, children should be older than ten.

Marc and his wife, Cheryl, are the parents of an eleven-year-old daughter and two boys, nine and seven, who all get along well. Recently, they started leaving the children for an hour or two in the early evening, but they are home early so the youngsters don't have to go to bed without supervision.

Marc has also made sure the children are familiar with getting out of the house in an emergency and how to call 911. He always writes down the phone numbers of the restaurant and several neighbors.

Jeff and his wife, Kelly, feel confident they can leave their three teenagers (sixteen, fifteen, and fourteen) alone, but they still call them periodically. They also have a friend stop by occasionally to "borrow" something and check on them.

Of course, *where* you live—an urban neighborhood, the suburbs, or in the country—will also color your decision on when your children are old enough to be home alone.

■ What alternatives are there to traditional baby-sitters?

Most early teens are convinced they can handle being alone. This is where you may have to get creative. One single mother paid an older neighbor to go into her house each afternoon and start dinner just as the children arrived home from school. Since the woman was helping around the house, the children didn't think of her as a baby-sitter.

Other mothers hire a college student to assist the children with homework after school. Another creative mother arranged to have her eleven-year-old daughter help with the preschoolers at their church day-care facility. The girl was able to spend time with the toddlers—an age-group that she enjoyed—and the mother knew she was safe.

■ Can you outline some rules I should have for my home-alone children?

Do you want their homework started immediately? Do you allow "wind down" time with the TV first? May they call their friends? Whatever your rules are, make sure the children understand them.

One midwestern mother, Leslie, told her two middle school children that when they got off the school bus in front of their house, they were to walk directly inside and start their homework. Leslie usually arrived home from work an hour after they did. Among her rules were these: Under *no* circumstance were they to cook, answer the phone, or open the door.

Leslie's children listened too well. The day came when Leslie forgot her house key. She banged on the door, shouting that it was their mother. The children were upstairs, so they couldn't hear her voice. Then she went to the neighbors to call them. On the third ring, Leslie remembered the rule about not answering the phone. Leslie's one hope was that the answering machine was still on. On the sixth ring, the machine picked up, allowing her to shout that it was OK to let Mom in. They heard her voice from their bedrooms and came downstairs to open the front door.

■ What should my children say when they get a phone call?

Of course, we don't want our children to lie, but they don't need to tell everything either. Thus, it's best to instruct your youngsters to say, "I'm sorry, but my mother can't come to the phone right now. If you'll leave a message, I'll have her call you back."

■ I'm a single-parent mom who can't get off work until six o'clock, and I know my children have some concerns about being home alone. How can I make it less painful for them?

For many youngsters, it's coming into a dark house in the winter.

To solve that problem, make a simple investment in an electric timer for the lights, which should take care of the problem. Many parents respect their children's feelings and won't leave them alone if they are afraid of the dark or are uncomfortable with younger brothers or sisters.

Another thing you can do to allay their fears is to make sure they have your work number. But insist they don't call to have you referee their squabbles.

■ As a working parent, how can I minimize my time away from the kids?

Can you seek out "flex time" at your place of work? When Melanie's husband died, she was suddenly thrust into the world of full-time work, and her two elementary school-age children were thrown into the world of latchkey kids. She didn't handle the trauma well at all, so she talked her situation over with her boss. Melanie was allowed to "flex" her work schedule so she could start work an hour earlier. This meant she could arrive home only an hour after her children did—a big difference for everybody.

By offering flex-time schedules, employers can help moms be available to their families. The company, at the same time, benefits by gaining an employee with greatly improved morale.

■ What advice can you give me regarding "home alone" teenagers?

Extend to your teens the same respect you demand of them. Mary Alice always expected her teens to let her know where they were, who they were with, and what time they were expected to be home. If any of those plans changed, they were to call her. Mary Alice, in turn, was to offer them the same courtesy.

However, Mary Alice still remembers one night when she goofed: She and some friends decided to stop for coffee after a special meeting at church. The restaurant phone was out of order, and it was inconvenient to find another one. She figured both teens would be in bed anyway by then, so why bother them?

When Mary Alice arrived home, sixteen-year-old Jay—who had

sent his younger sister on to bed—was still up, supposedly doing homework. His stern "Where were you?" and "Well, you still could have called" not only echoed her own earlier lectures to him, but it also let Mary Alice know that her youngsters worried about her just as much as she worried about them.

That's why you shouldn't forget to pray—a lot! You can't follow your children through life, clearing their road of every potential hazard. Instead, you must do what you can to provide for their safety and then leave the rest to the Heavenly Father. Be comforted by the fact that He loves your children even more than you do.

■ What happened to Diane Jones, the mother at the beginning of this chapter? Did she ever leave her children home alone again?

It was a year and a half before Diane had the courage to leave the children alone again. But one particular day she'd been especially busy with laundry, plus preparations for that night's church supper. Eighteen-month-old Spencer was studiously stacking his wooden blocks on the family room carpet while his eight-year-old brother, Daniel, read nearby. It was a perfect time to mail some bills at the corner mailbox before the five o'clock pickup.

She explained to Daniel that she was going to run down the street and would be back in just a couple of minutes. She left exact instructions that he was to watch his little brother's every move.

She quickly strode the half block, threw the bills into the mailbox, and walked back home. As she opened the door, Daniel was frantic.

"Mom, I'm so sorry," he sobbed. "I didn't mean for it to happen. I took my eyes off Spencer for just a moment. . . ."

Diane gasped, "Oh, no!" and rushed past Daniel, expecting to find Spencer sprawled on the floor, dead.

Instead, the toddler was standing by the kitchen table with chocolate brownie smeared all over his face. He was enjoying the dessert she'd prepared for that evening's church supper.

Poor Diane. She knew she could never leave any of her children alone again—ever. At least not until they're married.

This material is adapted from From One Single Mom to Another *(Regal Books) by Sandra P. Aldrich.*

5

How to Prepare Your Child for a Hospital Stay

. . . .

■ **My young son needs to have some surgery to correct his urethra. I can tell he's scared, and I am too, since the only time I was in a hospital was to deliver him. What can I do to prepare him for a hospital stay?**

Consider these two stories:

Four-year-old Timmy just checked into the local hospital for a tonsillectomy. He is led down a long hallway. It smells funny. Once in his room, strangers poke him with needles and weird-looking instruments.

They make him wear funny clothes and eat yucky foods—all without learning his first name or explaining what is going to happen to him. He goes to bed in a dark room with another child he doesn't know.

Contrast Timmy's first hospital experience with Susan's:

The night before surgery, five-year-old Susan is found in the hospital playroom. A staff member explains to her what tests will be done and what will occur in the surgery bay. Susan "plays hospital" by giving shots to her teddy bear and checking the heartbeat on her Raggedy Ann doll.

She and her hospital roommate are looking forward to drawing in their hospital coloring books after dinner—hamburgers and fries are on the menu tonight. Susan's mother will sleep beside her on a cot. Susan is actually enjoying this "adventure."

With a little effort and planning, you can avoid Timmy's trauma and provide a positive hospital experience like Susan's for your child.

■ What do I have to do to ensure that this happens for my preschooler?

No one knows a child's special needs—or fears—better than you—his or her mother. Besides, it cannot be assumed that the medical professionals will handle everything, no matter how excellent they are.

More than half of hospitalizations for children are considered emergencies. Therefore, you should begin now to prepare yourself and your child for an unanticipated hospital visit. Of course, any hospital stay should be treated seriously, whether or not it is considered an emergency.

Talk to your pediatrician to learn where he or she has hospital privileges, and ask if he or she prefers using a children's hospital or a general hospital with a pediatric wing.

A children's hospital focuses entirely on children and adolescents, whereas general hospitals don't. If no children's hospital exists in your area, find out if a nearby hospital has a pediatric wing or a pediatric emergency room.

■ I have a long, long list of questions. The first one is, Is there a preadmission tour?

Many hospitals offer a group tour; some even have a casual "get acquainted" part afterward.

■ Are there visiting hours? May siblings visit?

Many children's hospitals do not have formal visiting hours. Some have visiting hours between 10 A.M. and 10 P.M., while others have twenty-four-hour visiting privileges for parents. Siblings and friends may come when it's convenient for the child. Some innovative hospitals even allow pets to visit.

■ **Can I remain with my child for the entire stay?**

The fear of being separated from loved ones and familiar surroundings can be difficult for a youngster. A roll-away bed is usually provided for parents wishing to stay the night.

■ **How do I give input about my child to the health-care team?**

The health-care team consists of doctors, nurses, social workers, psychologists, therapists, and dietitians. These professionals understand that you know your child better than anyone, and they should welcome hearing about your child's specific needs (e.g., food, allergic reactions). Probably the best time to discuss your concerns with the medical team is at the preoperative session.

■ **If my child has a chronic disease or will be in the hospital for a lengthy stay, what do I need to know?**

You need to find out if there is a "Child Life" program and a playroom. Certain children's hospitals have a comprehensive Child Life program (or something similar) that is designed to minister to the medical and emotional needs of children under twelve and is staffed by professional educators and therapists.

Such a program includes a central playroom where group and individual activities are offered. The area offers a wide range of creative activities such as singing, drawing, writing, and games. Music tapes, which parents provide, also help create a relaxing—and therapeutic—atmosphere.

The playroom is a "safe retreat" within the hospital—no painful procedures are allowed there. The hospital normally absorbs the cost of the Child Life program. However, due to lack of funding, only about 35 percent of U.S. hospitals can afford a Child Life program. If no such plan exists, many nurses are trained in recovery therapy and can organize children's activities.

Here's a recap on how you can help prepare your child for the hospital:

▶ Attend a hospital tour or arrange for a private visit.

▶ Allow time for questions and discussion in order to clear up any misconceptions. Realize that you probably won't be able to answer all of your child's questions.

▶ A hospital stay gives parents a unique opportunity to explain to their children how the Great Physician walks with them in times of trouble. Bedside prayers and promises from Scripture will help soothe their fears and bewilderment.

▶ Find out from your doctor what procedures will be done and explain them to your child. Show your child by "playing through" the procedures with a favorite doll or stuffed animal—or even with you.

■ Hospital smells always freak me out. Can I leave my daughter once she's checked in?

No, you shouldn't. She needs you. Bring several of her favorite possessions from home and participate in the playroom activities with them.

Pediatric experts agree that a child needs to talk about hospitalization in order to cope with her fears. A child is usually more willing to open up when she is "doing something" with a parent or staff person. Play therapy and recreational activities provide that framework and are good methods for coping with anxiety.

Prayer and Bible study will help you and your child acknowledge God's provision and control over the situation. Remind your child that God goes before us to lead us and follows behind to protect and uphold us—even in the hospital (Isa. 52:12). We also have God's constant and comforting presence (Deut. 31:6), as well as His strength (Ps. 55:22). Another valuable insight is that there is purpose in suffering: the outflow of compassion for others who hurt (2 Cor. 1:3-7).

■ What if it's me who's struggling with fears and anxiety?

Don't be afraid to ask for support from your pastor or hospital chaplain. Also, seek out the fellowship of your friends and church body and let them know of your specific needs for prayer, babysitting, meal preparation, and transportation.

And as much as possible, appear confident before your child. He or she probably feels helpless, so it can be frightening for him or her to see a parent who appears to have lost her composure.

You can support your child by continually affirming that he or she can trust you. Never surprise your child. Do not allow anyone to perform a procedure on your child without first explaining it to him or her.

Always tell the truth—if a procedure is going to hurt, *tell* your child that it will hurt. Recognize that pain is often a part of the hospital experience. In addition to being honest about painful procedures, allow your child to cry and encourage him or her to talk openly about it.

Discourage others from talking about your child's medical problems as if the child were not present. Include your youngster in the conversation.

■ Anything I need to do when we get home?

When your child returns home from the hospital, continue reading hospital books and talking to him or her about her recovery. Especially after an emergency hospitalization, continue to allow the child to work through this time of trauma and any residual fears.

We are imperfect human beings, but we are the only flesh and blood models that our children have. In the chaos and fear of the hospital world, parents must strive to mirror the stable rock of Christ for their children. Your children will love you all the more for that—and they'll get well more quickly too!

This material is adapted from writings by Mary Ann Froehlich, who lives in Benecia, California and is a certified Child Life specialist.

Sibling Quibbling

. . . .

■ **My kids' squabbles are driving me nuts! Each evening it seems that all I hear is:**

"She got more than I did!"

"It's not fair!"

"Mom, he pinched me!"

Occasionally, they even get into actual fights. I've tried to reason with them, separate them, and punish them. But nothing constructive is happening. I'm sure every family experiences sibling rivalry now and again, but it seems as though my children are the only ones who are at each other's throats all the time. In fact, they even go at each other when we're under the greatest stress as a family, such as when our old dog died.

I would have thought they would have banded together, but it was just more of the same. What can I do to curtail their fighting?

"Sibling rivalry is an expression of our sinful nature. It's a competition for the prize—the attention and love of the parent," says Elaine McEwan, author of *"Mom, He Hit Me!" What to Do About Sibling Rivalry.* Some children will go to any length to establish their turf.

Often, it's no one thing that brings out the worst in your children, but rather a combination. Family position, for example, can create natural sibling rivalry. The firstborn may be a high achiever, and the youngest, a pampered child. Those children can frequently take center stage, leaving a middle child struggling for recognition and rewards.

Age is important, as well. If your children are ages six through twelve, they may have reached their prime fighting time. That period, called middle childhood, is when children most heavily vie for their special places in the family.

■ **I think I know what you mean. My children will choose to act out at the exact time the family is under greatest stress. I knew it was getting out of hand when it became extraordinarily physical or when children expressed cruel and hurtful words. Why does sibling rivalry happen that way?**

Elaine McEwan speaks not only from professional knowledge, but she has also counseled many parents during her nearly three-decade span as teacher, principal, and assistant superintendent. She also speaks from personal experience that saw the rivalry reach its peak during a family crisis.

"When my first husband died, our children were in college," she says. "While their father was terminally ill, they were wonderful, responsible, reliable, and thoughtful. But the minute it was just the three of us, they started going at each other's jugulars. In hindsight, I see that they were asking, 'Now that the family dynamics have changed, are you still going to love me the same way?'"

Elaine sometimes found herself simply wanting to dissolve in a heap of tears and say, "Fight among yourselves, and let the best person win."

"Parents have a tendency to fall apart at the seams," she admits. "They make mistakes in handling the rivalry and then wring their hands in despair when family reunions resemble Civil War battles more than Norman Rockwell paintings."

With fighting at its peak, Elaine would have settled for a happy medium. Even that, however, doesn't always happen on its own. That's when she remembered the "public place approach." As she had done earlier in her child-rearing years, Elaine took her children out to eat. A restaurant was one place she knew everyone could maintain control while talking out disagreements.

Over the years, Elaine has discovered many other ways parents can lessen sibling rivalry, and many ways they themselves contribute to it.

■ Wait a minute. Is she saying that my husband and I may actually cause the problem?

Cause it, no. Contribute to it, yes. Think about your family structure. Do you unwittingly play favorites? Do you expect the oldest to carry greater responsibility than the others?

Elaine says that playing favorites may be parents' most-difficult-to-avoid offense, especially if they have an older child who often is asked to carry more responsibility, especially when consistently asked to baby-sit the others. "Look for support from extended family or other networks," says Elaine. "You will need other people to get you through difficult situations, but if you lean on one of your children, you can expect the fighting to increase."

Another mistake any parent can make is assigning labels, especially within earshot of the children. Elaine recalls several instances when parents of her schoolchildren described a child as the "smart one" or the "troublemaker."

Other actions that may spark sibling rivalry are issuing verdicts of right or wrong during sibling fights, comparing your children, emphasizing gender differences, rewarding tattling, and being inconsistent with your actions.

■ OK, you've got my attention. I'll try to watch my unrealistic expectations of my children from now on, but what else can I do to stop the battles?

Your role as a parent with fighting children doesn't have to be limited to referee. There are specific steps you can take to make sibling rivalry more manageable. One of them is to give your kids permission to own their feelings.

"When a child says bad things about his or her brothers and sisters, we are so often tempted to not want to hear it, to argue with it, and to want to punish the child immediately," Elaine says. "But sometimes all they are doing is verbalizing the way they feel at the moment. Let them! You're better off trying to defuse it than deny it."

Among the dozens of other suggestions Elaine has found successful are the concepts of taking personal inventory, nurturing the family, creating a family team, and studying uniqueness. Let's take a closer look at each concept.

1. Take personal inventory. When considering the behavior of your children, consider too your own behavior. Do you often speak poorly of your husband or children? An immature child will pick up on what you are doing and model it, Elaine says. A mature child will use it as ammunition.

2. Nurture family. Take a proactive stand to help your children become nurturing, supportive siblings. Plan activities in which your children can work together, even though they may be different from one another. (See "How to Nurture Supportive Siblings" on page 133 for ideas.)

3. Create a family team. Creating a team atmosphere involves the sharing of decisions and responsibilities. Don't take this to mean a parent must give up his or her leadership role. Instead, he or she allows children to realize their significant place within the family.

To begin with, hold regular family meetings. These meetings give everyone the feeling that there will be an opportunity to talk about problems, complaints, and suggestions in a forum in which everyone listens, including the parents.

4. Study uniqueness. Think about the gifts each of your children brings to the family. What makes your child shine? Even if those talents are not ones you particularly prize, accept and value them. Find ways to draw them out without pressuring your children to develop them. Strive to make each of your children feel special and wonderfully unique.

"Trying to treat your children as equals rather than unique individuals will make you a crazy person," Elaine says. And you'll be disappointed in the results. "Many children spend their lives adding up the parental ledger, constantly looking for shortfalls," she says.

We have a child who has cerebral palsy and is considered a special-needs child. How do I handle him vis-à-vis the other children?

Parents of special-needs kids recommend managing sibling rivalry by

▸ Scheduling daily one-on-one times with each of your children

▸ Answering your children's questions about the special-needs child

▸ Helping siblings empathize with the special-needs child

▸ Involving your children with each other

▸ Affirming your children for the love they give to a sibling.

■ **Does sibling rivalry hit every family?**

Sibling rivalry will probably never be eliminated from a family, but it can be moderated. Your children will benefit for years from the unity you work to build now.

This material is adapted from writings by Peg Roen and Elaine K. McEwan, author of "Mom, He Hit Me!" What to Do About Sibling Rivalry. *Copyright 1996. Used by permission of Harold Shaw Publishers, Wheaton, IL 60189.*

HOW TO NURTURE SUPPORTIVE SIBLINGS

by Elaine K. McEwan

Even though I'd endured my own share of sibling battles with my younger brother and sister, I just knew that when I had my own children, everything would be different. I'd be able to raise perfect children who loved each other, seldom said unkind things, and almost never fought.

Of course, this was not the case. But I did find throughout my years of parenting that whenever I took a proactive stance, my days were happier.

The following are suggestions for nurturing supportive siblings. Choose ones that fit the needs of your family.

Strategy No. 1: More Cooks, Not Fewer

There's a saying that "too many cooks spoil the broth," but I haven't found

continued next page

that to be true in my kitchen. Preparing a meal together can illustrate for kids the adage that "many hands make light work." When siblings work side by side in the kitchen (or in the garden, or in the garage), they will learn to depend on each other and work together.

Strategy No. 2: The Family Bulletin Board

Our refrigerator functioned as the bulletin board when my children were growing up. It contained artwork, certificates, messages, special photos, and a calendar of upcoming events. Everyone got equal billing on the refrigerator, and we periodically changed the display to keep it fresh.

Strategy No. 3: Open for Business

Sibling relationships were always at their best in our house when my children were collaborating on a joint venture. Once or twice a year, they put together a lemonade stand. One time they collected their old toys and had their own garage sale. Other families work together on "real" money-making ventures such as team newspaper delivery, lawn-mowing services, pet-sitting, or housecleaning.

Strategy No. 4: Family Time Capsule

Put together a time capsule that includes a representative sampling of things from every family member. Store the items in a sturdy container and put it away for a five or ten years. Possible items to include are snapshots, handwriting samples, favorite candy wrappers, a short letter from you describing your children, a short essay from each child on "What I Want to Be When I Grow Up," or a list of favorite activities and friends. This is a good activity to do at the end of summer vacation or on New Year's Day.

Strategy No. 5: Room Redecoration

When siblings share a bedroom, rivalry can become especially intense. One way to alleviate some of this is to permit the children to rearrange and redecorate the room. Before you begin, develop some ground rules and help them negotiate the sticky points of the decorating project.

Strategy No. 6: Sibling Secrets

Whether it's planning a birthday breakfast in bed for Mom or decorating Dad's bathroom for Father's Day, kids love to surprise their parents. Encourage such teamwork and cooperation. Send them with a relative or trusted friend (who can supervise from a distance) to shop together for a single gift.

HELPING YOUR CHILDREN GET ALONG

by Naomi Clement DeGroot

Children have a natural bent for fighting and need instruction in *how* to get along, which begins with knowing what is expected of them. Otherwise, if left to their own direction, it's like the old story of the frog race. From the river-bank, the largest frog yells, "Ready! Set! Go!" and the others leap off lily pads in a dozen directions, not knowing where the finish line is. Racing frogs and families need rules.

The Golden Rule provides direction for all ages: "In everything, do to others what you would have them do to you, for this sums up the Law and the Prophets" (Matt. 7:12). Even preschoolers can understand that concept when it's applied to their experiences. "Brandon, do you want Jessica to bite you? Then you shouldn't bite her, right?"

A six-year-old can understand higher logic. "Wouldn't it be nice to live where no one is allowed to call you names or treat you mean? That's the kind of home I want for us. So I won't allow Jeni to be mean to you . . . and I won't allow you to be mean to her."

An effective house rule is **no name calling.** While our children are at school or playing in the neighborhood, we can't protect them from names that belittle. But in the home, we can guarantee them safety from verbal attack. Words such as "stupid" and "dummy" are not allowed.

An effective second rule is **no annoying each other on purpose.** Surely every parent has heard the backseat wail of "He's on my side!" Chances are, Mark is on Julie's side merely to pester her. When three children share the back seat, it *is* difficult not to elbow each other. Car seats and belts help define personal space. A book or small toy reserved for car time can divert each child from seeking amusement from an elbowed brother's reaction.

Establishing a few rules lets children know what is expected. Enforcing the rules isn't easy, since stopping an activity to enforce them takes time and effort. But it's worth it, especially when you consider the alternative: years of continual bickering.

7

When Counting to Ten Isn't Enough

- -

■ My precious two-year-old deserves a better mother. Recently she splashed in the bathtub amid suds and toys. "Time to wash your hair," I announced.

"No, Mommy. No wash hair," Jessica pleaded.

As I massaged the shampoo into her hair, she began rubbing her eyes and yelling, "It's in my eyes. It hurts!"

"Oh, it is not," I yelled back. "There are no suds near your eyes. Besides, it's baby shampoo. It doesn't sting."

She screamed louder. Without warning, exhaustion engulfed me. The pressures that had been mounting throughout the day overwhelmed my body. I turned on the faucet and jerked her to it, pushing her whole head under the running water. Soap flowed down over her face into the tub. She sputtered and coughed, but I didn't care.

Grabbing her arm, I yanked her out of the tub. I screamed, "The next time you'll hold still when I tell you." Anger boiled inside me like hot lava. Spanking her with my hand became an outlet for my tension and exhaustion until Jessica's hysterical shrieking brought me back to reason. I carried her into her room and dropped her into bed. Slamming the door behind me, I bolted down the hall sobbing.

"O Lord Jesus," I gasped. "I hurt Jessica again. I keep saying I won't do it anymore, but I can't control my anger."

What's wrong with me? I don't understand why God isn't answering my prayers for deliverance.

What you don't realize is that God does want to help you, but not instantaneously. You have begun the process of growth by facing the results of your anger, and good things will come out of this in time. In fact, author Kathy Collard Miller went through a process much like the one on which you are embarking. She not only discovered some causes of her parental anger, but she also decided on a five-step process for dealing constructively with it.

It all began when Kathy was nine years old and became so angry with her best friend, Irene, that she hit her in the nose. As Irene ran off crying, Kathy stood paralyzed in horror. *See what happens when you get angry?* she thought. *You had better never get angry again.* She concluded all anger was wrong and tried from then on to bury it.

Years later, she discovered Ephesians 4:26-27, which says: "In your anger do not sin: Do not let the sun go down while you are still angry, and do not give the devil a foothold."

These verses acknowledge that we are going to get angry and that the emotion itself is not wrong. But we should not let that anger become sin by allowing it to turn into wrong or destructive attitudes or actions by neglecting to deal with it.

Yet, if we believe all anger is sinful, as soon as we feel it we think we've sinned. Then we condemn ourselves and try to squelch the feeling. As a result, we become even more angry. As one young mother said, "I get angry with myself for being angry."

■ **That's exactly how I feel. But as a Christian I don't want to be acting this way.**

Nor did Shelly, a young single mother. "My parents were Christians," Shelly said, "and every time I expressed any unpleasant emotions, they told me I was sinning and should repent. When I married Greg, I couldn't tell him that his infidelity made me angry because I thought I would be sinning just as he was. As a result, I didn't confront him. Now I am learning that it's OK to challenge sin, even with anger, if it's done the right way."

■ **What are some other reasons mothers get angry?**

Displacement, or "the transference of an emotion to a logically inappropriate object," is another cause of parental anger. When Kathy looks back to that angry time in her life, she can see how she displaced her feelings. She blamed her daughter for her outbursts, thinking the child's disobedience caused her anger. Now she sees that other situations and relationships were involved, but she didn't see their influence or significance at the time.

The best way to prevent displacement is to deal with problems as they occur instead of storing them up. Also, by recognizing potential situations for displacing, mothers can stop spilling out other problems onto the children's misbehavior. They can ask themselves, *Am I actually angry at this present situation, or is something else bothering me?* Most of the time, the child's present disobedience is not the main cause of the parent's anger. By identifying the real cause and dealing with it, it won't be displaced onto someone or something else.

■ **That's scary. I gave up a great career in marketing because my husband insisted we start a family. I had Jessica, but then he pulled the disappearing act. Now he's never around to help me with the child he demanded we have. . . . This is starting to make sense. What else does Kathy say is a cause of parental anger?**

When we can separate our sense of worth from the behavior of our children, we are on our way to dealing with anger more effectively. As your child is having a temper tantrum on the grocery store floor, how do you feel? Mothers, in particular, are often embarrassed, angry, frustrated, and tense.

Those feelings indicate we are thinking our child is a reflection of us. Yet, the truth is, while we are responsible to train our children, we are not responsible for the decisions they make. We can and should consistently give discipline and training, but our children can still choose to disobey. Even if it were somehow possible for us to be perfect parents, our children would still act like children because that's what they are. In 1 Corinthians 13:11 we read: "When I was a child, I talked like a child, I thought like a child, I reasoned like a child." Why do we expect them to respond like adults?

The wise parent will follow through consistently in giving consequences, especially in public. Backing down because we are feeling embarrassed will only embolden our children to challenge our authority. As we tell ourselves repeatedly that *my child is not a reflection of my worth and value as a child of God*, we'll respond more calmly when that challenge comes.

If I'm really going to get a hold on my anger, what steps should I take?

Kathy suggests these steps:

► **Step 1: Realize you're feeling angry.** Recognizing early warning signs of anger gives you time to deal with your feelings before they become destructive. These red-flag warnings include feeling hot, cold, paralyzed, tightened muscles, churning stomachs, or a desire to cry. When you pay attention to your unique red-flag warnings, you can realize that your anger countdown has started.

► **Step 2: Distract yourself from your anger.** Anger always brings about physical energy. A distraction helps to relieve tension. A few distractions might include the following: taking a walk, running, hitting a pillow, taking a shower, singing, taking ten deep breaths, counting out loud, playing a musical instrument, reciting a Bible verse, telephoning someone, watching a funny TV show.

► **Step 3: Recognize the underlying cause of the anger.** Ask yourself questions about your physical condition first: *Am I tired? Do I need exercise? Have I been eating too much or the wrong kinds of food?*

Then ask questions about your psychological state: *Am I thinking negatively about something? Am I worried? Has my child mirrored a bad habit of mine?*

Finally, look at your spiritual status: *Am I not trusting God? Do I have unconfessed sin? Do I need to forgive someone?*

► **Step 4: Analyze your thinking for incorrect assump-**

tions. Many times we become angry because we assume an idea is true when it is not. These underlying assumptions warp our thinking, yet we believe we're basing our attitudes and actions on truth. Stopping to evaluate our thinking by examining Scripture and by sharing our ideas with others will help us identify wrong ideas. Once we do, anger will not have as much fuel to feed it.

Here are a few wrong assumptions:

- ► "Being financially secure will take away my problems."
- ► "If my husband would cooperate with me, I could be happy and content."
- ► "Since I've made so many mistakes, my children can't grow up to be emotionally healthy adults."
- ► "If I hadn't had children, I would be happy and have fewer problems."

► **Step 5: Verbalize anger appropriately.** This means using *I* messages instead of *you* messages. *You* messages express blame, as in, "You make me angry." As a result of *you* messages, the other person usually responds defensively and is not open to hearing our feelings or ideas for solutions to the problem.

One the other hand, *I* messages express how we feel without telling the other person what to do about it (unless he or she asks). *I* messages express our needs and may be more conducive to someone really listening. An example would be "I feel angry when my needs are ignored."

Besides watching the wording, we need to monitor our motives. We should not use *I* messages to try to subtly change the other person. Instead, we should honestly share our feelings while trusting God to control people and circumstances. *I* messages are most often effectively used with another adult, not a child. This will help us to avoid displacing our anger from an adult to a child. With children we need to used "consquences for their disobedience" in order to train them.

We can also verbalize our anger by calling a friend, professional counselor, or pastor. We could share our feelings within the safety of a support group or by writing them in a journal.

■ **There's a lot of theory here. Do these five steps work?**

Some time ago, Kathy applied these five steps when a woman broke a promise to her.

First, she realized that she was indeed angry. Even after she tried to understand her friend's viewpoint, she still believed she had been treated inappropriately.

Then she played the piano for a while to pound out some of the energy that her anger was creating. That was her distraction, the second step.

The third step, finding the real cause of her anger, was obvious. Yet, when she thought more about the situation, she discovered even more reasons why she was angry. For instance, her broken promise prevented Kathy from completing a project she had promised for someone else. Therefore, not only was Kathy angry because of how her friend had treated her, but because it damaged her reputation before others.

In analyzing her thinking for incorrect assumptions, Kathy realized that what she had regarded as her friend's "promise" had actually been intended as a "possibility." She had assumed they were communicating at the same level, but she learned she needed to be more assertive in determining someone else's plans and thinking.

Finally, Kathy verbalized her anger in a letter in which she let the fur fly. Then she edited it to make her words appropriate and acceptable. In the letter, she asked her friend to forgive her for her reactions and shared how she had hurt her.

As Kathy typed the final copy, she decided to wait a week before she mailed it.

By the next day, her anger had evaporated, and she knew she would not have to mail that letter. Verbalizing her anger, even on paper, had taken care of it, and she was able to forgive her friend. Today, she has no bitterness toward her.

This material is adapted from writings by Kathy Collard Miller. Her daughter, Darcy, now in her twenties and a college graduate, not only has forgiven Kathy for the way she treated her, but has also coauthored How to Be Friends With Your Kids *(published by Harold Shaw, 1997) with her. Kathy lives in Placentia, California.*

8

Fun Ways to Celebrate Valentine's Day with Your Kids

. . . .

by Susan Mix

On Valentine's Day, stores across the country will sell more than 100 million pounds of chocolate. Whether it melts in your mouth or in your hand (or even in the box), chocolate is considered one of the best ways to say, "I love you." But after all those heart-shaped boxes are empty and your kids' tummies are full, what's left? This February 14, why not give your favorite valentine a treat to remember? Try out one of these surprises, or think up your own.

- ▶ Surprise your children with a trip to the local skating rink (or pond). It's great exercise and you might even want to join them.
- ▶ Serve strawberry pancakes to the kids for a special breakfast in bed.
- ▶ Make a heart stamp. Cut a potato in half. Carve a heart in the potato. Press into a red ink pad and soon everything will be covered with red hearts.
- ▶ Buy a bottle of pink bubble bath for a clean, practical gift.
- ▶ Purchase removable wax from any craft store. With the wax, draw hearts and a Valentine's greeting on white cotton

sheets for your children's beds. Then dye the entire sheets with red dye. Remove the wax and your designs will remain on the cloth. It's easy for even a child to do. And your little ones will cherish their personalized Valentine's Day sheets.

▶ Tape-record a Valentine's Day greeting and follow it with your youngsters' favorite Bible story or nursery rhyme, read by you.

▶ Take a picture of your child's pet or his or her favorite stuffed toy. Have it blown up into a poster and sign the pet's (or stuffed animal's) name with red ink in the lower right corner.

▶ Buy an inexpensive bird feeder and watch your midwinter "guests" come along to entertain.

▶ Buy a small, blooming cactus and wrap it with a red bow. Many have red flowers and can be purchased for around $1.

▶ Find smooth rocks the size of eggs. Paint happy faces on them and little red-and-white outfits. You can make animals such as mice, kittens, or piglets, depending on the shape of the rocks.

4

<hr />

*Moms and
Their Teens*

1

"Can I Have the Car Keys Friday Night?"

. . . .

■ **What's the dating scene like these days? In my day, girls wrapped angora wool around her boyfriend's ring each night—to make it fit her own finger. But I have a sinking feeling that's as outdated as malt-shop waitresses on roller skates.**

It is. Kids still exchange class rings in some parts of the country, but many parents are putting the kibosh on that, saying, "I didn't pay that much for a ring just to have some girl lose it!" The *cool* thing for many girls these days is to wear her boyfriend's varsity jacket all day at school.

As for today's dating scene, it's still customary for a guy to ask the girl out, but in some parts of the country, as soon as she accepts the date, they will kiss—a move that certainly jump-starts any relationship. And casual dating is now called "seeing each other," while "going steady" is merely known as "going out."

Parents *should* worry about dating in this day and age of high school girls walking around in "outerwear" (frilly bras and girdles worn as public attire), classmates' heavy necking between classes, and the principal's annual letter asking parents not to rent hotel rooms for their child's prom night.

■ **I've heard all about that stuff, which keeps me on my knees. What else can I do to make sure my teens don't succumb to all those temptations?**

You might anticipate advice reminding you to keep children active in church. Yes, that's a given, but parenthood doesn't come with guarantees, even if we do all the "right" things. Besides, most youngsters don't need *more* activities; they need time with their parents. But today's busy lifestyles make that difficult for many families because of so many responsibilities outside the home.

Darrell Worthington, a Colorado Springs youth minister, said, "I'm convinced many Christian students have the same problems as non-Christians. They take their moral standards from movies and TV instead of the Bible. They don't know how to date and get to know each other. Often they date one night and immediately establish inappropriate commitments. They accept abortion and aren't concerned about AIDS because they think it'll never happen to them.

"Parents must *train* their children as well as commit them to the Lord. But they opt out of their responsibility, thinking that just enrolling them in a Christian school or putting them in a youth group will do the trick."

One thing you can do is talk to your teens about friends and acquaintances who have made inappropriate and even tragic choices over the years. Remind them not to live in a way they will regret later. Perhaps you've heard stories of teens who've given in to sexual pressure and then sobbed, "I want to go back to the way I was."

■ **My sixteen-year-old daughter was asked to go to the movies by a boy in her English class. I agreed on the condition that my husband and I meet her date when he comes to pick her up. She told me that would be a pretty "uncool" thing to do, but I'm not going to back down. Am I blowing all this out of proportion?**

Not at all. All parents of dating teenagers should start a little routine known as "The Talk." The Talk consists of having your daughter's would-be date answer pleasantly asked questions such as, "How long have you lived in this area?" "What do your folks do?"

and "Do you have brothers and sisters?"

Within a few minutes, you'll want to advance the questions to "What are you planning to study in college?" "What church does your family attend?" and "Do you have time to be very active in your church youth group?" Listen closely: The answers will tell you a lot about the young man's character, although you can never be too sure.

If the young man keeps glancing toward the stairway, it's probably because he's wondering when your daughter will be ready.

One of you should should smile and say something like, "It's OK. She'll be downstairs when this is over."

Then ask the young man to have a seat on the sofa. You should have his full attention now, and when you do, have your husband look him in the eye and say, "Even though we've just met—and you might think this is ridiculous—I can guarantee you that in about twenty-five years when a guy asks your future daughter out, you'll think of me and say, 'That ol' man was right!'"

Let the thought sink in before you jump in. Then say, "I know you two are just going out as friends, but we've lived long enough to know how quickly situations can change. So remember this: Treat our daughter the same way you hope some other guy is treating your future wife."

Look for his eyes to widen at this thought, and when they do, you'll know you hit your target. This discussion can be initiated by single mothers too. The important thing is to be involved in your children's social life no matter the makeup of your family.

Don't be surprised if your little "talk" gets around school. But an unexpected side benefit is that The Talk will give your kids cover. If a young man refuses to meet you, then your daughter has an easy "out" not to go out with him. The teen doesn't have to like it; he just has to do it.

■ What are a few things I can do to make this time less stressful?

▶ **Expect your teen to have high standards.** It's sad to hear a number of parents who *expect* their sons to be sexually active, even in this day of rampant out-of-wedlock conceptions and sexually transmitted diseases. As adults, we need to set high standards for our children—through our words as well as our actions—and let them know that *real* men and women do not act irresponsibly.

One thing you don't want to say is, "Be careful that your feelings don't run away with you." If you do, you're conveying the idea that sexual feelings are so strong they can overrule judgment. That's an incorrect message to give.

Sexual feelings don't have to be acted on any more than feelings of anger. One mother left this message on a three-by-five card in her teens' rooms: "You may not be able to control your feelings, but you *can* control your actions."

▶ **Express trust in your teen.** If not, your teen may do a rationalization number sounding like this: "If my mom's gonna accuse me of it, I might as well do it."

▶ **Anticipate problems.** Even while you're trusting your teen, you can't close your eyes to potentially dangerous situations. Most of us managed to survive the sexual temptations of our own early years because we were supported by a society, church, and family that shouted, "No!" and "Wait!"

Today, teens are hearing a different message from those same institutions—along with the media's siren song: "If it feels good, just do it." They need us to say, "No, you're not going there if his parents aren't home."

▶ **Talk with your teen.** Don't assume you know what's going on. In a nonthreatening way, ask if anything is troubling him or her about the relationship. Amy noticed that her seventeen-year-old son was withdrawing from family activities. One Saturday morning, over a leisurely pancake breakfast, she asked if he wished he could change anything.

"You bet, Mom," he said. "I wish I were older so Sheila and I could get married."

With all the calmness and candor she could muster, Amy talked to him about the sexual pressures he was facing and decided that the best way to help was by including his girlfriend in more family activities so they could spend time together without the temptations of intense dating.

▶ **Get to know your teen's date.** Think of the young man or woman not as the enemy but as a potential friend and (gulp) even future in-law. When Lynn's son, Paul, started seriously dating a non-Christian, Lynn knew she'd drive him away if she harangued him with admonishments about being "unequally yoked together."

Instead, while she patiently reminded Paul of God's concern for the future, she welcomed the girl and lovingly worked at getting to know her. As the opportunities arose, she even shared her faith, explaining why it was so important in her life and their family's. Because the young woman felt so comfortable with Lynn, she readily consented to attend church with the family. Two weeks before the young couple got engaged, Lynn had the privilege of leading her future daughter-in-law to the Lord.

When your children are in college, you know that you won't be able to counsel them before they go out the door. But know that your prayers will have a lot more power than your talks. As mothers—and especially as single moms—we may not get through this stage as well as we'd like, but by talking to our children, keeping them in a good youth group, and being ever watchful, we increase our chances of raising them to make sound moral choices.

Isn't that the goal of every mom?

This material is adapted from One Single Mother to Another *(Regal Books) by Sandra P. Aldrich. William R. Mattox, Jr. lives in Montclair, Virginia.*

IT'S FOUR O'CLOCK IN THE AFTERNOON. DO YOU KNOW WHAT YOUR TEENS ARE DOING?

America's teenagers don't talk a lot about going to "Lover's Lane" or "Inspiration Point" these days. Apparently, "parking" with a date on a Saturday night is a dying, or at least declining, custom.

The demise of "parking" has little to do with smaller cars or changing attitudes about sex. A new study by the Centers for Disease Control shows that more than one-half of all high school students have had sexual intercourse at least once. Forty years ago, only one-quarter of all females were sexually

continued next page

experienced by their eighteenth birthday.

Instead, the decline of "parking" is because even the most spacious and luxurious back seat of a car is not as comfortable as one's own bed. And there is growing evidence that more and more teens home alone after school are pursuing what some call "love in the afternoon."

A recent study in *Public Health Reports* shows that young boys whose mothers are employed full time have rates of sexual experience 45 percent higher than those for male classmates whose nonemployed mothers are home during the day. A 1994 study in the *Journal of Marriage and the Family* reports similar findings for young girls.

"Sex usually happens at home, either at the boyfriend's house or the girl's house," said social worker Pat Garrity in the *Chicago Tribune*. "Kids nowadays have an inordinate amount of time alone, particularly in single-parent households where children are left unsupervised during work hours."

The fact that "home alone" teens have higher rates of early sexual activity does not surprise psychologist Brenda Hunter. She says unsupervised latchkey youth are also more apt to smoke, drink, use drugs, view pornography, and engage in juvenile crime.

Dr. Hunter believes the "4 o'clock sex" problem serves to illustrate the need for flexible work arrangements that allow parents to work from home, to work part-time, or to organize their work schedules around their children's school schedules. "In many two-earner households, one parent will get the kids off to school in the morning, and the other will arrange to be home before the school bus arrives in the afternoon," Dr. Hunter notes.

Jim Sims, a pastor in Allentown, Pennsylvania who has worked with youth for years, applauds these strategies for increasing parental supervision in children's lives. But he is quick to remind parents that appropriate supervision is only part of the solution to curbing sexual activity.

"Teens must develop the personal conviction to do what is right, even when no one else is around," he said. "For parents, this means the best strategy for discouraging early sexual activity is still 'teach your children well.'"

Give Your Grad the World!

. . . .

■ **"I know I need to go to college, but I'm just not ready!"**
My eighteen-year-old daughter, Katie, appeared wistful. When my husband, Paul, and I looked at each other, we knew Katie wasn't emotionally mature enough to go away to college. What do you suggest?

Perhaps Katie could do something *different*—live with a missionary family for a while as a volunteer.

Katie's words recall the time when Christine Greenwald was feeling like a frustrated high school senior. Like your daughter Katie, Christine was not ready for college. Although Christine knew that one day she wanted to pursue some type of higher education, she felt directionless and unmotivated by a dream or goal.

Her godly parents observed her frame of mind and took action. Christine's mother wrote to a friend whose husband supervised operations for a mission organization in Europe. She asked her, "Do you have anything Christine could do for a year before college?"

Amazingly, five families—in five different countries—invited Christine to live with them as a "daughter," to sample life in another culture, and offer light domestic help and child care. Suddenly Christine had a dream! She chose to live in Sweden for seven months. Afterward, she returned to four years of college with new confidence and assurance in God.

■ Staying with a family sounds like something only young women should do, right? What happens if our son isn't ready for college?

You're right—spending six months with a missionary family taking care of young children is something your son probably wouldn't enjoy. But that shouldn't close the door for your son. There are tons of missionary families around the world who could use a helping hand around the house with chores or with farm animals. Another idea would be to find a family needing help with a building project. The possibilities are limitless, if your son is willing to be flexible.

■ What "year-out" options are available?

Some individual churches and many denominational mission agencies offer short-term service opportunities. Parachurch organizations such as The Navigators and Youth With a Mission also have programs in place to fit your teen. Your pastor or your youth director may know about other resources or contacts.

■ How far ahead should we plan?

Most teens don't decide to take a year out until six months before graduating in June. It will probably take you at least five months to make connections and put together all the pieces for a successful experience. Since colleges have deadlines for notifying them with your plans, realize that you will have a few anxious (make that *prayerful)* moments!

So start early. Whether or not you think your young person might want to "do something different" for a year before continuing his or her education, be sure to visit colleges or trade schools while he or she is a high school junior. Narrowing down the choices and getting applications in the mail by September of the senior year will allow time for adolescent indecisiveness, surveying the options, and choosing the best scenario.

If your teen opts for a foreign opportunity, obtaining passports and visas, making travel plans, fulfilling mission agency requirements, and getting his or her college enrollment deferred can all take time.

■ **Are colleges willing to defer enrollment? After all that work to get our teen accepted, I'd hate for a college to rescind its acceptance.**

Most colleges are willing to facilitate delayed enrollment. In fact, many admissions counselors acknowledge that a well-structured year out enhances academic and social progress when a student does enroll.

■ **What about my daughter? Won't a year out deter her from pursuing further education?**

Probably not, if she is already accepted at an educational institution and knows it is the expected next step. More likely, your daughter will gain a new sense of God's guidance. Again, time, planning, and clear communication will make the difference.

■ **What will it cost to have my daughter stay with a missionary family?**

Most short-term mission trips involve substantial sums of money for transportation, insurance, and personal needs, which can be raised through summer and after-school employment and/or fundraising appeals. Many mission

FOR MORE INFORMATION

▶ Call The Navigators' Center for Global Opportunity at (719) 594-2435.
▶ Call (206) 771-1153 and request a copy of *The Go Manual: Global Opportunities in Youth With a Mission,* YWAM Publishing, P.O. Box 55787, Seattle, WA 98155. Cost is $4, which includes shipping.
▶ Call (847) 570-5694 and request a copy of *The Great Commission Handbook or The High School Short-Term Mission Directory,* published by Berry Publishing, 701 Main St., Evanston, IL 60202. Cost is $3 and $5, respectively, which includes shipping.
▶ Call Greater Europe Mission (18950 Base Camp Road, Monument, CO 80132-8009) at (800) GEM-4488 and request a copy of their Eurocorps Summer Missions brochure.

agencies will assist your teen with this process. Host families often offer room and board in exchange for your teen's participation in ministry and family duties, and they will usually include your teen as part of the family for recreational activities, travel, and so on.

■ **What about health insurance? How will she be covered?**

Be aware that some health insurance plans cover nineteen- to twenty-three-year-olds only if they are full-time students. By law, however, your insurer must make a COBRA policy available to cover nonstudent young adults for up to eighteen months once they are ineligible under their parents' plan. Mission agencies can also tell you about special insurance plans available for short-term missionaries through internationally recognized companies. Be sure to ask your insurance company about procedures for submitting claims for out-of-country health care.

■ **So you think this is a good idea?**

With time, prayer, a heart open to God's leading and provision—and a lot of preparatory phone calls—you too can give your teen the world!

This material is adapted from writings by Christine W. Greenwald of Clymer, New York.

3

What Your Teen Is Reluctant to Tell You

. . . .

■ **My oldest, a sixteen-year-old son who walks around with his ball cap flipped around and T-shirts that should have landed in my dirty laundry hamper last week, has been a handful. I don't mean to imply that he's been a troublemaker, but he's moody, uncommunicative, and prone to sleep half of Saturday away.**

A few times I've been able to get him to open up, but most of the time he's tough to talk to. If he could squirm out of his shell and *really* tell me what he's thinking, what could I expect to hear?

First of all, teens have it tough. They act like kids but want to be treated like adults; they yearn for responsibility, but they want Mom to cook, clean, and iron for them.

At the same time, they are growing up, and rather quickly too. Teens sense this passage, but many have difficulty articulating where they are in life because of their lack of experience. But if you want to get into their heads and know what they are thinking, you need to walk a mile in their combat boots.

Every time your teens step out the front door, it's like walking into a war zone. You can tell them that sin's been around since Day

One, but they are growing up in a culture that is, morally speaking, spiraling down faster and faster.

When you were their age, at least kids knew they were doing something wrong. Their world, however, preaches that it's up to them to decide what's right and what's wrong. The only thing sinful in today's politically correct society is to not do your own thing or to be intolerant of someone else's lifestyle.

Some of their friends, even those from good homes and religious backgrounds, will tell your son, "Trying marijuana or booze is no big deal" or "If you're really in love, you can't fight that feeling. Sex is natural."

You have probably taught them that abstinence is the way to go, but they are receiving no support out there, unless they're involved in a great youth group at church. In other words, it's hard to be a PG teen in an R-rated world.

■ **What if my teen asks me if he can go to the most popular person's home for a big Saturday night party? What should I do?**

You need to remain firm in your resolve, but you also need to know that his holdout span is limited. When your teen asks you if he can go to a big party Saturday night, but you don't know the parents, a little alarm should be going off in your head. This is an invitation for trouble, which is why your teen needs to hear you say, "Absolutely not." Your strong stand will take the monkey off his back so he can tell his friends that his mom said "No way." Then he doesn't have to rely on some flimsy excuse.

The same thing goes when you have to ground your teen for missing curfew or messing up. Stick to your sentence. It shows you care. He may gripe about it (that's part of being a teen), but he'll respect you for exercising parental leadership.

■ **My daughter, a high school junior, recently won the lead in the school production of *The Sound of Music*. I'm so proud of her! When her grandparents were over, I asked her to sing one of the play's songs, and she nearly burst into tears as she**

ran to her room. What did I do wrong?

Your daughter was not being moody; it's just that she can't per-form on demand. Just because she's talented on stage doesn't mean she feels comfortable performing in the living room. Putting on stage makeup at the school auditorium gives her security. Maybe you could invite friends and family to the school play. She'll do a good job there, and you will be proud of her.

■ **But you should have seen how embarrassed she was when I just asked her to sing one song. Why didn't she respond the way I hoped she would?**

It's all part of growing up. You've forgotten how hard it is to field remarks like, "My goodness, Meghan, you're certainly blos-soming into a young woman!"

She may give an appearance that she has life together, but she has probably never felt so fragile. Everyone can see her zit-covered face and how her body's changing. That can be depressing to a teen.

Nor does she like being compared with others, especially within the family. She'll gag every time someone says, "Are you a tennis player like Hannah? *She is so good.*"

So what? That's Hannah, and regardless of what people may think, your daughters are not Siamese twins.

■ **One of the issues I struggle with as a parent is that I want my teen to enjoy the same things I do. I played tennis in high school, so I naturally want my son to have that experience as well. What's happening here?**

The plain truth is that life contains no guarantee that your son will enjoy the same sports or have the same interests as you. He may want to take tennis lessons, and that will be just fine, or he may end up playing another sport that interests him—like in-line hockey. The fact is that you can never tell which path teens are going to take. They may want to simply follow in your footsteps, or they may want to walk their own paths.

Either way, don't have a cow when he decides that he wants to get into photography. In fact, if you're the type of mom who likes to leave notes of encouragement on his pillow, now would be a good time to do that.

■ Sometimes my sixteen-year-old daughter acts like a little child. When is she going to outgrow this?

Every child sets out on a different path when it comes to maturity. But then again, many teens are in a no-win situation. Sometimes we adults treat them like children, so when they act like kids, we tell them to grow up and behave like adults. We say that they're hard to live with. Well, we can be difficult and set in our ways, as well.

Teens are torn between wishing they were eighteen and out of here to fantasizing about what it would be like to be a little kid again. Too bad God doesn't let them skip all those years between eight and eighteen. But as you know, those are some of the most exciting times we had growing up.

■ My teen son has been openly questioning whether he is a Christian or not. How do I handle that?

Don't be shocked when your teen questions everything you've taught him, especially about God, Christ, and faith. It's not enough to tell him that Jesus makes a difference. They really need to see it, as when Paul told Timothy to be an example "in speech, in life, in love, in faith and in purity" (1 Tim. 4:12).

Mom, know that raising teens is hard. They would love to tell you that, but they don't know how yet.

This material is adapted from writings by Coleen L. Reece, an author and editor living in Auburn, Washington.

4

Help! My Teen Is Breaking My Comfort Zones

. . . .

■ **Remember the terrible twos? I've tried to block out memories of my Cheerio-wielding, diaper-waving, legs-wobbling tyrant who demanded ice cream for dinner. No longer is he the drooling, defiant, dictatorial, despot toddler he once was. He has changed. Grown up. Matured.**

Now I have a teenager. Drooling. Defiant. Dictatorial. Demanding. Minus the diapers and Cheerios, he still has to be wooed to the dinner table with the mouth-watering aroma of a freshly delivered pizza—anything to get him to sit with the family. I thought I survived the epic drama of the tumultuous toddler years. Guess what? They're baaaaack!

Those who have worked for years with parents and teenagers stress this important point: *If you want to develop a closer relationship with your teen, you've got to get uncomfortable.* It seems as though teenagers are wired to break a parent's comfort zones. It's in their blood. It's in their brains. It's in their bones. You did it too, and now it's payback time.

So what's a comfort zone? You've got 'em. Your teenager's got 'em too. It's a thick layer of protective insulation that prevents you from touching or changing something about your life—even bad habits.

A spiritual comfort zone is an invisible, isolated cocoon where you can't be bothered by anything or anyone, even God. It's a tiny space for hiding from the dangers, risks, and difficulties of the person God is calling you to be. Comfort zones are spiritual prisons that keep you locked away from an intimate relationship with your Creator, preventing authentic spiritual growth.

Remember the old Shake 'n Bake TV commercials? Do you ever have days now when you feel like that pink lamb chop or bent chicken wing trapped inside the plastic bag? The moment you step through the door after a long day at work, your teenager sprinkles you with a golden sawdust of incessant pleas, demands, and wild requests. Tenderized and pulverized, your temper begins to sizzle.

Teenagers will shake you with their thundering, reverberating, indecipherable rock music. They will bake you with a pan full of buttered-up requests when you're at your weakest point. (It's a secret adolescent rite of passage.) They will do anything to shake, bake, break, and decimate your comfort zones.

It's hard enough raising a teenager, let alone having him or her break your comfort zones. There are days when you want to scream, "ATTENTION! ALL TEENAGERS IN THIS HOUSE! LEAVE HOME WHILE YOU STILL KNOW EVERY-THING!"

■ **That certainly sounds familiar. But at least I know our family isn't the only one going through this. I've talked with other Christian parents about the complicated issues affecting our teens' development. The constant questions include:**

"**How can we help our teens resist peer pressure?**"

"**How can we talk to our teen about sexuality?**"

"**What can we do to get our daughter to treat us with respect?**"

"**My son refuses to go to church with us. What can we do?**"

Before you start flipping through the Yellow Pages looking for the number to the local army recruiter, it's important to remember that teenagers have spiritual comfort zones that need to be broken down for them to grow in their relationship with God. Your job is to help them, but assisting your teenager through his or her spiritual development is not an easy task. It takes determined, intentional, and consistent effort poured into one of the most important investments of their lives.

But how is it possible to manage the never-ending roles and responsibilities you have as parents? Your teen probably thinks you are his or her personal automated teller machine. As chauffeur, you make more drop-offs and pickups than a New York cabby during rush hour.

Separating low-blowing, screaming, hair-pulling, kicking, clawing, and swinging kids, you've got the credentials to referee a heavyweight boxing match. Drying tears from your daughter's eyes after a breakup with a boyfriend and encouraging your son who's struggling in algebra, you become a trusted counselor, cheerleader, and head coach in an everyday drama. And as parents, you are the spiritual head-honchos with a God-given calling to do the best you can to stoke the spiritual flame in the fireplace of your teen's heart. Whew!

■ **Oh, my. Even though my husband isn't always around for the latest crisis, at least I'm not trying to do this alone. So what are some effective ways of dealing with teens? I'd love to have something crack open our son's comfort zones.**

Ponder these five strategies:

▶ **Know who you are in Christ**. By investing in your relationship with God, you will receive everything you need and more to invest in your teen's spiritual growth. In Jesus Christ, you are enough (2 Cor. 3:4-6). Meet with other parents of teens who will encourage you in your relationship with God. Ask them to pray for you and your teen.

▶ **Make time.** Spending time with your teenager is the foundation on which almost everything in your relationship depends. Invite him for a walk or to his favorite restaurant. You don't need a specific agenda. Casual conversation often leads to deeper levels when the teen feels secure.

Questions about God, dating, peer pressure, struggles at school, and their future will surface when they know you are available. When you make it a regular habit of spending time with your teen doing things he enjoys, his words, thoughts, and feelings will follow.

▶ **Set boundaries.** Though most teens will push the limits set by any parent, they need and even want boundaries. One fifteen-year-old lad said he wished he would have been grounded when he was caught drinking alcohol. Instead of putting her son on restriction, though, the mother did nothing. The son interpreted his mother's indifference as a sign that she didn't care.

BREAKING NEW GROUND

It is critical for you as the parent to look for creative ways to break new ground in your relationship with your teen. Just as you no longer raise your toddler on smashed peas, pureed beef, squished squash, and other assorted stomach-churning forms of baby food, your teen needs you to help guide your relationship with him or her in new, innovative directions.

Here are some creative ways to get started:

▶ Begin making a surprise memory album of your child's teen years. Collect photos, newspaper clippings, school calendars, and pictures of his or her friends. Have teachers, coaches, friends, and youth pastor write special notes to be included inside. Give it to your teenager at his or her high school graduation.

▶ Plan a special, inexpensive outing once a month.

▶ Find an activity you both enjoy and spend time doing it together.

▶ If you can't agree on something you both like to do, do something you've both never done. Take a one-day class on ceramics, painting, cooking, or using a computer.

▶ Hop in the car and start driving. Go to the beach, mountains, or lake.

▶ Ask your child how you can be praying for him or her.

▶ Find one spot during the week to spend time together as a family. Make sure to ask for your teen's input on activities.

▶ Get your teen involved in a short service or missions project with you. Help out with a canned food drive or volunteer at a local rescue mission.

▶ If you go on a vacation, go to a place that is teen-friendly. There is nothing worse for a teen than to go on a boring family time away.

▶ Write short notes—lots of them. Send them in the mail. E-mail them. Put them in his or her sock drawer or other fun places. Affirm your son for the Christian qualities you see in him. Write a special Bible verse and let your teen know how you are specifically praying for him.

Not only do boundaries protect teenagers from the physical and emotional dangers of drinking alcohol, engaging in premarital sex, and other hazardous behaviors, they also provide spiritual protection. Providing teens with boundaries helps them say no. "No way! My parents would kill me if I was caught drinking."

Develop positive boundaries for your teenager, such as going to church and attending midweek Bible studies and youth events. Don't fall into the trap of making family spiritual matters optional. As a parent, you must decide what the family "nonnegotiables" are. Though you can't make your son or daughter love God or grow closer to Him, you can set spiritual priorities and guidelines for your family. Boundaries provide teenagers positive comfort zones.

▶ **Ask for help.** Making your needs known is not an admission of weakness or inadequacy: it is a sign of strategic courage. Talk with your youth pastor. Let him know the unique needs of your family. Ask for teen devotional books or resources. Find out when the upcoming youth events and retreats are. Make it a priority for your teen to go to a Christian camp.

One week of camp is worth more than a year of Sunday School. The friendships, fun experiences, time alone with God, and positive memories that your teen will bring home from camp will stay with him or her for a lifetime. If finances are an obstacle, ask your youth pastor if scholarships are available. Seeking help for your teenager is one of the best spiritual investments you can ever make.

▶ **Pray.** Never underestimate the power of prayer for your teen. Prayer has an amazing way of breaking comfort zones. Like the Israelites who circled the walls of Jericho for seven days praying for the walls to collapse, God can do the same for those concretelike comfort zones separating you and your teen. Praying makes a silent investment in teens' lives that has eternal returns.

Breaking your comfort zones is a daily choice, a firm resolve, and a determined stance to be God's person with your teen. It's choosing God's way over your way or the world's way. It's looking past the momentary inconveniences and emotions and on to the eternal things of God. Breaking your comfort zones is an intentional step to walk with Jesus every day of your life. It involves a lifelong process of following Him where He leads you.

Jump-start your sluggish commitment to Christ and your family by breaking free from comfort zones. By doing so, you will discover the true, lasting joy of being a child of God—even with a teen.

This material is adapted from Joey O'Connor's book Breaking Your Comfort Zone *(Revell, 1996). Joey lives in San Clemente, California.*

5

Plugging the Holes in Your Teen's Moral Ozone

· ·

■ I can tell our two teens are closely watching my husband and me, but I also know that they are living in a world where kids are taught to disregard laws that they believe are silly or impossible to obey.

They see others run red lights with impunity and park in handicapped zones without a proper sticker and politicians play games with the truth. When our teens see all this going on, a hole is punched in their values. Do you have any tips to combat it?

Let's get down to the basics by relating this story from newspaper columnist Kathleen Brown, who once wrote about a fifteen-year-old girl's creative interpretation of her parent's rule "no cigarettes and no smoking."

"The girl would go to her bedroom, open the window, and invite the neighbor boy to meet her in the backyard. She would hang out the window while he offered her drags from his cigarette. Her mother asked about the pile of cigarette butts under her window. She said they didn't belong to her. She claimed she had no cigarettes in the house. She said she doesn't really smoke."

According to Brown, the loopholes could have been plugged if the teen's mom had said:

▶ "You are to have no cigarettes in your possession."

▶ "You are to have no cigarettes in the house."

▶ "And you will not smoke inside or outside the house."

A fifteen-year-old who has not learned honesty and truthfulness needs to be held accountable.

■ So, how can parents be reasonably certain their children will have the right values?

Teenagers develop virtues when their parents present a clear set of values about right and wrong, display those values by their own example, and encourage their children to decide which behavior exemplifies those values.

The moral principles found in the Bible are at your fingertips, and children who follow these values can have the courage they need to resist conforming to society's mold. Scripture gives us firm, unchanging values. With these values, teens can solve the moral and ethical problems they confront.

Besides, it takes time to cultivate a teen's values. You can help your teen develop creative solutions to tough problems by examining your family values and eliminating useless rules. To compare your family values and rules, divide a sheet of notebook paper into two columns.

▶ List the spiritual and moral values important to your family. Do you want your teen to develop self-control? To tell the truth? To value hard work?

▶ Jot down your family's rules. For example, you might want your teenager to come home on time, bathe regularly, and wear clean clothes.

▶ Add missing values you think are important to develop.

Now study your list of rules and eliminate useless ones.

Finally, ask yourself, "Do I model the values I want my child to learn? How can I improve?"

Telling right from wrong isn't impossible for most teens. Our responsibility, as parents, is to instill in our kids the moral strength to do what they know they should do. This happens when parents model values and motivate their teens to accept those values.

■ How should I respond when my teen challenges me on family rules or values?

The following quiz is based on some real-life scenarios. Read each one and choose the best response.

1. Alice is glued to the TV. In spite of your rule forbidding TV before her homework is finished, she isn't moving. What do you do?

a. Turn off the TV and escort her to her workplace.

b. Do nothing. Homework is her problem.

c. Threaten to restrict her for two weeks.

The best answer is a. Threats don't work. If you do nothing, Alice may continue to ignore you. Turn off the TV, and check to see if she has her books and materials. The rest is up to Alice.

2. Your son, Jack, is suspended from high school. The school counselor said Jack dipped a classmate's hat in the toilet, poured water on the boy's head and punched him out. You should:

a. Ignore the incident.

b. Talk to Jack and get his side of the story.

c. Call a school board member and complain about the poor teaching, counseling, and discipline at the school.

The correct answer is b. Talk to Jack and get his side of the story. Don't make accusations until both sides are heard.

3. Thirteen-year-old Jennifer doesn't like to shower. Each day she exits the bathroom combing her damp hair and leaving her clothes and a soggy towel in a pile. Suspicious, you find her reading a novel while the empty shower sprays hot water. Your reaction is to:

a. Blow up when she says, "I use deodorant. I don't need to shower every day."

b. Say: "The importance of a daily shower has been established as one of our family rules."

c. Talk to her about trust and truthfulness.

Was your answer b? This is a clear case of breaking a family rule. Also, talk to Jennifer about trust and truthfulness, two important values.

4. Josh and his friend are playing a game on the family computer. You overhear them talking about making and selling copies of the game. Josh knows what they are planning is dishonest. You should:

a. Ignore the conversation. It's Josh's decision.

b. Say: "You can't do that, it's stealing."

c. Lecture the kids on copyright law.

The correct answer is b. Josh knows that pirating computer software is wrong. Since honesty is an important value, you can't ignore what they are planning.

This material is adapted from writings by Wesley Sharpe.

6

Leading the Way Through the Maze

. . . .

Editor's note: In 1955, just before hula hoops and fender fins, Jay Kesler became director of the Youth for Christ chapter in Marion, Indiana. For the next twenty-eight years, he was a staff evangelist, regional director and, eventually, president of the organization. In 1985, however, his career took a new path when he became president of Taylor University in Upland, Indiana, where today he continues to help young people sort through life's decisions. Christian parents can be daunted by the problems they face raising today's teenagers, but they needn't be, says Dr. Kesler. The following is an interview conducted by Sandra P. Aldrich about the challenges today's teens face.

■ **You've worked with young people all your adult life. What's the biggest problem they face today?**

Jay Kesler: At the top of my list is their identity crisis. The normal struggle of "Who am I?" "What am I?" and "Why am I here?" is compounded by information overloading their emotional circuits. The expanding world with its expanding insoluble problems makes them feel even smaller.

Psalm 8:4 asks, "What is man that you are mindful of him?" We can either answer that with—as the next verse says—"a little lower than the heavenly beings" or—as the world says—"a little higher than the animals."

Our world teaches young people they are the result of impersonal evolution. But if we accept by faith that we are God's creations and part of an eternal plan, our life takes on a different meaning.

■ Has the secular attitude affected Christian youth?

Jay Kesler: Yes. While they live in a world created by God, and are themselves created beings, they have experience-based faith and try to work through dilemmas alone.

I compare the turmoil of today's youth to shell-shocked soldiers who, in the midst of bombardment, start across the field because they can't stand any more fear. Their circuits are overloaded.

Information comes to our youth in mosaic patterns—a splash of truth here, a splash of experience there. Often they can't absorb any more information because they haven't assimilated what they already have. As a result, many live glandular, sensual lives.

■ How do we change that attitude?

Jay Kesler: We need to help them develop a Christian worldview, based on the premise that we live in a created world and this is a visited planet—that God actually walked on it in the Person of Jesus Christ. Knowing Him and becoming committed to His teaching and work gives our lives meaning. Suddenly, we don't have to solve all the world's problems ourselves—God is at work. Our task becomes finding His will for our lives and settling into that spot where we can make a contribution.

This idea of making a difference offers emotional freedom for today's youth. Those who can't comprehend that run from their problems.

Most "typical" youth problems, such as drugs and casual sex, are actually symptomatic of deeper needs. That lack of purpose causes them to live for their stomachs and glands instead of weighing today's decisions against eternity.

■ **How do you reach someone who isn't thinking in such lofty terms but just wants to gratify desires?**

Jay Kesler: We have to meet our young people in a different way than we met them a generation ago. Back then, the church met them at the door of unbelief and debated God and evolution. Today the church is having to meet young people at the door of experience.

But we haven't taken that far enough. After showing them how to trust Christ as Savior, accept forgiveness, and have the joy of meeting God, we need to put some content to it. Teaching doctrine and the Bible helps them understand that the supernatural has many sides to it. It's not just the great amoebic force they see in the movies.

But most young people don't want to study doctrine. They want to have another party, thereby sensually experiencing God and Christ. The task of the church, then, is to take them from the door labeled "experience" and bring them to the door labeled "faith." And that's a belief system based on Scripture.

■ **How do we accomplish that?**

Jay Kesler: Parents and youth workers can't just leave kids to themselves; they have to set goals for the young person's spiritual growth. They can't be satisfied that the kids are coming to the youth meetings. The adults must ask themselves, "What are we trying to achieve in this group?"

Of course, kids need fun, but it can be wrapped around the truth, the way chocolate covers a peanut. I tell youth workers, "Do the fun things, but be aware that you're teaching—either directly as you share the Word, or through your life."

The pattern is in the Bible: As Jesus walked with a group of men, He taught them. That's what parenting and youth work is all about. We don't just walk, we walk and talk, integrating life and its meaning.

■ **Why isn't that happening?**

Jay Kesler: Middle-class youngsters usually live in large homes, each with his or her own room. They may have their own TVs, stereos, and portable headsets. They can control the input of their life by turning the dial off and on. Thus, they can become self-contained units, totally unsocialized, just living with this electronic input, and becoming its product. This isn't God's intent. He wants humans to interact and learn from one another.

The product of this media age is young people who are illiterate—not only about biblical and historical events, but about life itself—simply because they control the data. We need to find ways of breaking through that, including getting Christian tapes in their collection. The Gospel hasn't changed, but our methods of getting it to kids must.

■ Many parents today grew up during the permissive 1960s and the me-generation '70s. How has that affected their parenting?

Jay Kesler: In the general culture, we have a group of parents whose attitudes toward drugs, sexuality, and patriotism are vastly different from those of their own parents—even though they carry the same responsibilities.

Many parents assume the schools will rear their children. But a teacher rarely can help a kid whose parent is irresponsible, a thief, or a drug addict. Parental support has to be present too. Three things work together: the school, the home, and the church. And many kids have at least two of those unhooked.

That's one reason I shifted from youth work to the family. We have to appeal to the parents to escape their own adolescence.

■ What can Christian parents do?

Jay Kesler: It is possible for a parent to say, "Hey, I must have input into my child's life." We won't all agree on what that means—some parents choose home schooling, for example—but each parent has to direct what happens within the family. Even though our society is getting used to things we have no business getting used to, numerous Christian parents are finally saying, "Hey, that's enough! We're going to do something about that as a family."

It's the only way we're going to escape what the Scriptures call a "wicked and perverse generation."

■ **A Gallup poll revealed that a little more than half of churched youth are—or have been—sexually active, so the majority of Christian youth are no different from those "of the world." How do you respond to those statistics?**

Jay Kesler: They're frightening. The Christian kid's attitude toward sexuality is largely the same as the general population. Part of this is because our current youth work hasn't made a connection between behavior and theology. For many, faith is a way to go to heaven. We've soft-pedaled the idea of responsibility and the implications of the Christian life. Therefore, our youth look at sexuality like any other life process. Their attitude becomes "If you itch, scratch it." And they don't feel guilty about it.

■ **How has this happened?**

Jay Kesler: Christian principles haven't come to them from their churches or their families because they're concentrating on what they can experience: Knowing Jesus makes me happy. Knowing Jesus makes me free. Knowing Jesus fulfills my longing. It's like a bromide. The idea of God having a will for our lives and being concerned about how our lives and our behavior affects others hasn't been addressed.

Even at a Christian college, such as Taylor University, where I work, we've found that a major task is teaching young people the implications of sexuality, that it's not just about the physical body.

The condom isn't the answer to AIDS. The answer is Christian morality. Abstinence. Monogamy. But our society has given up teaching morality. The church needs to teach the value of abstinence and the virtue of virginity. Coming to marriage sexually inexperienced is not an act of naïveté or stupidity, but purity. We've failed our young people if we haven't told them that.

Some leaders are calling now for a last-ditch effort. It's like the Alamo—Santa Anna's out there with all of his troops marching closer, and we keep moving the sandbags in further and further until it's just Jim Bowie in some room with a knife. It's time we moved those spiritual sandbags back out to the perimeter and made our stand on biblical teaching.

■ Do parents feel pressured to be lenient?

Jay Kesler: Many of them. But the one who is laughed at by someone saying, "Oh, you're too protective. You've got to let them out and give them a chance," has to realize that what you're giving them a chance to do is become more deeply involved.

This is true not only of alcohol and pornography but of casual sex as well. When a young woman has had an abortion—or two— by age twenty, I contend her psyche is scarred. In the past, some parents gave their teens birth control information, ignoring the implications. But AIDS has changed that view. This isn't sowing wild oats; you've sown strychnine.

We need to teach our sons and daughters to be biblically oriented sexually. I think adults who don't believe that either don't have children and are talking about life in theory, or they've given in to these issues themselves and don't want to acknowledge their mistakes.

■ Do you know the definition of a conservative parent? It's a parent whose daughter just turned thirteen.

Jay Kesler: (Laughs). That's true. We become conservative when we have something to conserve. But we also don't want our children to be hothouse plants. The wrens that have a nest in our yard don't wait until the neighborhood cat is there to decide to give their little ones the acid test. They start by letting the babes take little loops around the nest. When they're able to fly well, they fly away.

This is what we're to do as parents. We teach our children to take these ever-enlarging loops until they can leave the nest. But many children are missing out on those trial runs because of absent parents—whether through divorce, alcoholism, abuse, neglect, or selfishness.

■ What are some of the loops we need to allow our children to try?

Jay Kesler: Children need experiences in responsibility. Staying overnight with Grandma or with trusted families is a good start. Later, handling money, even doing the math in the parent's checkbook for a couple of months, and caring for pets helps too.

If the first time a young man has been responsible for maintaining his room or money is when he leaves home, he may not handle it well. That's when people say, "Well, the army ruined him," or "She was never the same after college."

But the truth is, no independence has been built into them. Young people need to be increasingly trusted with responsibilities—such as the family car. But you don't do that in one big gulp overnight. You start it when they're small. Occasionally those little loops will include mistakes, such as spending money foolishly. But if they aren't given that opportunity, they have to learn the lesson in adulthood when their families will suffer.

■ Where's the line between teaching values and blind sheltering?

Jay Kesler: This is a question every parent must really think about and then come to a personal conclusion. We can't abdicate our responsibility in this two-pronged situation.

First, each young person either absorbs the two or three feet around him or makes the two or three feet more like himself. If he's an absorber, he needs a safe atmosphere until he develops his own autonomy. Parents need to ask themselves, "Is my child ready to make these decisions?"

Second, today's youth are facing more serious challenges than previous generations. Today's drugs aren't cornsilks smoked behind the barn, and drugs and pornography aren't things they outgrow. It isn't a situation in which everybody does a little bit, realizes it was foolish, and goes on. Some of these things can't be moved on from.

Taking the attitude that a young person can experiment because it's part of growing up is like saying, "We have to teach him about cars by letting him play in traffic."

■ Any final word for moms?

Jay Kesler: Be optimistic. God wouldn't ask you to do something you can't do. All too often you buy into the hand-wringing of "ain't-it-awful?" Don't fall for that. I believe that "greater is He that is in us than he that is in the world." And if you will put your

Christian faith to work—not just as a way to go to heaven, but as a way of life—then it becomes powerful. Christian families—and the church—don't have to give in to the world.

This chapter is based upon an interview of Jay Kesler that originally appeared in Christian Herald *magazine.*

5

. . . .

Moms and Their Homes

1

There's No Place Like Home

. . . .

■ **I want to make our home a special place that will create good memories for our children. But where we live now is small and always in need of repair for one thing or another. What can I do to make it more "inhabitant friendly"?**

"There's no place like home."

Why was is that Dorothy loved that little house in Kansas? It was a farm house, not even in the best shape. The paint was peeling. The front porch sagged just a little. With all of the chores to be done, the inside was less than sparkling.

If interior designer Terry Willits had to guess, she'd say perhaps none of this mattered. Dorothy loved her home because within its walls, she could count on many things, including the smell of Auntie Em's homemade rolls, the summer breeze as it moved the curtains, the taste of fresh cookies and milk straight from the cow, the view from her window of the sunset on the plains, and the sounds of the farm animals in the backyard.

How about you? If you think back to your childhood, what memories come to mind? Does it make you want to shut your eyes and go there? If you said yes, chances are it wasn't because of the architecture. In fact, it probably had little to do with the building itself.

After fifteen years of home expertise, Terry knows well the cliché that "love makes a house a home." She'd add something, though: "It's love and how that love is shown." Not only does Terry know how to create a "sense-sational" home, she has also made it the focus of many seminars and conferences.

One thing she stresses is that even though a house looks good, it's not necessarily a home.

"There's a lot more to it than that," she says. "What you do in your home can make a difference. I have been in huge houses that are perfectly decorated, yet they don't feel homey. I've also been in tiny apartments that may be modestly decorated, but somehow they exude warmth."

■ **How did Terry begin to explore exactly what it is that makes a house or an apartment a home?**

She drew on her own past and began to see how although God created beauty, He also gave us our other senses to experience life.

"I remember going to my grandmother's house in Maryland when I was a little girl," Terry says. "Her house smelled like moth balls, perfume, and whatever she was cooking. For some reason, it was a good smell. She always met us at the door wearing an apron. Music would be playing on the phonograph, and in the winter, she always had a fire going. You could hear the fire crackling. She wasn't a great cook, but we would sometimes have steak on the grill. It was just a combination of all the different things about her home that made it and us feel special."

Although Terry's grandma may not have consciously thought about making her home a sense-filled experience, that's exactly what she did—without investing a lot of money or time. You can do the same, and the rewards are great.

"To me, one of the greatest motivations for a parent is that she wants to give her child a positive home experience," Terry says. "The more sense-filled any experience is, the more we remember it."

Stimulating a child's senses does two things to provide that experience. First, it can create security in his or her changing and seemingly unstable world. Imagine a child who clings to a blanket. Touching and holding that blanket gives him or her a sense of security. Stimulating other senses repeatedly gives children a chance to become familiar with certain experiences—the smell of muffins baking every Saturday morning, the soft night light leading the way to the bathroom, a decoration that appears on a certain holiday. That familiarity produces security.

Keep in mind that a parent's touch is also important for creating security. Greet your children at the door with hugs. Hold their hands during mealtime prayer. It takes little time and no money, but the benefits are immeasurable.

■ **That's heady stuff—to think that my awareness and use of the five senses can create a more positive atmosphere within our home. What else will it do for my children?**

Over time, stimulating the senses creates memories. When you smell a fragrance, taste a food, or hear a song that is familiar, it evokes memories. In the same way, the senses that a parent incorporates into the home now are things a child is going to remember twenty years from now.

Children are not the only ones who benefit. You, too, can find satisfaction from creating a home full of sensory pleasures. You can be sense-sationally blessed by sitting down for a cup of tea, taking a bed tray up to your room for a late-night snack, taking a bubble bath, or lighting a scented candle while you are reading.

"Unless you replenish yourself," Terry says, "you don't have a lot to invest in your children."

■ **I'm misty-eyed thinking of things I remember from my childhood. I want my children to have those same good memories. So where do I begin?**

Beginning may be the most difficult part of creating a sense-filled home. But once you're over that initial hurdle, you're going to have fun. Terry suggests starting with fragrance. It is one of the easiest senses to appeal to and possibly the one with the most long-term benefits.

"There is a saying that a house becomes a home when good smells come from the kitchen," Terry says. "I'm not a big baker, so

I will often buy slice-and-bake cookies and put a sheet in the oven just so my house will smell like cookies. That's only one way to create a familiar scent."

Another way Terry loves to create a familiar smell is by using an inexpensive lamp ring. Place it on top of a lightbulb and add a couple of drops of fragrant oil. The heat helps the fragrance fill the home. This is an especially good tip for a parent with small children because lamp rings are safer than lighted candles.

Terry says simplicity is the key for the other senses too. "God has created a bounty of food for us to eat, and the closer it is to a natural source, the better it is for us," she says.

Don't feel guilty or overwhelmed because you cannot prepare a gourmet meal every night. Slicing a tomato in season and having grilled chicken for dinner is enough; it's also easy and good for your family's bodies.

As for sight, Terry says one of the least expensive ways to transform a room or any part of your house is with paint. Adding yellow or cranberry or whatever color you love to sterile white walls immediately gives a room warmth.

"I think the bottom line is everybody loves her home," Terry says. "I encourage parents to make those homes pleasing places, but the most important part is the heart of the homemaker."

So, as difficult as it is for a busy parent, you must find the time to replenish your relationship with the Lord and allow Him to fill your heart and mind. After all, "Out of the overflow of the heart, the mouth speaks" (Matt. 12:34). What we fill our homes with will be a reflection of what we've stored up in our hearts.

This chapter is adapted from writings by Peg Roen, who is creating a "sense-sational" home in Denver.

QUICK TIPS TO MAKE YOUR HOME SENSE-SATIONAL

Taste

▶ **Relish your refrigerator.** Use clear glass or plastic food containers to display foods attractively inside your refrigerator. Place fruits and vegetables in bowls. Enclose meats and cheeses in clear plastic bags.

▶ **Celebrate the seasons.** To know what is in season, look for what is plentiful, healthy looking, and reasonably priced. Cool months call for hot apple cider, pot roast, citrus fruits, or vegetable soup. Warmer months welcome fresh lemonade, corn on the cob, melons, or sliced tomatoes.

▶ **Make it better with butter.** Butter always adds a burst of rich flavor. For a terrific taste, flavor butter by sprinkling jalapeño, onion, black pepper, basil, and parsley onto a stick of softened butter. Mix all the ingredients together, roll them into a log, then wrap and freeze for use on broiled meats and fish or to stir into vegetables or pastas.

▶ **Go nuts!** Enhance salads with a handful of nuts or sunflower seeds. Try walnuts, pecans, almonds, or peanuts, toasting them lightly to bring out their flavor. If you don't have young children in your home, place a wooden bowl filled with different sizes, shapes, and flavors of nuts in your living room. Leave a nutcracker in the bowl so family and friends can help themselves.

▶ **Top off your hot chocolate.** Enhance a steamy mug of hot chocolate with a tasty swirl of whipped cream and a sprinkle of cinnamon sugar or chocolate shavings. At Christmas, add a candy cane stir stick. For a cool hot chocolate sundae, add a small scoop of vanilla or chocolate ice cream and top it with small marshmallows, sprinkles, and a maraschino cherry.

Sound

▶ **Tie one on.** Tie a bell or string of bells to your entrance doorknob with a pretty piece of ribbon. The welcoming jingle will become a familiar greeting to loved ones stepping inside.

▶ **Serve foods that sound scrumptious.** Try crispy chips, crunchy vegetables, popping corn, or sizzling steaks. Pleasant-sounding foods enhance the satisfaction and memory of a meal.

▶ **Say please.** Set a good example for your children by using the word "please" as part of your everyday vocabulary. "Please" softens a statement by turning it into a respectful request.

▶ **Tick, tock.** Place a beautiful clock with pleasant-sounding chimes in a prominent spot in your home. The familiar sound will ring "home" every time it strikes.

continued next page

▶ **Have a "get-well bell."** Spoil a sick child with a designated get-well bell beside the bed. Whenever he or she needs something, a simple ring will let you know. This soothing sound and a little TLC is sure to help cure any mild illness.

Smell

▶ **Keep closets fresh as a forest.** Use cedarwood hangers to hang outerwear in your coat closet. They will repel moths and mildew while pleasantly scenting your garments. For an extra whiff of fragrance, hide a cedar block on the top shelf of the closet.

▶ **Simmer a scent.** Simmer apple cider with cinnamon sticks, cloves, and orange peel for a spicy, fragrant beverage. If you don't have cider on hand, use boiling water. Although you can't drink it, the smell is just as enjoyable.

▶ **Share a cup and saucer of scent.** Drop a scented votive candle into a pretty teacup. Place it on a saucer in a spot looking for a touch of fragrant charm.

▶ **Mist in menthol.** For a menthol treat, tie a bouquet or wreath of eucalyptus to your shower head. Moisture from a steamy, hot shower will release its stimulating scent.

▶ **Sprinkle your sheets.** Before turning in on a warm summer night, turn down your sheets and sprinkle them with a fragrant body talc. The perfumed powder will absorb moisture, delighting your nose while keeping your body dry.

Look

▶ **Make your front door friendly.** Your front door is an outsider's first impression of your home. A pot of flowers, a wreath, a welcome sign, a fresh coat of paint, or a pretty doormat all say welcome.

▶ **Store memories by the bowlful.** Put a big bowl or basket on your coffee table and fill it with family photos that haven't yet been filed into albums. Not only is it a fun and easy accessory, it's a great conversation starter or memory jogger.

▶ **Brighten chores with friendly faces.** Hang an attractive bulletin board filled with photographs of family and friends above your washing machine. Their faces will brighten your day as you do laundry and will remind you to pray for them.

▶ **Light up the night.** Turn on your front porch lights at night for a friendly glow. Use pretty night lights in all your bathrooms to light the way for children, guests, and even yourself.

continued next page

► **Decorate down under.** When accessorizing a sofa table, don't forget to decorate beneath it too. Use large plants, stacks of big books, baskets, old leather luggage, or anything unique that will add warmth and charm.

Feel

► **Plop onto floor pillows.** Keep two or three jumbo pillows stacked on the floor in your living room, playroom, or children's bedroom. They are great for those who want to sit on the floor to watch a movie or lounge in front of a fire. With zippered coverings, they can be easily cleaned.

► **Reach out and touch.** Hold hands while praying at mealtime or any time. Give hands an extra "I love you" squeeze at the end of the prayer. Pamper with a powder puff. Apply a favorite perfumed powder all over your body with a big, fluffy duster. Use the powder puff on young children after a bath. They'll treasure its touch as it tickles their bodies from head to toe.

► **Collect spoons in all shapes and sizes.** Smooth wooden spoons make stirring, sautéing, or tossing food a delight. Collect a variety of them and store them in a decorative canister within easy reach of the stove.

► **Roll out the rugs.** Colorful cotton rag or braided rugs soften a hard, cold floor. They are comfortable, reasonably priced, and reversible. Scatter small ones in places where you stand frequently—in front of your shower, tub, or kitchen sink, and at the front and back doors. Do not use rag rugs on top of carpet where they might get wet and stain the fibers.

2

Hard to Keep Your House in Order?

■ I don't know how this happened, but the clutter in my home has moved from "the lived-in look" to "natural disaster area" decor. I have one of those cute little wall plaques hanging in the entryway that says, "If you come to see me, come anytime. If you come to see my house, please make an appointment," but living like this is not funny.

I want my children to be comfortable bringing their friends home, but I've noticed that only a select few come through our doors now. In the past, I would occasionally invite friends over for a company dinner as an incentive to do major cleaning, but even then I just stashed most of the junk in the hall closet. The situation has gotten way beyond that remedy now, however. I don't know where to begin, but I've got to get a handle on this.

Let's have a little fun: Look around your home and imagine it as an 1800s western town. The Clutter Gang has spread onto every countertop and lurks in every corner. You know you must face the enemy one last time. Exhausted, you're tempted to surrender to the relentless varmints. Instead, you strap on your six-guns of determination and organization. You're ready.

Your first step is to round up a posse. Choose four strong-looking boxes. Their names are Throw-Away, Put-Away, Give-Away, and Store-Away. You can't ask for better backup.

At the break of dawn, you and the boys are going to face the enemy head-on—for thirty minutes. It may take weeks to separate and destroy individual piles of clutter until all are gone for good. But remember that those critters are only target practice. The real desperado will still be at large until you face a showdown with the closet.

When that time comes, face the closet door and swallow hard. Have your gang behind you, ready for action. Take a deep breath and turn the knob. There in the stillness of the dark closet, you'll face the enemy. You'll be up to your eyeballs in clutter.

But take heart: Within moments, debris will begin to fly. Sweat will bead on your brow in anticipation of each move. But you'll be quick on the draw, delegating remnants of clutter to Throw-Away, Put-Away, Give-Away, and Store-Away without hesitation.

It may take an entire week for your gang and you to hog-tie this outlaw. But by the end of the seventh day, your boxes will be filled with mittens, shoes, game pieces, toys, half-finished craft projects, and sewing items.

The Clutter Gang and their sidekicks, Chaos and Confusion, have been driven out of town. Neatness, peace of mind, and a warm hearth had taken their place. Your homestead has become a restful watering hole for the soul.

■ **You almost make it sound as though I can tackle this wild disorder that has invaded our home. Is there hope?**

Sure, there is. Think about clutter. It visits all of us from time to time: papers, toys, pins, clips, coins, books, and thousands of other household items. It causes irritability, confusion, and exhaustion. As busy parents, we need to make our lives as irritation-, confusion-, and exhaustion-free as possible. With all of the balls we juggle, we don't want to be dragged down by this enemy, and chances are, neither do you.

Some clutter is visible to the naked eye and distracts from the more pleasant characteristics of a room. Other clutter hides and waits in drawers or closets, ready to inflict distress and frustration on all who approach. No matter where your clutter gathers, it needs to be faced, rounded up, and taken away.

■ **I like the idea of looking at this mess as a gang of Old West varmints. So how do I drive them out of town?**

Use a three-step plan called "Face the enemy," "Round 'em up," and "Take it away."

▶ **Face the enemy.** To find your clutter, grab a notebook and take a tour of your home. Step inside the door of each room and write down all the distracting, disorganized areas. Then write down drawers, closets, and other areas hiding debris that you want to organize. Since you will be referring to this notebook periodically, make a point not to add it to one of the piles.

Next, strategize. Choose a room. Then select one clutter area in that room. You will need four boxes (or three boxes and one trash bag). Label them 1) throw-away, 2) put-away, 3) give-away and 4) store-away. Set aside fifteen to thirty minutes each day and sort your clutter into the boxes. Don't burn yourself out on a two-hour clutter-clearing binge. A little work daily will make a big difference.

After you clear one area, move on to another in the same room. Make sure to finish one location before going to another room.

▶ **Round 'em up.** The throw-away box or bag is easy to deal with. Just fill it, then toss it. The put-away box works best when you actually put away its contents each day.

Things that haven't been used for a year or more should be given or thrown away unless there is good reason not to. If you're one of those people who finds it difficult to get rid of things, use the "one year or out of here" rule. That will help you ditch things you are tempted to keep, including the gift neon orange blouse you keep thinking you'll someday wear.

As you begin your quest for a clutter-free home, you may not have the time to separate all of the items to be stored away into their own boxes (such as winter clothes in one box, crafts in another).

So here's a new system: a junk tracker. At the end of your allotted sorting time, number the store-away box. Also number an index card to correspond to the box. It will take five minutes to list all the items in your store-away box, then file the index card in a recipe container. When you need that extra phone, you can go through the index file and find the numbered box in which it is stored. Then you can venture to the basement and pinpoint the exact box.

▶ **Take it away.** Laundry is the clutter king in many homes, especially when there isn't room for dirty laundry or drawer space for the clean clothes. Here are some ideas to make dirty clothes less intimidating:

   ▶ Designate one area in the home or in each bedroom for dirty laundry.
   ▶ Train everyone, including yourself, to pick up his or her own dirty clothes.
   ▶ Make everyone put his or her own clothes away.
   ▶ Sort clean laundry as soon as possible.
   ▶ Use pillowcases for laundry bags.
   ▶ Assign one dresser for no more than two people.
   ▶ Discover hangers. They really work.

> **CREATIVE LAUNDRY BAGS**
>
> Have the kids create their own laundry bags. Purchase inexpensive pillowcases with large hems. Cut holes near the opening of the pillowcases and feed cords through the hems to create drawstrings. Allow kids to decorate their bags with fabric paints. Hang the laundry bags from hooks, nails, or bedposts. Be sure the bottom of the bag rests on a floor or other flat surface to support its weight.

■ **I'm starting to get the hang of this showdown with the Clutter Gang. What else can I do to run these "varmints" out of my home?**

Try some creative decluttering. In other words, learn to be creative with your clutter. Train your mind to think that if there's a purpose for it, there must be a place for it. Find a "home" for all important items. Sometimes you have to be creative. But with a little imagination and some effort, you can find a place for all the items you need. Here are a few ideas for getting your clutter-zapping juices flowing:

- ▶ **Shelve it.** In many homes, shelves rule. You might install one wall-length shelf and two smaller ones in your children's room. Use sturdy boxes, or fruit boxes from your local grocer for the toys, and place them on the shelves. You might also use stained shelves above your desk and over the children's project table. You can also put one more shelf in each closet to better use the space between the existing shelf and the ceiling.

CREATIVE SHELVING

Shelves can add character and charm to your home with a few creative touches:
- ▶ Cover with material or printed self-adhesive paper
- ▶ Paint to match your color scheme
- ▶ Stencil patterns on your shelves or frame around them
- ▶ Use a glue gun to put lace or ruffles around the edges
- ▶ Cover shelved boxes with printed self-adhesive paper

- ▶ **Hang it.** Some items can go on the wall or ceiling. Hang your son's toy space vehicle from a hook over his bed, and mount his kite on the wall above his dresser. Hang your daughter's frilly pink umbrella on the wall next to a picture. Electronic games and card sets can hang on hooks on the side of your child's shelves to give the room a playful toy store appearance.

    Hanging baskets add character and storage space to any room. In the kitchen you can store your bread, cookie cutters, or fruits and vegetables in hanging baskets. Hang your plants or potpourri in the living room. The bathroom or bedroom makes a great place for hanging hair ties and beauty supplies. Action figures or those tiny toys from fast-food restaurants hang well in the kids' rooms. By hanging items from the ceiling or walls, you free up other space that can be used more effectively.

- ▶ **Group it.** Another great way to minimize clutter is to group items that belong together. Keep books, tapes, CDs, and videos with their own kind. This system works for all items in your home, not just clutter. Put craft items in attractive storage containers. Drawing paper, coloring books, crayons, and other kid-friendly art supplies need a home as well.

▶ **Delegate it.** Kids love order, despite how much they moan and groan when we tell them to put things where they belong. The benefits outweigh the complaints. Who knows? The kids may find clutter-free rooms pretty handy when they're searching for their baseball gloves or homework.

Remember, clutter didn't just ride into town one night and decide to take up residence. Your odds and ends took months, years, and maybe even decades to settle in your home. So start small and work your way back through the piles. As each cluttered area is conquered, you will regain control of your home. And that's enough to make any *hombre* smile.

This material is adapted from writings by Cindy Jacobs, who remains at her homestead in Mishawaka, Indiana.

CREATIVE STORAGE

Finding a home for everything can be challenging and fun. Here are a few different ways of storing things.

▶ Plastic bags that seal. These are great for storing game pieces, cards, and other small items that might scatter around the house.

▶ Sturdy boxes. Since they come in all sizes, boxes store tools, sewing items, crafts, hair ties, videos, and clothing. For an added touch, cover them with self-adhesive paper to correspond with your decor.

▶ Shoe bags. Besides holding shoes, these can be used to hold stockings, lingerie, scarves, mittens, or jewelry.

▶ Video storage units. These hang securely on the inside of closet doors and provide excellent organized shelving for your movies.

▶ Under-the-bed storage units. Great for toys or bedding.

▶ Large envelopes. Store your children's important items. Write their names on the envelopes and keep their certificates, ribbons, artwork, report cards, and other achievement records inside. Use another envelope to hold their birth certificates and Social Security cards.

3

Let's Talk Turkey (and about Christmas)

. . . .

■ I love being a classroom volunteer for my son's kindergarten class. As part of a Thanksgiving Day assignment last year, I walked around the classroom and wrote down things the students were thankful for.

Naturally, with the holidays fast approaching, Christmas was mentioned by many of the boys and girls. When I asked several students if they knew whose birthday was celebrated on Christmas Day, they had no idea. Not only was that sad and shocking, but it opened my eyes to their ignorance of our culture.

What can I do when public schools turn Thanksgiving into just another multicultural event and flat-out ignore Christmas?

There are a few things you can do, but at least in your son's school, the teacher still emphasized being thankful during Thanksgiving. But from Plymouth, Massachusetts to Santa Claus, California, millions of public school students are being miseducated about Thanksgiving and Christmas. More frightening is that some teachers are being threatened or intimidated into censoring any mention of the religious side of the holidays.

Robin Woodworth of Boothwyn, Pennsylvania was shocked at the censorship in her son's classroom. He came home from school one day explaining that when he wrote "Merry Christmas" on the chalkboard, the teacher made him erase it for fear she would get in trouble.

One kindergarten teacher in Charlotte, North Carolina said that the Christmas program at her school was changed to "The Five Senses of Winter" and the word Christmas was not allowed to be uttered at school.

■ It's so sad to see little ones who don't have a clue about why we celebrate Christmas. How did this happen?

Very slowly, but the secularization of religious holidays is nearly complete. Schools now have "winter concerts" instead of Christmas concerts. Caroling is out, Christmas trees are taboo, and even red and green colors are banned from bulletin board during December in some schools—lest someone think Christmas is being promoted.

The move to completely secularize Thanksgiving and Christmas has come about for two reasons: misconceptions about court rulings on how to handle religion in public schools and deliberate attempts by some to alter our culture.

The National Association for the Education of Young Children, which is composed of thousands of preschool and elementary teachers, publishes an "Anti-Bias Curriculum" that attacks the holidays.

For Thanksgiving, this organization encourages teachers to focus on the plight of Native Americans. The association suggests that teachers use the holiday to confront bias against the Indians: "Talk about what is fair and unfair, what helps us learn about Native Americans, what hurts their feelings."

In outlining her approach, a preschool program director in Pasadena, California sent the following message to parents: "To many Native American peoples today, Thanksgiving is a day of mourning because it is a reminder that in return for their help, knowledge, and tolerance of original European settlers, they were 'repaid' with the theft of their land and the genocide of their people."

What her students will not learn is that during the first Thanksgiving—celebrated in 1621—the Pilgrims feasted, prayed, and sang songs of praise to God for three days. They will not learn that in his Thanksgiving Day proclamation in 1789, George Washington said, "It is the duty of all nations to acknowledge the providence of Almighty God, to obey His will, to be grateful for His benefits, and humbly to implore His protection and favor."

Nor will they learn that Abraham Lincoln established Thanksgiving in 1863 as a national holiday specifically to give thanks to God for the blessings we have received during the previous year. Thanksgiving was never intended to be a history lesson about the "invasion" of the Pilgrims, and nowhere was it established to be a multicultural lesson about the plight of Native Americans.

Yet the trend is to distort Thanksgiving—and Christmas as well. For the latter, the "Anti-Bias" handbook suggests three options:

▶ Integrate December holidays from several cultural groups into one nonreligious celebration.

▶ Observe December holidays other than Christmas.

▶ Don't observe December holidays at all in the classroom.

The teacher-trainers fail to see the hypocrisy of suggesting an obvious bias against Christmas and Christians in their "antibias" handbook. In fact, many teachers give lessons about Hanukkah in December, but steer clear of Christmas. When challenged on this, educators claim that teaching about Hanukkah is multicultural, while teaching about Christmas violates the separation of church and state.

■ **In the midst of these cultural attacks, is there any good news to report?**

Many parents and teachers are beginning to gently restore traditional holidays to their schools. The movement to guard the holidays from censorship is just beginning, but it is growing and gaining momentum.

Eric Buehrer, a former public school teacher, knows that the best way to restore the holidays to the classroom is to convince educators that it is not only legal, but it is the right thing to do as well. It is not enough to simply change the school district's policy. We must help the teacher see the holidays as important cultural lessons.

Due to the widespread discrimination against Christmas, Buehrer wrote "A Gift for Teacher"—an eight-page Christmas card that parents can give to their children's teachers. It expresses, in a nonthreatening way, how public school teachers can *legally* teach about Jesus' birth without violating the Constitution and how the ACLU even lost a landmark case when it tried to stop a school district from having a very permissive policy for teaching about religious holidays.

At first the card was a local project, and Eric and his wife, Kim, distributed about 500 cards in Southern California. But the idea caught on. In the last few years, parents and teachers across the country have ordered more than 50,000 cards! Their goal now is to inform every public school teacher, administrator, and school board member how religious holidays can legally be taught (see page 203).

■ How can teachers legally teach about Thanksgiving and Christmas?

It all stems from an incident in 1979, when the Sioux Falls (South Dakota) school district was sued by the American Civil Liberties Union because of its policy that permitted the observance of religious holidays. In 1980, the U.S. Court of Appeals for the Eighth Circuit upheld the constitutionality of the school policy, and this ruling has not been overturned. The policy reads as follows:

It is accepted that no religious belief or nonbelief should be promoted by the school district or its employees, and none should be disparaged. Instead, the school district should encourage all students and staff members to appreciate and be tolerant of each other's religious views. The school district should utilize its opportunity to foster understanding and mutual respect among students and parents, whether it involves race, culture, economic background, or religious beliefs.

In that spirit of tolerance, students and staff members should be excused from participating in practices that are contrary to their religious beliefs unless there are clear issues of overriding concern that would prevent it.

The use of religious symbols such as a cross, menorah, crescent, Star of David, crèche, symbols of Native American religions, or other symbols that are a part of religious holidays are permitted as a teaching aid or resource, provided that such symbols are displayed as examples of the cultural and religious heritage of the holiday and are temporary in nature. Among these holidays are included Christmas, Easter, Passover, Hanukkah, St. Valentine's Day, St. Patrick's Day, Thanksgiving, and Halloween.

■ What is it about the "Gift for Teacher" cards that make them work?

Hearts and minds are best changed in the context of relationships, which is why Bev Remillard, a mother of two in Laguna Hills, California, used the card to open a dialogue with her children's teachers.

"The card was a nonthreatening tool for expressing what I felt," she said. "It made it easier for me to approach my children's teachers knowing I had documentation to back me up."

Leann Havekost of Mazon, Illinois gave her son's first-grade teacher a card. "She really enjoyed it," Leann said. "She just didn't realize she could teach so much about Christmas. And this is in a school that is fairly friendly toward Christian issues!"

Another mother said she and a friend handed a card to each of their children's teachers. "One of the teachers said that because of it, she would teach the real Christmas story for the first time in her ten years of teaching," this mother recalled. "The other teacher said that while she has always taught that Jesus was born on Christmas, she didn't feel liberated to have the children sing Christmas carols until she received the card. When my neighbor and I heard this, we jumped up and down and wept!"

WHAT THE CARDS ARE ALL ABOUT

The Thanksgiving Day card "Talking Turkey About Thanksgiving" tells the humorous story of a talking turkey who visits a public school teacher and explains the real purpose for the holiday. He explains the history of Thanksgiving and why it is a national holiday.

For Christmas, "A Gift for Teacher" is a nonthreatening eight-page card that expresses how public school teachers can teach about Christ's birth. The card tells the lighthearted story of Santa visiting a public school teacher on Christmas Eve, only to learn that the instructor doesn't teach about the real reason for the season.

To order Thanksgiving and Christmas cards, write to Gateways to Better Education, P.O. Box 514, Lake Forest, CA 92630, or call (800) 929-1163. You can order any combination of Thanksgiving and Christmas cards (envelopes included) for $4 each (minimum order two cards), 10 for $35, 50 for $150, or 100 for $275 (shipping and handling included). California residents, please add 7.75 percent sales tax.

■ **Do the teachers have to do the teaching on Thanksgiving and Christmas, or should they bring in a church pastor?**

No, you don't want to invite a pastor into the public school. But when teachers don't want to teach about the holiday themselves, they can invite parents to visit the class and explain to the children what the holiday means to them. Carolyn Strickland of Raleigh, North Carolina said, "My success amazed me. Last year I told the Christmas and Easter stories in my child's public school classroom."

Virginia Olson of Wichita, Kansas wrote: "I gave a card to both my children's teachers, and one teacher responded by inviting me to tell the biblical account of Christmas in her third-grade classroom. She had cleared it with the principal, who had no objections or cautions, so I used a flannel graph to tell the Christmas story." The teacher later told Virginia that in her twenty years of teaching, she had never had a parent come in and tell the Christmas story to her class.

■ **I can imagine that the Christian teachers are overjoyed to learn something about these cards. Is it because no one ever told them they could legally teach about Thanksgiving and Christmas?**

You've got it. "Before I received my card," one teacher said, "someone had posted one in the teachers' lounge under the caption: 'Do you know your rights?' Nativity pictures have come out of the bottom drawers where they have been hiding for years!"

Fourth-grade teacher Karen Mutschler of Irvine, California read aloud to the class the Christmas story from the Bible, had her students listen to and discuss Christmas carols, and finished up with an art project in which the students made Nativity scenes. Isn't it refreshing to hear what teachers will do when they really understand the law?

■ **What can the teachers teach about Thanksgiving?**

Teachers need to know that it is perfectly legal—and constitutes an important cultural lesson—to explain the real history and purpose of Thanksgiving. The Supreme Court recognizes the holiday as a national religious celebration, and previous U.S. Presidents have called on Americans to use Thanksgiving Day to express appreciation to God for His blessings.

This material is adapted from writings by Eric Buehrer, president of Gateways to Better Education in Lake Forest, California.

4

Taming the TV,
Deciding What's Right

....

■ One evening during the Christmas holidays, our family gathered in the den to watch television. The kids had played all day outside in the snow, and I had done my Christmas baking in the afternoon. We were all bushed and prepared for a relaxing time of entertainment.

Bud's flicker landed on one of those Thursday night sitcoms, and it soon became apparent that all the jokes had to do with masturbation. Click. The next show showed two lesbians in bed. They weren't doing anything, but we didn't wait around to find out what would happen next. Click. We landed on one of those reality-based cop shows, which showed bad guys sticking guns into people's ears and pulling the trigger.

We've always limited the kids' TV viewing, so it had been awhile since we took a chance and decided to see "what's on." Normally, all we watch are sporting events or rental videos. Will the TV ever be safe for the family?

Probably not, if you rely on the standard network fare of sitcoms and made-for-TV movies. And if you get a "premium channel" like HBO or Showtime, you can figure that anything on after 8 P.M. is rated R for steamy sex scenes and blood-soaked violence.

For TV to be safe, you'll have to be as sly as a fox in determining whether the upcoming program will be suitable for your family. You'll have to read broadcast descriptions, interpret newspaper reviews, and preview some of these shows yourself.

If you do, you can pretty much write off any of the networks' "situation comedies." They use humor to bring down your defenses, all the while standing on a soapbox and preaching: Homosexuality is OK. Premarital sex is cool and exciting. Parents don't know anything. Dads are dolts.

"Movies of the week" can be hit-or-miss affairs, however. Some, like ones presented by Hallmark, are noted for their high production values and respect for traditional morality. A story might be about an 1850s frontier family trying to get its wagon to California before the snow flies or a family dealing with a deadly disease. Those two-hour presentations can lift the spirit and are worth watching.

But you have to be vigilant about network "docudramas," which might be the two-hour story about a gay elementary school teacher who fights "prejudice" in his small town. Believe us, these shows have an agenda—i.e., homosexuality is normal and anyone who's against gays and lesbians is a religious nut, homophobe, or bigot.

You may not know this, but TV writers are taking you and your values on, as are the producers of network newsmagazine shows such as ABC's "20/20" and NBC's "Dateline." Rarely are Christian values held up as worth emulating.

■ That's depressing. So what should I do?

The easy answer would be to not watch TV. This would be an extreme step for many families. For those who have junked the idiot box, however, they say that they could never go back. But that approach is not realistic for many families, which we expect is the case for you and your family.

While TV has the awesome ability to change a culture, it also provides a window to the world. There are many worthwhile things to watch on TV, especially news and sports. If you are going to have a TV and want to keep viewing under control, do these two things:

1. Have no more than one TV in the home. Some families have TVs everywhere you look: the kitchen, master bedroom, family room, kids' bedrooms, and basement. But having one TV forces the contraption to be a *family* TV, so that when it's on, watching it becomes a family activity and gives everyone a bit of accountability. You don't want the kids running off to their TVs because you and your spouse give up control of what they watch.

2. Make your TV time count by watching good shows. Here's the rule: No casual viewing or sitting around surfing through the channels, just to "see what's on." Simply put, TV viewing should be intentional. It should be for a predetermined time. *Jason, you can watch the second half of the basketball game, but then you have to finish working in the yard.*

Begin by looking in the *TV Guide* or your local newspaper to see what's on. Read the program descriptions or upcoming previews. If the reviewer gushes that a certain program "breaks new ground" on the issue of gays in the workforce, you can be sure that this would not be a program suitable for family viewing.

■ Is cable TV worth $30 a month?

The short answer: Yes. The four networks—ABC, NBC, CBS, and Fox—produce plenty of raunchy programs. Not that cable TV is much better, but investing in cable or satellite dish TV means you can pipe in the History Channel, the Family Channel, Discovery, Arts and Entertainment, and other channels that often have entertaining shows the entire family can enjoy. A new channel—called the Food Network—shows different chefs whipping up delectable delights twenty-four hours a day.

If you have a lot of boys in the household, sporting events are usually safe, although the players seem to be using more bad language than ever.

Another idea is to use the VCR to your advantage. You can rent movies or tape something decent on TV for later viewing. For instance, let's say an interesting program on the rise of Adolf Hitler is on the History Channel. Nobody wants to watch it at 2 in the afternoon, but you can tape for viewing that night.

Make the technology work for you. You don't have to be a captive audience for standard network fare.

■ **I have a neighbor down the street who's on the local school board. She's liberal on social issues, and she knows I'm conservative. We both like to walk our dogs, and lately we've been walking together and discussing what our children are exposed to in movies and television.**

I've been trying to be nonconfrontational yet firm in where I stand. Every time I talk about not letting my children see the latest episode of a controversial show she says that I'm "censoring" shows for my teenagers, and that I'm selling their "education in life short."

I don't want to be argumentative, but I need some calm, reassuring points that will help her see where I'm coming from. Got any tips?

We're glad you asked. Let's do a little role-playing here. The boldface type will be your neighbor using the standard liberal point-of-view on the media. The regular type can be your response:

"So, not letting your teens see a controversial show is just the same as censoring it. Do you believe in censorship?"

When you hear this question, simply turn it around and ask her, "Well, do you believe in censorship?"

She will answer, "No, I do not."

Then say, "Well, do you believe it would be OK to show a child being molested on television?" Unless your friend is totally devoid of morals, taste, and common sense, she will have climbed into her own trap.

Point out that ever since communication began, there has been censorship. Every word ever printed, every word ever aired has been censored. It all depends on who is doing the censoring. Are you for government censorship of usual programming? No. But since other people decided they were going to produce and air that raunchy episode, you have the right to decide whether or not your children will see it.

"But I don't think we should shield our children from life's realities. Sex is part of society, and people can say whatever they want."

Some people would like to see a film on child pornography. Shouldn't they have that right? That some people would like to see something on a movie screen is no reason that the film should be made. Say that it is your family's desire that all programs add to or make a positive contribution to our cultural, social, mental, emotional, and spiritual heritage in an informative and entertaining manner. There's no compelling reason you see for a film or program to exploit our prurient nature.

Yes, our media should deal with the real world. But love, truth, compassion, beauty, and other positive values are also part of the real world. Why should films and TV programs dwell primarily on the ugly and ignore that which is beautiful?

"But what right do you have to tell me what I can watch?"

None. But at the same time, you don't have the right to tell me what I *should* watch.

"So if you don't like what's on television, turn it off. That will solve the problem. Just don't tell me what I can and can't watch."

It's not as simple as you make it out to be. Would you also say to me that if you don't like crime in the streets, stay in the house? Would you say to me if you don't like drunk drivers, stay off the streets?

Here's a case in point. A few years ago, a mother and her young daughter watched an exceptionally good movie on television titled *Born Free*. When the same network (NBC) carried a movie titled *Born Innocent*, the mother and daughter thought it might be the same type of movie and began to watch.

Very early in the program, there was a graphic scene of a young girl being raped with a plumber's helper. The mother immediately flicked to another program. The mother said such scenes should not be permitted because some child could be negatively impressed and commit the same act.

Two days later, her nine-year-old daughter was raped with a beer bottle by a gang of children and youth. They were imitating the movie they had seen on television.

Then there was the movie that showed young people lying down in the middle of the street playing "chicken" with cars. Not until there had been one or two "copycat" deaths did the film studio pull the movie.

The fact is, we live in a society, not as a group of isolated strangers. I care deeply about our society, about our families, and about my neighbors. I want our community to be the best possible environment in which to live, work, and raise our children. The fact is that impressionable young people can be influenced to act on what they see. I don't see that as a positive for our society.

"Watching films or television never corrupted anyone. Look at me, I turned out fine."

Using that argument, then films and TV never helped anyone. The truth of the matter is that good shows project good images and poor shows project poor images. We should remember that all media are educational, and we need to ask ourselves what the media are teaching us.

The way I see it, popular films and TV programs teach that sex has no morals attached, that violence is an acceptable way to solve conflict, that profanity is acceptable language, and that homosexuality is OK. That is not what I'm teaching my children.

"But you can't legislate morality."

On its face, this cliché is absurd because every law legislates morality. Every law sets some standard for its citizens, and every citizen must ultimately make the moral decision to obey or disobey.

This chapter is adapted from The Home Invaders *(Victor Books) by Donald E. Wildmon, founder of the American Family Association in Tupelo, Mississippi.*

5

Supermarket Sweep

. . . .

■ **I just came out of the grocery store with only six bags of groceries but $127.34 lighter in my checkbook. And I know I'll be back at the end of the week to shop for the weekend. How can I save money at the supermarket?**

The high cost of groceries is frustrating, but chances are, with a little planning and know-how, you can buy much more than you're buying right now without spending more. You need to be flexible and buy what's on sale, purchase store brands rather than more-expensive name brands, buy in bigger quanitities, and stock up when there's a big sale. In other words, you have to be rather intentional about what you do in the supermarket.

To get the most out of your hard-earned dollars, you begin by taking charge of your grocery shopping. Set a realistic limit on spending. Could you get by with $125 a week instead of $175? If so, that's an extra $200 a month in your pocket! Go to the store rested and well-fed, with a list and a general menu plan in mind, but as mentioned before, you have to flexible to snap up those bargains. Of course, it helps to know prices so you're not getting fooled. Don't let supermarket displays manipulate you into buying what you don't need.

Second, shop the cheapest store in your area, and you won't know *for sure* which one that is until you comparison shop. Take a price notebook with you and shop a different store each week until you've hit all the supermarkets in your area of town. Write down prices of staples that usually land in your cart: milk, cheese, veggies, bread, cereal, juices, meat, and desserts. When the results are in, you can make an intelligent decision on where to purchase the least expensive food.

■ **But that's too much work, writing down so many prices. Can't I just buy what's on sale?**

Of course you can. Each supermarket advertises "specials of the week" or "buy one, get one free" that can really stretch your food dollar. Plan your menus around these specials. In other words, if chicken fryers are on sale for 39 cents a pound but your family is hankering for sirloin tip at $4.59 a pound, you should be eating barbecued chicken and stir-fry that week. You have to learn to go with the flow.

■ **When my husband goes grocery shopping, it's always a disaster. He fills the cart with every kind of chip known to man, "comfort food" such as Hostess Twinkies, and expensive Häagen-Dazs ice cream. How can I convince him that he just blew our food budget for the month?**

By showing him—right on the receipt—the high cost of convenience foods. Anytime someone else does the baking, cooking, or cutting, you're going to pay extra. Convenience food prices are 50 percent, 100 percent more, but you, as a smart shopper, can find cheaper substitutions. For example, instead of expensive name-brand cereal for breakfast, substitute oatmeal, whole wheat pancakes, muffins, or scrambled eggs.

■ **Cereal. Why does it cost $4.59 for twelve ounces of flakes and flavoring?**

The main culprits: packaging and advertising. But there are ways to beat the high cost of name-brand cereals. These days, supermarkets routinely sell "knock-off" versions of the same cereal—and for 30 to 40 percent less. For instance, you can buy a cereal that looks like Post Grape Nuts, smells like Grape Nuts, and tastes like Grape Nuts, but it will be called "Nutty Nuggets" and be sold under the house brand.

Look for the little displays that say "Compare to the national brand and save!" If you can get over having to purchase what your kids see advertised on Saturday morning cartoon shows, you can save tons of money.

But name-brand cereal makers are fighting back. Recently, some manufacturers have begun selling their cereal in resealable bags, cutting packaging costs and knocking a dollar or two off the price of the cereal. But generally speaking, you're right: cereal prices are too high.

■ What are some other tips about navigating the grocery aisles?

Let the store personnel help you. Invariably, you'll find the staff friendly and eager to please. Let them point out some of the deals of the week. The produce manager can tell you which fruits and vegetables are in season and cheapest. And did you know that you can ask for discounts on bruised fruit? If you're going to make a batch of banana bread, you can purchase overripe bananas for pennies on the dollar.

Butchers can recommend good, inexpensive cuts and suggest ways of tenderizing and cooking the meat. Some butchers will even sharpen your cutting knives for free!

■ I'm afraid I never learned to cook, so I feel inadequate in the kitchen. I know how much take-out food and restaurants cost us, so I'm determined to give the kitchen another try. Where do I start?

You might consider the "15-Minute Cooking" program devised by Rhonda Barfield, a home-schooling mom of four children in Missouri. Her system is pretty basic: assemble a good, home-cooked dinner in short sessions, one in the morning and one right before the evening meal.

■ This sounds great. How does it work?

For example, start a chicken-and-vegetable soup in the slow cooker first thing in the morning, along with making a Jell-O dessert. That evening when dinner rolls around, prepare meatloaf and cornbread, which takes only ten minutes. While they cook in the oven, dice some carrot coins for your veggies.

On another morning, mix up poppyseed muffins and later that afternoon, you can bake a chicken in the oven while rice cooks on the stovetop. Assemble a lettuce salad, and voila, you have a nice meal.

Under Rhonda's system, mealtime is more relaxed because everything is organized ahead of time. You won't be tempted to eat out as much. But best of all, this way of cooking will encourage your family to sit down together at evening meals because you really have something to look forward to.

■ I don't think I'm sold on this 15-Minute Cooking. You're going to have to do better than this.

OK, consider these benefits:

► Much-lower-than-average grocery bills, even with growing children
► Fresh food, hot entrées, homemade breads, tasty salads, and luscious desserts
► Once-a-week grocery shopping (no more last-minute trips for ingredients)
► Healthier meals that consist of foods lower than average in fat, sodium, and sugar
► Plenty of food left over every day to serve for tomorrow's breakfast and lunch
► Stockpiled foods in your freezer: your own tasty, low-cost convenience foods

With a little practice and imagination, "15-Minute Cooking" is an excellent way to wisely manage both the time and money God gives us.

This article is adapted from writings by Rhonda Barfield.

6

What's Cooking Tonight?

. . . .

■ **Picture this: It's 5:32 P.M., and I've just walked in the front door. Work was demanding, I'm exhausted, the boys will be home from practice soon, and my husband will pull into the garage in twenty minutes. Becky has to baby-sit in an hour, and Annie needs help with her math homework. And I have to think about dinner.**

This is a typical scene at our house. Often, my frustrating dinner choice is between popping some frozen entrees in the microwave or bringing home fast food, which is lower in quality and more expensive. Short of hiring a cook, what can I do?

There is a solution to your dilemma: cooking systems such as the "15-Minute Cooking" program that was discussed in the last chapter. But Rhonda Barfield's cooking system isn't the only one out there. There are two others that offer detailed, step-by-step plans for daily meal preparation that can be especially helpful in meeting the needs of busy parents.

Generally speaking, cooking systems concentrate your preparation time into blocks, saving precious minutes and even hours in your day. They also save hundreds—sometimes thousands—of dollars annually because they help you avoid a cart full of convenience foods during a last-minute trip to the supermarket. Finally, cooking systems help you shop smarter and cook more nutritious meals.

In addition to the advantages of saving time and money and enhancing nutrition, cooking systems also offer different styles to fit your family's needs.

■ **Cooking systems? I'm open to any suggestions that will help me with this dinner-hour crisis.**

Let's take a look at three systems—once-a-month cooking, mega-cooking, and 15-minute cooking—so you can decide which, if any, could work for you.

Once-a-month cooking. Mimi Wilson, who wrote the book *Once-A-Month Cooking* with Mary Beth Lagerborg, says: "I developed this plan because I felt I had to do something drastic to squeeze more time into my day. I had three young children, a busy husband, and guests at our home two or three times a week. I used time studies to see where I wasted the most minutes, and I found it was in making meals from scratch every day."

Mimi also wanted to reduce food waste and have a ministry of spontaneous hospitality. So once-a-month cooking enabled the both of them to reach their goals by cooking a month's (or two weeks') worth of dinner entrées in a single day, then freezing them.

In their book, Mimi and Mary Beth have taken care of the planning for busy cooks. All you have to do is choose a menu that includes low-fat fare, company dishes, and plenty of good "kid food." For your part, you will need to set aside a couple of hours of supermarket shopping and a *really* long day of cooking—perhaps into the evening. But the result is a month's worth of entrées. As Mary Beth points out, "When it's done, it's *done*."

All thirty entrées, some packaged in plastic bags, will fit into a refrigerator freezer when the preparation is complete.

The *Once-A-Month Cooking* book does all the planning for you, outlining exactly what dishes to prepare and when. Mary Beth and Mimi also detail tips for shopping, cooking, freezing, saving money, and adapting the system to your own recipes. In addition to recipes for entrées, there is also a chapter of "More Recipes to Enhance Meals."

■ **I'm not sure I'm ready for once-a-month cooking. Right now I can barely stand the thought of being in the kitchen for an hour at a time, so cooking all day is beyond me. What's my next choice?**

Well, you're probably not going to like this one either. It's called mega-cooking, and you prepare six months' worth of entrees at one time—another long period in the kitchen.

The idea was cooked up by Jill Bond, who, along with her husband, Alan, and their four children, work together for most of a weekend preparing about 180 entrees. They cook huge batches of chili, sweet-and-sour meatballs, chicken entrees, and thirty to forty other kinds of dishes—all divided into dinner-sized servings and frozen for later use. This system differs from once-a-month cooking in that many batches of the same dish are all prepared at one time.

Mega-cooking, especially when preparing nearly 200 meals, can seem overwhelming for the beginner. "It doesn't have to be," Jill says. She suggests you start small, perhaps with something as simple as tripling tonight's lasagna recipe and freezing two portions.

Dinner's in the Freezer is Jill's home-management book describing her cooking system. More than fifty sample recipes are included, but readers are encouraged to use their own favorites. Her book provides several blank forms, such as "Tasks to Be Done" and "Sample Timing Chart," as well as plenty of good advice and interesting anecdotes.

■ **I like the idea of making a double batch of meatloaf or lasagna, but there's no way I'm going to make 200 meals for the freezer. What's your third suggestion?**

Rhonda Barfield, whose "15-Minute Cooking" was introduced in the last chapter, says her cooking system breaks food preparation time into two short, daily sessions. The evening meal is started in the morning (or the night before), then finished right before dinner. Quantities are large to allow for some leftovers for breakfast and/or lunch the next day. Once a week, on Day Five of each menu, a "leftovers meal" (soup, casserole, etc.) is featured, so little food is wasted.

■ **The 15-Minute Cooking plan would appear to be the best one for me right now, but what else do I need to consider before I make a decision?**

Each cooking system has its strengths and weaknesses. It all depends on how you prefer to manage your time. If you prefer meal preparation in large blocks, once-a-month cooking or mega-cooking are better choices for you. If you like to do a little cooking each day, then go with 15-Minute Cooking.

Obviously, mega-cooking shopping has the lowest cost per meal because food can be bought in mega-quantities. You can buy "warehouse club" portions of beef and chicken at Sam's Club or Costco, as well as large tins of canned vegetables and fruits.

■ **So, which system is best for me?**

Actually, that decision is up to you, but there's no reason why all three couldn't be used by the same family chef. Busy families need to save every bit of time, money, and energy they can muster. Cooking systems can help on all counts.

This material is adapted from writings by Rhonda Barfield.

RESOURCES FOR FURTHER READING

Dinner's in the Freezer by Jill Bond is available in Christian bookstores nationwide. Or call the publisher, Great Christian Books, at (800) 775-5422, to order.

Once-A-Month Cooking by Mimi Wilson and Mary Beth Lagerborg is available in both Christian and secular bookstores nationwide. Or call Focus on the Family at (800) 232-6459 to request a copy.

15-Minute Cooking by Rhonda Barfield is available by calling Great Christian Books at (800) 775-5422 or by ordering directly from the Barfields at Lilac Publishing, P.O. Box 665, St. Charles, MO 63302. Cost of the book is $12.95.

TIPS FOR HEALTHIER EATING

Tacos: Skip the meat altogether. Substitute beans or refried beans. Season rice with picante or taco sauce.

Cornbread: Substitute half whole wheat flour plus half white flour for all white flour. Substitute 1/4 cup applesauce for 1/4 cup oil. Substitute 4 egg whites for 2 whole eggs.

Graham cracker desserts: Serve graham crackers with sugar-free fruit spread.

7

Never
Pay Retail

. . . .

■ I was standing in the ladies' dresses section of an upscale department store. It was a few minutes before 8 o'clock on a Saturday evening, and a couple of dozen women and I were anticipating the next "dress riot," a ten-minute clearance sale on specially marked clothes.

"Why do you call these 'dress riots'?" I casually asked one of the salepeople.

"Oh, we don't like to use that term, but that's what they really are," she replied. "You should have seen the dress riot this afternoon. Two women grabbed a $229 navy-and-white Pendleton ensemble at the same time, and then began fighting over it. It was marked down to $19.99. You should have seen them rolling on the floor, trying to pull the dress from each other's grasp. Finally, our store manager took a bullhorn and announced, 'Ladies, if you don't stop right now, I'll have to call security.' "

I was a little surprised. Do things get that crazy at these big sales?

They sure do. If you ever want to witness all-out, aggressive shopping, then watch a couple of dozen women—and a few brave men—when clerks wheel racks of expensive dresses onto the floor, all marked down to pennies on the dollar. Bedlam is sure to break out, and you can even expect to see some shoppers brusquely sweep everything off the rack—twenty or more dresses at a pop. The feeding frenzy can leave the clothes racks resembling goldfish carcasses stripped by a school of piranha.

■ Dress riots don't sound like my thing because I'm not into any of those "moonlight madness sales"—the sixteen-hour, shop-until-you-drop bargain bonanzas.

That's OK, but know that some women really get into the big sales, finding good buys in everything from women's accessories to dresses to casual wear to shoes. One supershopper in Colorado, Lou Gage, took all of her buys home and laid them out on the living room floor, where she added up the receipts and compared them to the original retail amounts.

On one particular shopping excursion, Lou spent just over $500, but the regular retail amount would have been $3,085, an 83 percent savings. Actually, this was a down day for Lou. "I've never done worse than 82 percent, and my best is 90 percent," she said. "It's gotten to be a challenge: *How much can I get off?*"

■ Well, how much can you get off when shopping for clothes?

First, you need to get a lay of the shopping land. Granted, most of you aren't going to buy five hundred dollars worth of clothes at a clip, and you may not have dress riots in your town. But Lou's experiences are a reminder that those who seriously shop department store sales can purchase high-quality clothing at a fraction of the original price.

But department stores aren't the only shopping game in town, no sirree. (And that's not even taking into consideration yard sales, consignment stores, and thrift shops.) Let's take an overview of the retail family:

▶ Perched at the high end are **department stores** such as Neiman Marcus, Nordstrom, Hudson's, Saks Fifth Avenue, and Dillard's. They sell merchandise at a full markup but pride themselves on customer service and shopping assistance. Best of all, they have liberal return policies.

▶ **Power retailers,** such as Sears, JCPenney, and Montgomery Ward, have the financial muscle to buy in huge quantities and push vendors for discounts, which can be passed along to consumers. A small markup keeps prices low.

▶ Next we have the **moderate-priced stores,** such as Mervyn's and Miller's Outpost. They buy lower-priced clothes but still sell at a full markup. Customer services are good.

▶ **Discounters** include Target, Kmart, and Wal-Mart, which sell medium-quality clothes at a lower markup and offer fewer shopper services.

▶ Stores such as Ross Dress for Less, Marshalls, and TJ Maxx are called **off-pricers.** They buy from a variety of manufacturers and vendors—or closeouts from department stores— and work off a smaller markup. The selection may be limited and the styles a few months behind. Few special services are offered.

▶ **Closeout stores** include Pic 'n Save (also known as MacFrugal's) and off-site department store outlets, such as Nordstrom Rack and Macy's Clearance Center. They dispose of unsold inventory and returns at rock-bottom prices.

▶ **Warehouse retailers** such as Sam's and Costco buy in huge quantities from manufacturers willing to cut them a good deal. Selection is limited, but with minimal markups, prices are excellent. You won't find a fitting room, however; you have to take the clothes home to try on.

▶ **Factory outlets** have sprung up outside many major cities. Manufacturers such as Nike or Eddie Bauer sell surplus production, returns, and discontinued merchandise in these stores.

■ So how do I play the shopping game with all these choices?

Nearly every retail store has a selling system that boils down to this: move the end-of-the-season merchandise when the next season of clothes arrives. Because stores have to make room for their hot-selling profit-makers, *no one should ever pay retail for clothes.* Someone is always having a sale or just about to have one. Be patient.

■ **But I have to buy a dress for my daughter's eighth-grade graduation, and I've got to buy it soon.**

You will just have to work at it. You start by getting familiar with the way clothing stores sell things. If you can invest a few hours, then you can find *what* you want at a *price* you can afford. You do this by buying clothes off-season or during the stores' big sales three or four times a year.

An example of buying off-season would be walking into Mervyn's a couple of weeks after Labor Day. The summer merchandise has got to go since the fall and holiday stuff is arriving. That means you should buy your children's shorts or short-sleeve shirts after Labor Day—not in the spring, when they're sold at full retail. The same goes for other seasonal items, such as winter coats, gloves, and beach sandals. Although it may seem funny buying a ski jacket in April, you'll be glad you did the following November.

Many people don't shop at department stores because the clothes are expensive. That's understandable when you're paying retail. But if you wait for their once-a-quarter sales, you can purchase high-quality merchandise at 50 percent off or more. Remember, high-quality clothes last longer—and look better.

As for buying on sale, you do that by

► Shopping the department stores' "doorbuster" sales three or four times a year.
► Keeping an eye out for sales at the off-price stores, such as Ross Dress for Less and Marshalls. Many of them are not advertised.
► Checking out the clearance racks.
► Looking for closeouts at the clearance stores.
► Knowing prices so that when a deal comes along, you can pounce on it.

■ **But I have to tell you that I am skeptical of department store sales just because they are so expensive in the first place.**

Yes, but those huge department store chains sell clothes for dimes and nickels on the dollar to rid themselves of excess inventory headaches. You will see great prices on leather handbags, shower curtains, towels, small area rugs, kids' shoes, linens, bedspreads, and pillows—items hard to buy on discount.

■ **Before attending a big department store sale, how do I get adequately prepared?**

► **Check your expenditures for the month.** Do you have enough set aside to do some clothes shopping?

► **Know what you want to buy.** Does your husband need some new dress shirts? Do your teenage son's Levis have holes? Make a list.

► **Go the night before when the markdowns are being made.** Typically, all the advertised markdowns are made between 6 P.M. and closing. If you find something you like, you can usually buy it at the next day's discounted price. All you have to do is ask.

► **On the morning of the sale, the first thing you should do is ask for the ten-minute special sheet and the ad for the "doorbusters."** You can usually find these at the store's information counter. If the salespeople say they don't make these sale sheets available to the public, ask to look at them. They generally will not refuse such a request. Be sure to take notes of the ten-minute specials' "batting order."

► **Scan the ten-minute special sheet and figure out which ones you can skip.** You can use that time to run things out to the car, get a bite to eat, or visit the restroom.

► **Don't carry a purse; use a fanny pack.** You need freedom and flexibility as you hurry from one ten-minute special to the next.

► **Arrive five minutes before the store opens.** Early birds really do get the best worms, especially at the doorbusters which run from eight to eleven in the morning. In blowout sales, the size selection is often skimpy.

▶ **Follow the ten-minute specials.** These are the extra markdowns made on clearance merchandise that has already been marked down several times. You have to be fast on your feet.

▶ **Shop for classic styles.** Buy jackets, slacks, skirts, shoes, belts, and purses to match basic color schemes of beige, white, or navy. Don't buy fad items. Buy classic, tasteful color schemes so replacements are easy to find. You can always add an inexpensive accessory to update the style or the color.

▶ **Leave the kids at home.** They'll get bored and you'll get on each other's nerves. Plus, you need to concentrate on the task at hand.

▶ **Taking your husband along can be a two-edged sword.** On the one hand, he can help stand in line at the cash register while you go on to the next special. Then again, he can be a pain.

▶ **Keep your cool.** Like a shrewd Las Vegas poker player, have a spending limit in mind and stick to it.

This chapter is adapted from Saving Money Any Way You Can *by Mike Yorkey. Published by Servant Publications, Ann Arbor, Michigan. Used by permission.*

RATING THE RETAIL OUTLETS

To give you a better overview of the clothes shopping landscape, each retail outlet has been given a "bargain rating" on scale of one to five shopping carts (five being the best). The bargain ratings take into consideration the following variables: the final sales price; quality in comparison to other stores; frequency of sales; selection and size of the inventory.

Some stores are lumped together into one category, some are rated on their own. Keep in mind that we are talking about clearance merchandise and loss leaders. We'll begin with department stores, which are rated as a group since they are regional.

Sometimes major retailers will send merchandise that doesn't sell to other parts of the county or state where the economy is not as strong and the people are poorer, with the assumption that those shoppers will be less picky. If you

continued next page

live in a rural area, for instance, you might find your local Kmart sells dresses and shoes for less than the big-city Kmart.

Department stores

(Macy's, Hudson's, May Co., Marshall Field's, etc.)

Name of sale: varies.

Frequency: three or four times a year.

Best buys: clothes, luggage, silverware, jewelry (not fine jewelry), and household items.

Downside: it's crowded; the hours are long; the doorbusters start early in the morning.

Comment: If you play your cards right, department stores can be a great dollar-for-dollar deal.

Bargain rating: five shopping carts (for a ten-minute special or a doorbuster).

Power retailers

These are separate ratings for the "big three" in this category: Sears, JCPenney, and Montgomery Ward.

Sears

Name of sale: The Great Take-Off, 50 Percent Off Red Tag, or Baby Days.

Frequency: three or four times a year.

Best buys: children's and infants' clothes, baby furniture, paint, and Craftsman tools.

Downside: fashion styles are not on the cutting edge

Comment: Sears has been around forever, and it usually won't hassle you with returns. While not flashy, the chain is dependable.

Bargain rating: two shopping carts.

JCPenney

Name of sale: Red Tag Sale.

Frequency: three or four times a year.

Best buys: ladies' and kids' clothing, accessories, and shoes.

Downside: sales lack variety and certain sizes because you're dealing with end-of-season merchandise.

Comment: JCPenney will take an extra 30 to 50 percent off its clearance price.

Bargain rating: two shopping carts.

continued next page

Montgomery Ward

Name of sale: Clearance Plus.

Frequency: three or four times a year (depending on the volume of seasonal merchandise on hand).

Best buys: apparel.

Downside: limited selection, variety, and size.

Comment: Montgomery Ward doesn't usually take more than 40 percent off the clearance price, and it never features housewares and other hard goods.

Bargain rating: two shopping carts.

Moderate-priced stores

Mervyn's and chains that sell teen clothing represent this category.

Mervyn's

Name of sale: Super Weekend Sale or the 50 Percent Off Clearance Sale

Frequency: twice a year (end of January and late fall).

Best buys: school clothes, nightgowns, lingerie, towels, sheets, comforters, pillows, napkins, and cookie jars.

Downside: limited selection.

Comment: Mervyn's frequently holds sidewalk sales, but you're better off waiting for the Super Weekend Sale.

Bargain rating: three-plus shopping carts.

Miller's Outpost, The Gap, etc. (chains that sell teen clothes)

Name of sale: varies.

Frequency: not very often.

Best buys: Levi's and Dockers.

Downside: The infrequent sales never take more than 25 percent off.

Comment: Occasionally, these stores have clearance racks where you can find slightly damaged items. If your teens are looking for hot fashions, this is the place to go.

Bargain rating: One shopping cart.

The discounters

National chains such as Kmart, Target, and Wal-Mart are the best known stores in this category.

continued next page

Kmart

Name of sale: Blue-Light Specials or After Christmas Clearance.

Frequency: after each season (back-to-school, Christmas, end of summer).

Best buys: family clothes, accessories, shoes, and infants' clothes.

Downside: You have to be willing to buy out-of-season, and variety and selection are limited. And yes, those flashing blue lights are pretty silly.

Comment: You never know when Kmart is going to run a blue light special. You may arrive ten minutes after the last one, and it won't run another one just for you.

Bargain rating: three shopping carts.

Target

Name of sale: Red-Tag specials.

Frequency: quarterly.

Best buys: shoes and toys.

Downside: a reluctance to mark down clothing more than 40 to 50 percent.

Comment: "Tar-zhay," as some folks call the store, has improved its shopping ambiance in recent years, but the chain is reluctant to sell clothes at low, low prices. Its weekly advertised specials, however, are still good deals.

Bargain rating: three shopping carts.

Wal-Mart

Name of sale: Seasonal Clearance.

Frequency: seasonally and after each holiday period.

Best buys: children's clothing, shoes, Christmas toys, and nonperishable food items after holiday periods.

Downside: Wal-Mart doesn't clearance-price household items, hardware, automotive, appliances, and electronics.

Comment: The nation's biggest retailer isn't number one for nothing. You need to drop by often because it offers many "Manager's Unadvertised Specials."

Bargain rating: four shopping carts.

The off-pricers

Chains such as Marshalls, TJ Maxx, and Ross Dress for Less have carved a niche in the market by always selling at a discount.

continued next page

Marshalls

Name of sale: Down-and-Out.

Frequency: two or three times a year (usually February, August, and October).

Best buys: ladies' apparel, shoes, children's clothing, men's sweaters, and some housewares.

Downside: At the beginning of Down-and-Out sales, merchandise is plentiful but the discounts are low. At end of sales, discounts are high but pickings are slim. Selection is depleted daily.

Comment: The Down-and-Out sales last until the clearance merchandise is gone, and that might be one week or three weeks. During that time, the staff is constantly marking down merchandise.

Bargain rating: four shopping carts.

TJ Maxx

Name of sale: Red-Tag or End-of-Season Clearance.

Frequency: seasonally.

Best buys: all apparel.

Downside: TJs is reluctant to take deep cuts like Marshalls. One theory is that each outlet ships the stuff they can't sell to other TJ Maxx stores, where the market is better for that particular line of clothes.

Comment: TJ Maxx does not advertise its sales. Its clearance philosophy is to take the regular merchandise and mark it down only 20 to 30 percent. That's why you should wait a couple of days until the second or third markdown.

Bargain rating: two shopping carts.

Ross Dress for Less

Name of sale: Red-Tag specials or End-of-Season Clearance.

Frequency: seasonal.

Best buys: name-brand separates for men and women, shoes, accessories, and fragrances.

Downside: limited selection and sizes.

Comment: Ross does not advertise its clearances. Occasionally, it will take an additional 20 to 30 percent off at the cash register without your asking for it—at the manager's whim.

Bargain rating: three-plus shopping carts.

Clearance or closeout stores

Pic 'n Save represents this category, which includes stores such as

continued next page

MacFrugal's and Harry and David's.

Pic 'n Save
Name of sale: none.
Frequency: whenever.
Best buys: brassware, candles, baskets, toys.
Downside: Selection is poor, and you have to be careful about the quality of the merchandise. The Buster Brown clothes may be seconds.
Comment: Pic 'n Save buys endlots and closeouts from other retailers. But on some items, quality doesn't make any difference (e.g., candles and baskets).
Bargain rating: two shopping carts (depending on quality).

Department store "racks" outlets
Name of sale: none.
Frequency: all the time.
Best buys: designer-label merchandise, shoes, and accessories.
Downside: They never have two of the same item.
Comment: The "rack" stores are stocked with unsold goods and returns from the parent stores. Because of their liberal return policies, you might find twice-worn pumps for $20 instead of $115.
Bargain rating: three-plus shopping carts.

Warehouse outlets
(Sam's, Costco, and BJ's)
Name of sale: none.
Best buys: leather jackets and sneakers.
Downside: no place to try on slacks or pants, and selection is limited.
Comment: Bargains here, but some people are turned off by the shopping "experience." If you don't mind seeing other women trying on blouses over their own clothes while you scan the racks, good deals can be had. Shoppers never have any problems returning clothes they purchased and tried on at home. Just be sure to keep your receipt and not cut the tags.
Bargain rating: four shopping carts.

Factory outlets
(Laura Ashley, Geoffrey Beene, Toy Liquidators, Book Warehouse, Carter's, Nike, etc.)
Name of sale: none.
Best buys: anything!

continued next page

Downside: Most outlet malls are located an hour or two from metropolitan areas—or in another state. If you're traveling, ask the local tourist information office if an outlet mall is in the area.

Comment: Outlet malls are good places to shop while you're on vacation. Discounts can vary. Watch out, however, for the tendency to loosen the purse strings too much while on holiday.

Bargain rating: three shopping carts.

SHOPPING AT HOME

If you have cable TV, then you've probably come across QVC and the Home Shopping Network. Seventeen percent of Americans say they have purchased something from a shopping channel. QVC sells over a billion dollars worth of goods a year, and this phenomenon shows no signs of disappearing.

The shopping channels sell home furnishings, jewelry, electronics, clothes—just about anything. The prices are generally good. Markups range from just 30 percent for camcorders and VCRs to 50 percent on jewelry. You might be able to buy clothes by fashion designer Diane Von Furstenberg for half what a department store would charge. But many of the fashions sold on TV appeal to larger women who prefer to shop anonymously and not in a crowded mall.

But buying clothing through QVC and Home Shopping Network is fraught with potholes. You can't touch or feel the merchandise, which means quality is an unknown. More importantly, you can't tell how the clothing will fit. And although the Von Furstenberg dress many seem like a good deal, don't forget the shipping and handling charges. Yes, the return policies are liberal, but you pay the freight for the return.

You're not going to find any "doorbusters" or "red-tag" specials. The same warning applies to those who purchase by mail-order catalog. Unless you're a difficult size to fit, stay local. You'll usually save money.

8

The Honey-Do List

. . . .

■ **My husband is a truck driver and seldom home. My neighbor's husband is in the army and is stationed in Korea for the next year. Both of us have a "honey-do" list a yard long, and we can't afford to hire repairmen. We're both feeling very much alone in this situation. Short of robbing a bank to pay for home maintenance and repair, what can we do?**

Undoubtedly, you both are much more competent than you are giving yourself credit for. Why not consider doing the simple repairs yourself? Lots of women maintain their own homes.

In fact, Susan Gragg, a widow, surprised herself with newfound abilities after she was forced into the role of "home repair person" three months after her husband's death. The chores she faced were discouraging and overwhelming. The temptation to procrastinate and let things slide was strong, but she knew that allowing her possessions to deteriorate wasn't wise financially and could be downright depressing as she faced watching her house and car fall apart.

Oh, sure, tackling those chores at first presented a challenge. In fact, she ignored the box containing the new water filter for several weeks. She could tell from the label that it held the new water filter she had ordered, but she had no idea what to do with it. Changing the filter herself was not appealing.

Her only experience with home maintenance was making the "honey-do" lists for her husband and then picking up the miscellaneous gadgets and doodads upon completion of the chores. But try as she might, she finally saw no way but to replace the filter herself. The family's water was tasting pretty bad.

■ Replacing a water filter would intimidate me all right. What did she do?

First, she read the directions. They seemed simple enough, so she turned the filter canister over and saw a label. There in her husband's script was the date of the last filter change almost one year before. Below the date, he had written the words "I love you." Evidently, his illness had caused him to contemplate her future honey-dos, and he wanted to encourage her. He did.

In that moment, she realized she was going to have to add a "hard hat" to the collection she had worn over the years. That thought was disheartening. Then she decided that instead of getting discouraged, she was going to put that hat on her head and find a way to look good wearing it!

In the process of fixing that filter and several things since, Susan discovered five essential tools she says she now keeps in her belt:

▶ **Have a positive attitude.** Your role is tough. It's hard to walk evenly (never mind poised) with nine hats piled on your head. Sometimes a positive attitude is the only difference between failure and finesse in your daily balancing act.

Susan realized she needed this tool when she was given an end table for her den. It was new and nice. The problem? The table had been assembled wrong and was damaged. It had to be taken apart, fixed, and reassembled. Susan was in trouble.

She stared at the table, totally perplexed and tempted to pity herself. Then she remembered that God had promised to be a husband to the widow (Isa. 54:5). She prayed, "Lord, this is what my husband would be doing if he were here, so would You please show me how to fix this table? Thank You."

After she prayed, she got her screwdriver. She figured what she lacked in skill she would make up for in logic. She examined the table and saw that one of the legs had a screw in sideways. With tool in hand, she took off the good legs, set them aside and went after the wayward screw. It wouldn't budge. She was going to have to enter uncharted territory— the tool shed.

She opened the door to the shed, wondering what she was going to do inside. She couldn't tell a wrench from a socket. Summoning her resolve, she remembered sixth-grade science class and something about leverage. She searched for a tool that looked sympathetic to her need. After a few tries, she stumbled upon a sophisticated tool that did the trick. She later found out it was called a *pliers*.

■ **This story is a hoot! You mean she didn't know what pliers were?**

Hey, at least she admits it. Her first attempts with the pliers brought only frustration. It appeared she was going to need what she didn't have: physical strength. So she asked for help: "Lord, I'm not as strong as my husband was. What am I going to do?"

His answer was to give her the determination to try again. She cranked down on the pliers with all her strength, saying to herself over and over through gritted teeth, *I can do it, I can, I can.* She'll never forget the moment that screw came loose. She shouted, "Ha! There's nothing this woman can't do!"

With that statement, she firmly placed a positive attitude into her tool belt. She accepted that there would be many more honey-dos for her, but she knew that she could positively find a way to get them accomplished.

■ **Both my neighbor and I know how to use pliers already, so maybe we're closer to learning how to do our own repairs than we think. What was the next "tool" Susan added to her home maintenance belt?**

It was **courage,** and this tool was the result of another gift, a lamp. She placed it proudly on her newly repaired table, but discovered it was broken. Her first inclination was to throw up her hands and throw out the lamp. Then she remembered her positive-attitude resolution and decided to throw her energy into fixing the lamp instead.

She thought it was logical to replace the switch mechanism when it wouldn't turn on. The switch itself was missing. She remembered seeing those switches in little packages at the grocery store, so she bought one. She felt powerful buying it, almost as if she knew what she was doing.

She felt a little scared too. This wasn't a simple filter change or a harmless screw. This was electricity! There was also her reputation to consider. What if she failed? No problem, she decided. If she couldn't fix it, she would set it on her table and tell everyone that she received it broken. If she actually ruined the lamp beyond recognition, she would explain that she threw the lamp out because it didn't work. Yes, this was the time to take a risk. She could cover her tracks no matter what the outcome.

She fixed the lamp. She says she also discovered a secret men don't want women to know: *it was easy.* She read the directions and fixed the lamp in less than fifteen minutes, impressing all her friends along the way.

This experience reminded her that we usually fear the unknown. Each time we resolve to face a new challenge, it pays off. A little courage leads to a little more. Fixing a broken lamp can lead to repairing a light fixture. In fact, before long, changing the lock on the front door can be easier than mopping the floor. Really, Susan says!

■ **All right; I have two of the necessary "tools" in my home maintenance belt. What do I need next?**

It's **prayer.** As with every area of our lives, God cares about our broken blinds and our stopped-up sinks. He wants us to deliver those burdens to Him in prayer. This tool is free for the asking.

Susan learned that as she chose to take her honey-dos to the Lord in prayer, He always proved faithful to provide for her needs. Sometimes that provision came through strength to turn the screwdriver once more. Other times, it came through an offer of help at just the right moment. She says that prayer also reminds her that she is yoked with the Lord Jesus Christ. Our burdens are His, and we are not alone.

Susan further has learned that praying for hard-hat help has taught her there is nothing too small to pray about, no prayer too small for God to answer, and no time in her life when she'll ever be alone.

TOP TEN TOOL LIST

1. Think maintenance. Handle jobs as they come up.

2. Keep supplies on hand. Stock light bulbs, batteries, various kinds of tape, air conditioner and furnace filters, and vacuum cleaner belts and bags.

3. Put together a simple toolbox. Some suggested contents: several screwdrivers (both flat head and Phillips), pliers (both open and locking), wire cutters, nails, picture hangers, scissors, assorted screws, a drill with various bits (cordless is best), hammer, utility knife, and tape measure.

4. Go to a hardware store and ask questions. Most of these places have friendly hardware people for the do-it-your-selfers.

5. Shop around for outside help. Look up repair services in your phone book. Make sure the handyman is licensed and insured; don't take his word for it. Check with your municipal building department to verify references.

6. Work with the same people. When you do hire someone, keep his name written on your receipt and keep it in a file. If you use the same company again, you can request the same person.

7. Barter. Do you have a skill or a product? Trade it for services you need.

8. Find out basic information about your home in case of emergency. Where is the breaker box and how does it work? Where is the water main and gas main, and how do you turn them off?

9. Check things out. Make sure all tools and equipment, such as power cords and ladders, are in good condition before using them.

10. Turn on the TV. Watch those "This Old House"-type home repair shows on cable and public television.

■ **Yes, prayer definitely is a powerful tool. What else does she carry in her home maintenance belt?**

Susan says it's **perseverance.** This tool comes in handy when a lack of time and money demands that you find additional help with home maintenance. You can purchase this tool with prayer, courage, and a positive attitude.

Besides a lack of time and money, there are other reasons you will need to find additional help around the house. These are the times when you can turn to your support system for help. Neighbors, friends, deacons, family, and care groups at church are all examples of people in your support system.

Susan has had a neighbor charge her car battery, friends set up her computer, and deacons fix her broken windows. All for the price of a thank-you card.

■ **But when my husband is out of town, I don't have a support system. We haven't lived here long enough.**

Remember, the tool of perseverance can be purchased only with prayer, courage, and a positive attitude. Your positive attitude will be your cheerleader. Courage will help you pick up the phone and make the contacts. Prayer will remind you that ultimately your help comes from the Lord (Ps. 121:1-2).

If the thought of asking your neighbor to come unstop your garbage disposal makes you tremble, then start by asking him how much it would cost to get it fixed. This will give you valuable information when you seek to hire someone. It also gives your neighbor an opportunity to offer help.

In fact, this is good policy for all repairs and maintenance. Nelda, a beautician who faces her own maintenance at home and in the shop, asks her male clients questions while they're a captive audience. As she shampoos, they answer questions about the latest noise her car is making. Way to go, Nelda.

■ **Now that's an angle—and benefit—I hadn't considered. What's the final "tool" Susan has learned to pack in her belt?**

It's called **common sense.** This tool is like a screwdriver: No matter what job you're doing, it should be at your side. In other words, don't try to be Super Repair Woman. Some jobs are meant for the pros.

If your positive attitude inspires you, your courage moves you, your prayer empowers you, and your perseverance helps you, then let common sense guide you.

With these five tools in your belt, you'll find that honey-dos aren't always the huge obstacles they seem. Often, they are a blessing in disguise. You can handle many tasks quickly and cheaply. But even if you and your neighbor occasionally pay for outside help, you'll have peace knowing you have been a good steward of the home and money God has given you.

This material is adapted from writings by Susan Gragg, who lives in The Woodlands, Texas.

9

Packing Up Is Such a Moving Experience

. . . .

■ **My husband told me last weekend that his company wants to move us from Boston to San Francisco. This will be a major move for us. Can you give me some hope?**

Once upon a time, a pastor had to move to a new church. His old congregation had decided to surprise him by arranging to have flowers waiting at his destination. A loyal church worker was chosen to make the purchase.

"I'd like to buy flowers for my minister," she told the florist.

"Very good," the florist said. "What is the occasion?"

"Oh, didn't you hear? We lost him. We're simply heartbroken."

The florist heard the real truth a few hours later—just in time to keep the pastor from being welcomed to his new community with a large floral wreath and banner reading, "Deepest Sympathy."

There are times when a funeral wreath would seem to be an appropriate gift for someone faced with the task of moving to a new community.

■ **You can put that large floral wreath right in my living room. I hate moving. Is there any way I can have a smooth move this time?**

Like you, Denise Turner cringes at the very thought of moving, something she has done with her minister husband and family four times in twenty years of marriage.

Recently, she was faced with the prospect of moving 2,000 miles cross-country to Idaho. On this particular move, she was toting along a preteenager who was unhappy doing anything that didn't involve loud music, and a toddler whose favorite expression was "I didn't do it; my hands did."

Denise quickly became convinced of the need to find some way to put a little more joy into the experience. She began her search by dividing the move into several areas according to subject matter.

■ How did she prepare her family for the big day?

Denise began by finding lots of books eager to tell her how to move. None was able to tell her how to enjoy it. "Unpack boxes and check for damages immediately so you can file the necessary claims" was the kind of advice the books offered. But who has time to do that? Denise still had three boxes left to unpack from the *last* time they moved. Or as her friend Beth put it, "As soon as I learned where to shop, my husband got transferred."

Still, she always felt that good preparation is the best way to ease the pain. And that usually translates into spending time getting the children ready—by talking to them and listening to them—long before moving day.

When Denise and her husband told the kids about their prospective move to the mountains of the Northwest, they braced themselves for an unpleasant dose of culture shock. They were moving to the beautiful gateway of the Tetons and Yellowstone National Park, but the only thing her kids wanted to know was how far they would have to drive to the nearest McDonald's.

The most important thing to remember when preparing children for a move is that their perceptions of the idea are going to be almost totally dependent on their ages.

Infants, of course, are the easiest to move. They handle it fine as long as you keep them fed and comfortable—and as long as you have a big enough car to tote 110 pounds of baby equipment with you at all times.

Toddlers are a bit more complicated. You need to keep reassuring them that they, their beds, their toys, and their pets are going along too. In fact, Denise's toddler was so happy about this last move that he spent the first five minutes in his new house giggling hysterically—until she found out he was standing next to the toilet bowl splashing water on the bathroom walls.

Grade school children, according to popular opinion, sometimes feel a little unsettled by moving. Still, you can often appeal to their instincts for liking things that are new and exciting. Denise handled her ten-year-old by the guidelines laid out in the aforementioned books on moving.

"Let these children help pack and unpack their belongings and decorate their rooms," the books said. And it did help. It's just hard to expect someone who is allergic to order to pack anything neatly into a box or stack it on a shelf. Eventually, she gave up and closed her ten-year-old's bedroom door.

■ But I have two teenagers. How do I prepare them for a move?

The only hope in this situation is to help your children make new friends quickly—by planning social events at the house or by encouraging school acquaintances to visit. If you move during the summer and know some families in the area, call the parents and organize a swim party for all the teens. Knowing a few faces *before* school starts will help those first-week back-to-school jitters.

■ What happens if you have to move during the school year?

Experts contend that a child who has at least fair grades can be moved during the school year and live to tell about it. Look at it this way: at least he or she doesn't have to spend the summer alone. One sociologist even pinpointed spring as the ideal time to move a family, since teachers are so much less hassled at that time of the year.

It also helps to visit the new city and schools ahead of time, even to arrange a pen pal project through your child's new teacher so that there is at least one built-in friend upon arrival.

■ **How do you find a home, work with a mover, and get there from here?**

Most moving companies have colorful brochures on these subjects. Just don't believe everything you read. Especially the pictures. All of them feature freshly scrubbed families gazing peacefully at their perfectly labeled cartons.

One brochure even suggests taking pictures of the contents of each carton to tape on the boxes for future reference. This advice is being directed at moms who never even got around to taking pictures of their third child.

Let's face it. People don't really enjoy the logistics of moving (i.e., calling early for estimates, deciding who will pack the china, planning a garage sale, preparing appliances, checking out loss-and-damage protection, and inquiring about state laws on moving house plants). A recent poll revealed that 70 percent of all women hate cleaning out closets. And no one has ever been able to figure out how to move without doing that.

Then there is the matter of searching for the perfect new house in the perfect new neighborhood. Not to mention the matter of getting your perfect old house into shape to sell—the one with the drippy basement and the termite colony camped in the walls of the master bedroom.

And there are the related matters of banks and affordable mortgages and resale values. It's hard to find much joy in that sort of paperwork—even for the most seasoned of movers.

Denise Turner will never forget that first day in a new house in Ohio. She thought they had done everything right. But, when they arrived with the moving van, they found a leaky water valve (for which no one has yet come forward to accept blame) and a flooded living room carpet.

Three neighborhood children and a Siberian husky were waiting with that grim news. As Denise mopped and wept, a freckle-faced kid with a Popsicle kept telling her she should get a new carpet. Thanks.

On Denise's move to Idaho, she decided, once again, to do everything by the book. She figured she was bound to get it right sometime; and even if that didn't bring her great joy, at least it would make life tolerable. So she subscribed to the local newspaper of their new city and scanned the classified ads. They worked with a Realtor and established credit at a local bank.

Then they decided to take everyone's advice and rent for a few months before buying a house (a good thing to do as long as you can trick yourself into forgetting the fact that this means you will have to move twice).

All went well until the moving van set off toward Idaho. That is when Denise panicked. "What happened to the two boxes labeled 'car'?" she screeched at her husband. Those were the boxes the moving brochures always remind you to take in the car because they contain certain important items that you should keep with you at all times. These include valuables you cannot replace, such as family photos, financial papers, and jewelry.

"Oh, *those* boxes," her hang-loose husband replied. "I guess the movers took them."

C'est la vie.

Every night on the way to Idaho Denise had the same dream. She dreamed their moving van was rolling off a cliff—and she could see the two boxes labeled "car" tumbling down a ravine. That is when she finally realized why moving ranks so high on the stress charts.

■ What's the best and quickest way to plug into the new community?

Well, you're home at last. Time to call the local Welcome Wagon and seek out clubs to join and consult with pastors and teachers and community agencies about activities in which to get the family involved.

The first thing you should do when the boxes begin to trickle in is to start thinking about plans for an open house. Otherwise, you could spend too much time waiting for new neighbors to bury you with invitations to come over.

Often, you can combine the open house with a short dedication service, during which you can ask your new neighbors to join you in a prayer of dedication.

And that is the real key to moving. Though there are bound to be some negatives and some painful good-byes involved in every move, this is a crucial time to remember that we serve a God who is able to give us much more than can ever be taken away from us.

■ What's the best thing about moving?

You get to be a new you. You won't have neighbors dropping by and telling the kids, "I remember when your mom was seven years old and narrated that Christmas pageant, and she introduced the three kings as the three wise hens. Everyone howled!" Meanwhile, you've spent your entire life trying to forget the incident.

Your present neighbors don't know what you looked like at sixteen. They didn't hear you narrate that pageant, either. Maybe there is something to be said for mobility after all.

This chapter is adapted from writings by Denise Turner of Twin Falls, Idaho.

TIPS FROM A SUPER MOVER

Facing a move, whether across town or across the country, can be both a physical and an emotional challenge. To make the transition smoother, try these tips:

1. Make moving an adventure for yourself and your children. Your family will reflect your attitude. If you go looking for something good, you're sure to find it. The reverse is also true.

2. Ask the Lord to take away the desire for whatever you're leaving behind. Perhaps it's a dream house, a job situation, or a certain pattern of living. You'll find it is possible to painlessly give up a dream. The relinquishing process can be an opportunity to walk closer with the Lord, completely turning over your life to Him.

3. Look for the Lord's definite leading in the place you will buy or rent. Your choice may determine the schools your children will go to, the friends they'll make, perhaps the church you'll attend. In buying, don't be swayed above the amount you've determined you can afford.

4. Accept the fact that moving is a lot of work. Plan your move to make settling in as easy as possible. Sort and pack nonessential items as you can, but don't tear your home apart until you have to. Don't let precious weeks of your life seep away in long-extended upheaval.

With a heavy pen, mark an "X" on all sides of two or three packing boxes.

continued next page

These are your emergency boxes. In them, pack soap, toilet paper, dishwashing liquid, dish towels, rags, paper towels, sheets for every bed, and towels for each person. Include anything you'll need the first day in your new home.

Leave another box open until you've spent the last night in your old place. Into it goes all the bedding for the first night in your new home.

Label all boxes as to what room they go to. Also mark each one with a big "1", "2", or "3." Boxes with a "1" are everyday dishes, silver, glasses, pots and pans, towels, and sheets. When these are unpacked, the kitchen is functional and you can stop eating out.

Boxes labeled "2" are the best china, crystal, and other things not needed for a while.

Boxes marked "3" are Christmas decorations, out-of-season clothes, and items that can wait until the sheets are off the windows and drapes are up.

5. Go over your furniture with the movers. Double-check them as they number each item and mark down scratches. This way you'll have recourse if something is damaged in the move.

6. Don't go into the new place at night—things always look better in the morning. Even if you have to stay overnight a few miles from your destination, postpone arrival until morning.

7. When the movers arrive, direct them to put furniture and numbered boxes in the right rooms. For your own peace of mind, check off numbered items as they arrive.

8. Start living as soon as you arrive. Go to church the very next Sunday. The church may be larger than your previous one, or smaller. Just make sure the Lord is there. It won't be long before people will ask you to take responsibilities, and you will feel at home.

9. Learn to be flexible. Don't insist on what you had in the last place. It's never the same. Find a Bible study, exercise class, or hobby group where you can continue your interests. With confidence, look for what the Lord is going to do through you in this new place.

This material is adapted from writings by Margaret Hess and is based on suggestions by Dorothy Jenkins, who—with her executive husband—moved twenty-five times during her first nineteen years of marriage.

10

Getting Your Finances Under Control

· ·

■ **Every year, my husband and I vow to get our finances under control. And every year, we look at the chaos and say, "Maybe next year." Can you help us with some straightforward advice?**

First of all, don't despair. The fact that you're asking for help shows that you are closer to achieving financial control than you may think. The following four steps from financial expert Larry Burkett will help you sort through your financial chaos.

First of all, you need to learn how to live within your means. No matter what station in life we hold or how much money we have in the bank, we all must learn to live a lifestyle that matches what we can afford. To work toward the goal of living within your means, first get wants, needs, and desires in their proper relationship.

God has promised to provide our needs, not our wants or desires. Although He takes our wants and desires into consideration, He provides only what is best for us. Many times we are unhappy because we don't see the difference between luxuries and necessities. The following will help explain those differences:

▶ **Needs.** These are the purchases necessary to provide your basic requirements, such as food, clothing, housing, and medical coverage.

"But if we have food and clothing, we will be content with that" (1 Tim. 6:8).

► **Wants.** These involve choices about the quality of goods to be used: designer clothing versus plain, durable clothing; steak versus hamburger; a new car versus a used car.

"Your beauty should not come from outward adornment, such as braided hair and the wearing of gold jewelry and fine clothes. Instead, it should be that of your inner self, the unfading beauty of a gentle and quiet spirit, which is of great worth in God's sight" (1 Peter 3:3-4).

► **Desires.** These are choices according to God's plan that can be made only out of surplus funds after all other obligations have been met. When you learn to give your wants and desires to God, He changes your perspective. When you begin desiring what He wants for you, He often supplies much more than you need.

"Do not love the world or anything in the world. If anyone loves the world, the love of the Father is not in him. For everything in the world—the cravings of sinful man, the lust of his eyes and the boasting of what he has and does—comes not from the Father but from the world" (1 John 2:15-16).

Here's the action point: On a piece of paper, list your family's needs, then your wants, and then your desires. If you're honest, the answers should be illuminating.

Next, ask yourself: Where does all the money go? You need to know, no matter how much or how little you make. It's important to divvy it up correctly, remaining in control at all times.

► **God's part.** The word *tithe* means one-tenth. It is the *minimum* portion that a Christian should give to God. In the Bible, people usually gave much more than 10 percent of their income or harvest. The tithe's purpose is to be a testimony of God's ownership of everything. We, as good stewards (or managers), give back to Him a small portion of what we have. The *first* part of your income belongs to God.

"Honor the Lord with your wealth, with the firstfruits of

all your crops; then your barns will be filled to overflowing, and your vats will brim over with new wine" (Prov. 3:9-10).

▶ **Government's part.** There's a legitimate role in God's Word for government, and we should honor the authority that God has put above us. The taxes we owe the government should be paid.

"Then He said to them, 'Give to Caesar what is Caesar's, and to God what is God's'" (Matt. 22:21).

The portion available after tithe and taxes are paid is called "net spendable income."

▶ **Your part.** God commands us to provide for our families (housing, food, and clothing).

"If anyone does not provide for his relatives, and especially for his immediate family, he has denied the faith and is worse than an unbeliever" (1 Tim. 5:8).

▶ **Creditors' part.** God says you should pay your debts.

"The wicked borrow and do not repay, but the righteous give generously" (Ps. 37:21).

▶ **Others' part.** Faithful management over a period of time will yield a fifth portion, which means you may have more than you need. This is a major goal for any Christian. It is the surplus that allows you to respond to the needs of others, and it provides the flexibility to meet emergencies without credit.

"At the present time your plenty will supply what they need, so that in turn their plenty will supply what you need. Then there will be equality" (2 Cor. 8:14).

When considering the five divisions of income, you may fear there will not be enough money to go around; you may think you are a failure if you can't provide for your family's needs yourself. Pray, set priorities, and trust God to provide.

■ **I keep waiting for you to add "make a budget." But I need to say that hard-and-fast rules don't work for us. We don't like being ruled by a logbook.**

Compare starting a budget to starting on a trip: You cannot set a course without first determining where you are and where you want to go. So, come on in. This water isn't as deep as you think.

Let's start by figuring your net spendable income and your present level of spending.

First figure your gross income per month. Divide annual amounts by twelve for a monthly average. This includes salary, wages, tips, commissions, bonuses, self-employment income, alimony, child support, public assistance, rent subsidy, Social Security, disability, tax refunds, and veteran's or retirement benefits. Note: Figure amounts on income before taxes are deducted. For irregular income, average several low-income months. You should also include food stamps, regular money gifts, or anything not added in "income."

Next, figure your net spendable income per month by subtract into your tithe and taxes. This includes federal, state, local, Social Security, FICA, or self-employment taxes.

You need to know what you spend. To figure the amount you are currently spending, you must know your *fixed expenses* and your *variable expenses*. Fixed expenses are those that do not change from month to month. Variable expenses are those that may change from month to month or are not due every month. The following will help you figure both kinds of expenses.

Fixed expenses:
▶ Housing expenses: all monthly expenses necessary to operate the home, including taxes, insurance, maintenance, and utilities. The amount used for utility payments should be an average monthly amount for the past twelve months.
▶ Automobile expenses: payments, insurance, gas, oil, maintenance, and depreciation (money put aside to replace the car).

Variable expenses:
▶ Auto repairs.
▶ Food: grocery expenses, including paper goods and nonfood products normally purchased at grocery stores. Include milk, bread, and items purchased in addition to regular shopping trips, but do not include eating-out expenses.
▶ Outstanding debts: all monthly payments on credit cards, loans, or other obligations, except home mortgage and auto payments.
▶ Insurance: payments for health, life, disability, or any insur-

ance not associated with the home or auto.

► Entertainment/Recreation: money spent on vacations, eating out, camping trips, club dues, sporting equipment, hobby expenses, and athletic events. Don't forget Little League expenses, booster clubs, and similar activities.

► Clothing: the average annual amount spent on clothes for your family divided by twelve.

► Medical expenses: includes insurance deductibles (the amount that you must pay per year on your medical bills before some insurance benefits begin), doctors' bills, co-pays per office visit, sliding scale fees, treatments, tests, eye exams and glasses, prescriptions, dental work, or orthodontic treatments. Add only the amounts you actually pay that are not reimbursed. Divide the annual amount by twelve for the monthly amounts.

► Savings: Every family should allocate something for savings, no matter how small.

► Miscellaneous: specific expenses that do not seem to fit anywhere else, such as pocket money, miscellaneous gifts, Christmas presents, toiletries, haircuts.

► School and child care: This is the amount you spend for child care; preschool; after-school care; or tuition for private schools, technical schools, or colleges. Include related expenses, such as field trips and snacks. Remember, if you figure the amount on what you spend each year, divide that by twelve for your monthly cost. All other categories will have to be reduced to provide for these funds.

► To determine what you spend: Go through your checkbook for the previous year and find what you spent according to categories. You can also keep a diary for at least one month listing everything you buy by category. Include any expenses that are not paid every month, such as car repairs and clothes.

Finally, compare income versus expenses. If total income exceeds total expenses, you will have to implement only a method of budget control in your home. If expenses exceed income, examine each spending category to discover what adjustments can be made. You may find that it will be necessary to make lifestyle changes.

The Bible says that a borrower is a slave to the lender. If you are not able to pay your debts according to your agreements because of lack of money or overspending, you are in financial bondage. True financial freedom, however, comes from learning to become a *good steward*. A steward cares for something that belongs to someone else.

Since everything you have really belongs to God, being a good steward means managing well the money God has entrusted to you. It is possible, even if your income is low, but it's possible only if you look at your situation realistically and *plan ahead*.

A good spending plan, or budget, requires action and discipline to make it work. It may require sacrifice. But if we fail to plan, we are planning to fail. So begin the planning now!

This chapter is adapted from The Financial Guide for the Single-Parent Workbook *by Larry Burkett. Copyright 1997, Moody Bible Institute of Chicago, Moody Press.*

Get Rich
Slowly

. . . .

■ **My husband says we shouldn't count on Social Security—**
"Social Insecurity," as he calls it—as we plan for retirement.
Actually, I don't know why he's thinking about that already;
we're only in our early thirties. But just in case he's right,
how can we safeguard our financial future?

First, the bad news: "Unless the client is fifty-five or older, we
don't use Social Security in retirement calculations," says Chris
Jones, financial strategist at WMA Securities in Provo, Utah. "If
you are older than fifty, we think you will receive some benefits,
perhaps $300 a month in today's dollars. If you are forty to fifty,
you may get a token, perhaps $150. Under forty, forget it."

Now, the good news: Today's planning and adherence to godly
financial principles can secure a bright financial future for young
families.

Congress is considering several new Social Security scenarios for
the under-forty crowd. Privatization is one of the most likely solutions. This plan would allow individuals to contribute to their own
accounts, much like individual retirement accounts (IRAs). But
regardless of the changes, Social Security was never intended to
meet all of our retirement needs. It's become clear that we will have

to rely more on our own devices to fund our golden years.

■ **Oh, dear. So our early thirties isn't too soon to begin planning for retirement. So how do we prepare for those "golden years" when we don't have any gold?**

First, commit your finances to God in prayer. Remember, "God will meet all your needs according to His glorious riches in Christ Jesus" (Phil. 4:19).

Second, pay attention to the advice of Proverbs 13:11: "Dishonest money dwindles away, but he who gathers money little by little makes it grow." Saving even small amounts of money will add up over time. And the sooner you start "gathering money," the more you'll have later on.

Financial strategist Jones puts it another way. "A twenty-five-year-old thinking of saving $100 a month at 12 percent loses $130,000 in cash at age sixty-five if he waits only one year to start."

When it comes to retirement, the old cliché rings true: Time is money. The reason is that, over time, the power of compound interest transforms even a little bit of money into a tidy sum. So if you don't have a savings plan, start one today. The following process will set you on your way.

Get professional financial help. While savings decisions are ultimately yours to make, a financial consultant can help you wade through the unfamiliar jargon. Oftentimes you don't even have to pay for the service: Most financial advisers receive their commissions from the investments their clients choose.

Jones offers these guidelines when choosing a financial adviser: "Get someone who has licenses for securities, mortgages, and insurance," he says. "This person should also be familiar with estate planning. He or she should be willing to help you work out a budget, should have access to a large number of competing companies, and be familiar with their products. Finally, he or she should be able to show you how well his or her counsel is working for you."

■ **Where do I find a such a person?**

Start by asking around. Get recommendations from friends,

coworkers, and church members. If you belong to a credit union, check there since many offer financial planning services to their members. Or look in the Yellow Pages under Financial Planning Consultants. Be sure to shop around. Many consultants offer free "get-acquainted" interviews. Ask for one.

Taking the time to locate a capable adviser might be the most practical financial decision you make. His or her counsel will help guide you through the other retirement planning steps.

■ **That's helpful; I guess I never thought of regular people like us having a "financial adviser." What are the next steps?**

Set savings goals. How much should you save? Even though *Money* magazine reports that the average family saves 4.5 percent of its income, most families could afford to save more. It's easier than you might think.

"Most of us can cut out quite a bit," says Lisa Kopp, an investment research analyst at Frank Russell Company in Tacoma, Washington. "Buying a cola at work every day or getting a latté every time you walk by the espresso stand adds up quickly. If you're spending $10 a week on things like this, it becomes almost $50 a month. That's $50 you could be saving."

What dollar amount should you save? As a rule of thumb, Jim Owen of NWQ Investment Management Company in Los Angeles, tells his clients that they will need 80 to 90 percent of their current annual earnings to live comfortably for each year of retirement. Your adviser can help you calculate how much you should save now to retire at that level.

■ **What are some ways I can increase our savings? It seems too hard to sock any money away.**

Find a higher-paying job. To boost income, turn a skill into a marketable item. Clarissa gives piano lessons, June hangs wallpaper, and Connie baby-sits. Or, you may have to change jobs or take on additional schooling.

Cut living expenses. Decide if you can do without cash-draining possessions, such as new cars or electronics. Some families may even consider living with aging parents. Not only will you be able to keep housing costs down, but you will be able to care for your parents on site, thus saving time as well as money.

Invest your money. For retirement, stocks make the best investment. Even though stocks are a risky financial vehicle, most observers agree that the pros outweigh the cons. "It's the only asset category that outperforms inflation," Owen says. "CDs don't, and neither do bonds."

Mutual funds—a pool of investments managed by financial experts—is one of the safest way to invest in the stock market. With the help of financial publications and your financial adviser, pick a fund with a long-time fund manager and proven returns over time.

A word to the wise: Pick a "stock" mutual fund. Unlike other types of funds, stock funds (also called "equity" funds) invest *all* your money in stocks, the best return for your investment.

Once you've made your choice, put your monthly retirement amount (the figure you calculated in steps two and three) into your fund each month. Have your 401(k) or IRA automatically deduct this amount from your checking account. Since these retirement options are tax-advantaged, using them may cut your taxes now while saving for your later needs.

When you invest in stocks, be prepared to buy and hold. "Flavor-of-the-month is a bad investing strategy," Jones says. "The stock market has returned more than 12 percent on average per year for the last seventy years. But investors' return has only been about 5 percent. People switch horses too often. Every time they do, they lose money in fees and taxes."

■ **I'm not sure my husband and I are ready for the stock market. Do we have any other options?**

The best answer is simple: **Avoid debt.** Debt can cripple families in three ways. First, debt can force parents to work longer hours to make payments, infringing on family time.

Second, using debt ignores God's priorities. Matthew 6:19-21 says, "Do not store up for yourselves treasures on earth. . . . But store up for yourselves treasures in heaven. . . . For where your treasure is, there your heart will be also."

In *Taming the Money Monster*, financial counselor Ron Blue agrees that pursuing earthly treasure leads to discontent and debt: "Many things cause discontent. Reading and believing ads is a common cause. Another is browsing in shopping malls, which can raise your level of discontent to the point that it becomes almost impossible not to yield to the temptation to buy."

Third, debt is expensive. Debt basically makes the power of compound interest work against you. A recent survey found that 70 percent of U.S. credit card holders carry balances averaging $3,900, and 70 percent of them make only the minimum payment. At an 18 percent interest charge, it will take these debtors *thirty-five years* to pay up. Total interest cost per family: $10,000.

Given these findings, you might think that you should always avoid credit cards. But there *is* a proper place for them. Jones recommends using them carefully to build up a good credit history. Credit cards are also a good way to make the most of the money in your checking account. Using credit cards for purchases allows you to keep your cash in the bank longer, where it can earn money in an interest-bearing checking account. These strategies, however, help you only if you pay your credit card bills in full each month. If you can do that, go ahead and flash the plastic. Just be cautious.

Finally, remember that your retirement plan is an individual matter. "General principles apply," Jones says, "but every plan is unique." Nonetheless, heeding Proverbs 13:11 and saving "little by little" can help boost any family's future nest egg.

Best of all, savvy saving benefits extend beyond retirement income. "God asks us to be good stewards of all that we have," Kopp says. "When we manage our money responsibly, we have more left over to do His work."

This material is based on writings by twentysomething Katherine Scott of Seattle. She and her husband have already started saving for their retirement.

6

. . . .

Moms and Their God

Here's the Church,
Here's the People

. . . .

■ **How essential is the local church in developing strong, godly families?**

How essential? How about very essential? Planting your family's roots deep into your local church can have generational ramifications for your family long after you're gone. Being part of a church family means you are being fed with God's Word and growing in your Christian faith.

But platitudes aside, every Christian should attend church regularly, follow the prescribed procedures to become a member, observe the Lord's Supper, and inform the church leaders that his or her desire is to become an active member.

■ **A neighbor has three sons who are great baseball players, and since we live in Phoenix, they play in leagues nearly year-round. The family has six ball games every weekend, which means they get to church once a month, if they're lucky. I was having coffee with their mom, and while I know they believe in Jesus Christ, I gently asked her why church wasn't a high priority for them. She replied that at this stage of their**

lives, the kids' sports were very important, and besides, they were Christians anyway. I didn't know how to respond. What should I have said?

There are Christian parents who go through life in which church definitely takes second or third place in their list of priorities. They tell themselves, "Family has to come first," but all they are doing is fooling themselves. They are not fooling God, who reminds us in Hebrews 10:25: "Let us not give up meeting together, as some are in the habit of doing, but let us encourage one another—and all the more as you see the Day approaching."

Then there are those who have money, health, and all the comforts of life, and with those items in their hip pockets, feel they don't need to fellowship with other Christians.

But when the storms of life hit—and they will—those families will suddenly find nobody's there. As Dr. James Dobson has said on the radio many times, don't expect him to come visit you in the hospital during an illness. No, the person to come to you in your hour of need will be the local pastor. If you remain shallow in your relationship to your local church, you will lose out on the support of other Christians when you need it most.

On the flip side, when you neglect to minister within your local church, you also cause other Christians to lose out. The Lord Jesus says that He is the Vine, and we are connected to Him as branches. As a result, through Jesus, we are connected to each other. We are members of one body, the church.

■ **If we are going to plant our family's roots deeply into our local church, as you recommend, where do we start?**

First, make a commitment to your church. Luis Palau, the internationally known evangelist, is an active member of Cedar Mill Bible Church in Portland, Oregon. Although he travels widely through the United States, Europe, and Latin America to speak at evangelistic crusades, he knows that he is not excused from taking part in his home church and being subject to the elders. He feels it's important to consult with the elders on major decisions involving his family, and sometimes even his entire evangelistic team.

When you have an important decision facing the family, ask your elders for advice. Once, a young wife lost her husband. After the insurance settlement, she didn't know what to do with the money. Should she invest it? If so, where? Should she move into a new home because the present one contained so many memories? And if she moved out, should she rent or buy another home right away?

She sought out her elders for advice, and after much prayer and discussion, they suggested that she stay in her present home for at least six to nine months to see how she felt. They also put her in touch with an excellent financial adviser who would invest her lump sum payout in a conservative money market fund. By submitting herself to the elders' leadership, she did not make any rash decisions she would later regret.

■ How can I minister within my church?

You contribute to the body of Christ through your involvement. Remember, "to each one the manifestation of the Spirit is given for the common good" (1 Cor. 12:7). It isn't enough to know that we have spiritual gifts—we must use them!

Beware of the mind-set in looking to see if the church will meet your needs. Since when is the church a country club where you pay your dues until you find something more exciting to do?

Instead, the attitude that should characterize us as Christians is love—a love that gives. The Lord Jesus said, "All men will know that you are my disciples, if you love one another" (John 13:35). When your family is ready to leave for church, leave any expectations about what you want to receive with the dog. Consequently, everything you do receive is a blessing.

Another thing: Even though your church is certain to have faults, don't allow yourself to develop a critical spirit. Your church is your "family" in Christ. Defend it! When others grumble about something, remind them to take the matter to the elders, not to the rest of the body. Let your children hear you talking about "our pastor," "our elders," "our Sunday School," and "our women's retreat." This will help them claim the church as their own as they grow older.

■ **How much should we be giving to financially support our church?**

Although the New Testament doesn't give a fixed percentage for what we should give, it does emphasize the importance of regular giving. In 2 Corinthians, Paul explains that we should give proportionately, abundantly, purposefully, and cheerfully.

Although some may be able to give 10 percent of their income to the Lord, others may give much more, depending on their resources and the needs of the church. The Lord looks at our reasons for giving and our sacrifices to give, not the amount. If you teach your children to tithe from a young age, their small contributions may not seem important at the time, but they will discover how giving can become a regular, exciting part of their lives.

■ **What are some ways we can participate in the church body?**

Have you ever invited missionaries to join your family for dinner? Try it! Missionaries can be fascinating to chat with around the dinner table. They will share tales of what life is like in their country, what the locals eat, how they dress, and what their customs are. Don't be surprised if you hear a miraculous story or two.

You can also meet the physical needs of your fellow church members. Whatever we do for the least of God's family, we actually do for Him. Don't wait until someone asks you to help. Take the initiative and make that casserole dinner with chocolate cake for that financially hurting family. Offer to pick up their kids at school or sports activities when their mom works outside the home.

In closing, many of us face tremendous pressure to limit our participation in our local church. But Scripture tells us that if we keep our commitments to our families and our churches, we will be the winners in the long run.

This material is adapted from writings by Luis Palau of Luis Palau Evangelistic Ministries, which is based in Portland, Oregon. Nancy Hoag lives in Bismarck, North Dakota.

A WIFE GIVES THANKS

by Nancy Hoag

I watched my husband critically as he stood inside the main entrance to our church in his red usher's jacket, greeting people, passing out bulletins, welcoming newcomers.

Glancing at him as the service began, I thought, *How I wish he wouldn't wear that old tie. And why did he have to get his hair cut so short?*

Just then, our pastor called the ushers to the altar. Four came—without my husband. He was fumbling under a seat for the basket that he'd set down while talking to a new family who had just entered the sanctuary. Hastily, he retrieved the basket, stretched his steps, and caught up with the others.

I watched him with the same impatience I'd felt so often lately—wishing he were different, wishing he enjoyed traveling, wishing he'd learned to play tennis, wishing he'd been promoted, and wishing we'd be transferred "back home."

"Honestly," I muttered under my breath, "why doesn't he get with it."

That's when I heard a voice within my heart, a voice telling me to read Job 14:3.

"Lord, why don't I look it up at home? Our pastor is speaking and getting ready to lead us in prayer."

Again, I felt the command: "Read Job 14:3."

I hurriedly flipped through my Bible and located the Scripture: "Must you be so harsh with frail men, and demand an accounting from them? " (TLB)

Tears filled my eyes. I looked up toward the altar as the pastor began reading the Scripture for the day. I watched my husband amble up the aisle with those long, slow strides of his. Except for my pounding heart, everything in me became still.

Although the pastor was just introducing his sermon, the Lord had already tutored a delinquent churchgoer in need of direct instruction.

As my spouse slipped into the pew and squeezed my hand, my heart cried out, "Father, forgive my silent sins against my husband. He didn't hear me, but You did. Thank you for helping me see what I was doing."

But I knew I had more to pray about.

"And Father, thank You for the love he shows when he sets out for the bus stop with his lunch cooler, even before the sun has risen. Thank You for the brushing he gives the dog I hauled home from the pound. Thank You for the hours he spends at the kitchen table, helping our daughter with math, paying

continued next page

bills for orthodontists, prom dresses, and puppy shots.

"Thank You for the times he cared for me while I was so desperately ill. Thank You for the bird feeder he built for me outside the kitchen window. Thank You for all the hours he spends with me at garage sales, loaded down with good deals that I was unable to resist. And for the times he escorted me to plays and baseball games, just because I love the theater and ballpark hot dogs.

"Thank You for hikes, shared picnics beside a mountain stream, and wanderings in the moonlight to glimpse a herd of elk grazing in the long summer grass.

"Thank You, Lord, for this unique man—quiet, patient, dependable. Most of all, thank You for letting me see in him a small reflection of the sustaining, unconditional, protective love You have for us.

"Thank You, Lord, for helping me to appreciate him just the way he is."

2

The Art of Family Devotions

....

■ **A year ago, we asked friends in our church what was the most important factor in their decision to follow Christ. We were surprised—and troubled, too—that "family devotions" was the most common answer.**

The response disturbed us because at that time we were not successfully having daily devotions with our children. This is a routine that I would love to see our family do. How do we get started?

It really depends on the age of the children. You can never "start" too early, in the sense that you can read Bible stories to infants who can sit up. Toddlers and preschoolers have a short attention span, as everyone knows, so devotions must be short and sweet.

■ **Wait a minute. What are "devotions"?**

To those new in the faith or depending on the denomination you grew up, the word "devotions" can sound like Christian jargon. Also known as "family altar" or "family prayer time," devotions are a time when you take a small slice of the day and talk about Christ with your children. Sometimes you read out of the Bible, sing a song, or describe what you've learned from God's Word. Usually, devotions finish with conversational prayers for needs in the family—or praises.

■ When should we start having devotions with our children?

Those moms with children who have varying age differences— three, five, seven years—may want to consider scheduling individual devotional times for their children. For very young children, all you need to do is share the love of Jesus. You'll find it natural to cuddle, to coo, and to have eye contact with your precious baby. Researchers believe that these types of parent-child interactions enhance early development.

You can read Scripture, sing hymns, or pray out loud with your infant or toddler in your arms. Verbalize your faith by talking about what Jesus means to you and how He gave you a special gift—your child! If you play an audiocassette or CD of rhythmic praise songs in the background, don't be surprised if your baby starts clapping and giggling. Babies love upbeat music, and introducing them to Christian music will be great.

■ My toddler daughter can't stand still for five seconds, let alone rest in my arms. What am I supposed to do?

You should interest your child in books with brightly colored pictures; you know the kind: those big sturdy books in which she can point at someone or something in the story. Repetition is key, and keep the story interesting by asking questions: "And this is Noah, who God told to build a big, big ark. Where's the ark?"

Let her point out the big ark. Old Testament stories—such as Jacob putting goat skins on his arms to get the firstborn blessing from his father—are vivid and allow you to impart a lesson. If you can find a book that comes with an audiocassette, you can put your child to bed and put the tape in. She'll ask for it every night because she thinks she's postponing her bedtime!

■ **When should we start asking our children to join us in prayer?**

Whenever they are ready. For some children, they may have the verbal skills by the time they are three years old. For others, it may be another eighteen months or so. When they have the ability, let them try to construct one-sentence "popcorn" prayers, like praying for Grandma's upcoming visit or a friend's sickness. Let them learn to close their eyes, and if you hold hands, that touch increases the warmth between you and your young child.

Sunday School take-home papers are a good source of ideas for activities that complement a preschooler's church-school instruction. For instance, you can play with clay while discussing Creation; search for hidden pennies after talking about the "lost coin" story; and if you really want to go all out, build a campfire as the setting for recounting how Elijah confronted the prophets of Baal on Mount Carmel. At such events, God becomes the center of some of our most meaningful family times.

The most attractive family devotions, however, will fall short of encouraging children to worship regularly if the parents neglect their own worship routine. It is healthy for children to see Daddy and Mommy studying God's Word and praying. When you and your husband are having regular quiet times, you will see your little ones imitating your behavior. Don't be surprised if your son plays "Devotions" with his stuffed animals or your daughter "reads" a devotional book to herself.

Spontaneity is also an important factor in instructing preschoolers. Experts say that children constantly mix secular and sacred thoughts. And as the parent of a talkative tot, you'll believe it! Questions like "Did God make mosquitoes?" and "Does Jesus have a bathroom in heaven?" will let you know that your children are sometimes thinking about Jesus when you're not.

Children often reveal some astounding ideas that can set the stage for on-the-spot devotions. You can capitalize on the "teachable moment" by expanding on something that catches a child's interest. These educational techniques will work well for parents who are attentive to their preschoolers' immediate interests.

■ **Having regular devotions with each child individually sounds time-consuming. Can't we do it all together?**

By all means, yes! What's important is that you communicate to your children that daily time with God is important. Regular worship can help a child know Christ as the eternal King who deserves reverent praise.

Too often in establishing devotions, parents concentrate only on teaching right behavior or expanding biblical knowledge. Especially for small children, it is important that devotions be associated with positive, happy feelings. Harsh statements like "Can't you just sit still for five minutes of prayer!" can make devotions a dreaded time for both child and parent. Don't use your devotional periods for preaching, correction, or grueling types of instruction. You can look for ways to praise your children for the right behavior they show during devotions, but your emphasis is on making each time together an encounter with the living God.

> **A FEW THINGS TO REMEMBER ABOUT DEVOTIONS**
>
> ► Devotions should be a regularly scheduled activity.
> ► Devotions should take place with the majority of the family present.
> ► Devotions should be interesting and meaningful.
> ► Devotions should be centered around the Bible or a relevant life situation.
> ► Devotions should build godly character and habits.

■ **I'm afraid my husband is not interested in leading—or having—devotions in our home. He's always "too tired," and sometimes he's still working when I'm putting the kids to bed. Do I go ahead without him?**

Afraid so. Your children's hearts are wide open to the love of Christ at this age, and religious training can't wait. If Dad is not going to assume spiritual leadership in the home, you must pick up the slack.

But be of good cheer. Integrating worship into your children's daily lives is an exciting endeavor. Be drawn to the words of Deuteronomy 6:6-7 (NKJV):

"And these words which I command you today shall be in your heart. You shall teach them diligently to your children, and shall talk of them when you sit in your house, when you walk by the way, when you lie down, and when you rise up."

This chapter is adapted from writings by Denise Williamson of Birdsboro, Pennsylvania.

3

To My Daughter on Her Dedication Day

. . . .

by Carol Daniels Boley

Your father holds you as the three of us approach the altar, this day of your dedication. Your lacy white dress can't hide your chubby knees, and I smile inwardly as I struggle to quiet my pounding heart.

In just a moment, I will say publicly the words I have cherished privately for months, words that acknowledge my devotion to God and to you. A dedication is a sacred event, a holy moment. I am aware your father holds a miracle.

A part of my own body for nine months, you now are a person apart. It is my heart's newest delight to watch you day by day; today the baby, tomorrow the toddler, all too soon the vibrant young woman of God I know you will become.

I blink back tears and try to keep my mind from wandering to all that lies ahead.

What talents and gifts await nurturing within you? Will you be musical? Already you enjoy tapping piano keys and plunking guitar strings. Will you become an author? Even now you enjoy snuggling on a warm lap to read Bible story books. Will you sing your praises? I listen to your infant voice join mine and watch you clap for yourself in delight.

Your abilities will contribute to your uniqueness, but your character will point to the God behind it. Character—that is what I most desire to nourish in you.

The possibilities of society in your lifetime only peak like an iceberg on the horizon. Who knows what challenges await you? Change rockets you toward lifestyle and career options I cannot even imagine; I am frightened for you.

Yet, I must prepare you for this world unknown, to fortify you to love and serve God and your generation. And so, you are a baby with a mission: You must carry on the cause of Christ into your world—strong, vibrant, joyful!

A large majority of your peers will grow up in broken homes, be raised in day-care centers—some will be molested, neglected, abused. I pledge to provide you with stability and plenty of love to sustain you, even as you venture out on your own.

Like all mothers I want to spare you from every hurt, every tear. But do not fear the hard times, my little one, for as surely as they come, they will pass, leaving you stronger and more loving if you will allow God to deeply penetrate into your soul.

What kind of woman will you need to be, my child, to face such a world with love?

You will need to be God's excellent woman, as He describes in Proverbs 31: *industrious, caring, wise.* You will need compassion. You will need to know the blessedness of silence; of listening without comment or judgment. You will need to understand the healing that comes through a touch or a smile. You will need wisdom—to know your own heart and mind, and how to keep them under the control of the Lord.

Like ripples in a pond, your words and actions will affect others as well as yourself. You will need to learn responsibility and accountability, to accept the consequences of your actions. Your influence for good or evil can be infinite.

I want your personality to shine and your heart to resemble that of Jesus Christ. I want you to grow into a gracious, loving lady who reflects Him in all thoughts and actions, who thinks of others and deals gently with them.

I want you to laugh easily and often, to enjoy this brief life. I want you to keep a balanced perspective and view yourself properly; as a wise professor once said, "to take God seriously, but yourself, not at all."

In all of these areas, you will need a mother who models these characteristics. How I pray that God will enable me to show you by example what patience looks like, how mercy behaves, why love forgives.

To achieve my goals will require constant prayer and fellowship with other believers. How precious are the people who witness our commitment today!

Of course, I will fail at times. Because I am not perfect, I ask your forgiveness now, as I will then. And I pray that you will learn forgiveness by living in our home, with imperfect people who know that the loving and forgiving cannot be separated.

I smile now to see your resemblance to me physically; I tremble to know you will someday bear my likeness in your character.

My heart joins with Hannah in 1 Samuel 1:27-28 (RSV): "For this child I prayed; and the Lord has granted me my petition which I made to him. Therefore I have lent [her] to the Lord; for as long as [she] lives, [she] is lent to the Lord."

Having this responsibility from God to be your mother is a gift so great I can never repay Him for the honor. So I just hold you close and say with my heart, "Thank You, God. It is to You that I commit my daughter today."

Carol Daniels Boley lives in Phoenix, Arizona.

Small Groups Pay Big Dividends

. . . .

■ **We recently started attending a church that is big on "small groups." Our old church never had them. Why should we get involved in small groups at our church?**

Because they will become a lifeline for you. If you're still skeptical, then listen to what several moms told San Diego writer Elaine Minamide: "We were newlyweds, then new parents," said Debbie. "The people in our small group were people we respected. They were older in the Lord and had stable marriages. We not only developed close friendships with them, but we also learned how to grow as Christians."

Doris, another young mom, said, "We were friendship-empty," which is why she and her husband joined a couples' group at their church. "You get to know other people. Then you begin to care for them and pray for them. It's hard to develop this kind of relationship by going to church once a week."

Then there was Sonja. "We moved to California from the East Coast," she related, "and it was like a foreign land. I desperately needed friends. Couples in our new church reached out to us and befriended us. When our third baby nearly died at birth, members of our home fellowship group rolled up their sleeves and went to work, cleaning our house, baby-sitting, making meals. I don't know what we would have done without them."

■ **But I'm not sure I could feel comfortable in a small group setting. And my husband doesn't want us to make another weeknight commitment.**

God didn't create us to go through life in a solo effort. Personal involvement with other believers fosters spiritual growth by providing an environment of intimacy, encouragement, and accountability.

Need more arguments? Small groups are biblical. Look at Jesus and His disciples. His whole ministry centered on twelve men. Look at the early church in the Book of Acts. Paul went from house to house, teaching. The first Christians broke bread together in their homes. Small groups help us fulfill the biblical mandate to be "devoted to one another in love." It's absolutely vital for Christians to have relationship connections with other believers in some capacity.

All of us—even the staunchest loners—need relationships. That's why most of us wind up getting married and starting families, and that's why we should gravitate to friends or companions. Spiritually, we need relationships too. We were born into a family when we became Christians, fused into the body of Christ.

■ **Yes, but we're busy, and we get to church every Sunday and read our Bibles during the week. Isn't that enough?**

Though weekly church meetings reflect this unity to a certain degree, opportunities for personal involvement are limited by logistics—so many people, so little time. We assemble together for a little while, then go home, often not gathering again until the following week.

According to some statistics, up to 60 percent of churchgoers come merely to observe. Consequently, a majority of believers never engage in personal relationships with others outside their immediate circle of friends. Yet without those relationships, they may not arrive at their full potential—growing spiritually, and as a result, becoming more Christlike. That's why many church leaders strongly encourage Christians to get together on a regular basis with small groups of other committed believers.

■ **I'm not familiar with the term "small groups." Is it something like home fellowships?**

Yes, it is. Small groups, known is some denominations or parts of the country as home fellowships, care groups, or accountability groups, represent a vital part of a healthy, growing church. Typically, most groups meet together weekly for fellowship, Bible or book study, and prayer. Besides offering opportunities for friendship, small groups provide a safe haven in which we can know others and be known, where we can pray and be prayed for, where we can ask questions (when was the last time you raised your hand in church?), and where we can overcome practical barriers to living out our faith.

In addition, small groups present opportunities for service that otherwise might not occur. For example, a person may have a spiritual gift that's not being exercised simply because he or she is handicapped by sheer numbers at the church. A small group setting allows us to use our gifts more effectively because we can see specific needs around us.

■ **If I want to get involved in a small group at my church, what should I look for?**

▶ **Relationships.** One of the objectives of small groups is to foster intimacy among believers. Initially, look for people with whom you're comfortable. Are these people you enjoy and respect? Are you relaxed with them, or do you feel strained and uneasy? "It's like trying on shoes," one pastor says. "Walk around in them a bit. Not all small groups fit."

Many groups consist of people at similar life-stages— young married couples, families with small children, empty-nest couples, singles, widows, and widowers. Certainly groups like these meet needs on a practical level. However, don't assume it's necessary to search for a group of people at the same stage as you. Mixed groups that include all ages, from newlyweds to great-grandparents, provide a dimension often lacking in specific lifestyle groups. The younger give meaning to the older, and the older encourage the younger.

▶ **Safety.** Our natural tendency is to isolate ourselves. We avoid getting intimately involved with others because of the emotional risks. Ideally, a small group is a sanctuary, a place where we can pour out our souls, become transparent, even vulnerable, and still emerge emotionally unscathed. Those who participate in the group should feel confident that others involved can be trusted, and that personal matters will remain confidential.

▶ **Commitment.** How often will the group meet? Once a week? Once a month? Keep in mind that small groups aren't intended to evolve into cliques. A healthy group is terminal.

While a group leader may sign on for a year, participants may choose to stay for only part of that time. It's fine if you stay longer, but the bigger picture should include a vision for evangelism and reproduction. In other words, new people should be coming in, while longtime members theoretically should be mature enough to lead a group of their own.

▶ **Purpose.** What are the group's goals? Each is different, based on the needs of its members. For example, one may gather in order to encourage members to become better parents. Still another may seek primarily to pray or to minister practically to needs in their church. Some groups help keep each other accountable to personal commitments, such as weight loss or some other area of personal struggle. Married couples may get together to study books on relationships; men may meet to equip each other for leadership; older women may mentor younger women in accordance with Titus 2:4. Depending on your objectives and circumstances, search for a group whose purpose corresponds to your needs.

■ **Once again, tell me why it's worth it to rearrange my schedule, step out once a week, and get involved in a small group?**

Talk to anyone who's been in a good small group, and you'll hear him or her say, "Yes, it's worth it." In John 13:34-35 (NASB), Jesus said, "A new commandment I give to you, that you love one another, even as I have loved you. . . . By this all men will know that you are My disciples."

True discipleship is seen in our love toward other Christians. And what better way to demonstrate that love than in the intimacy and familiarity found among Christians who know, pray for, and serve one another? Small groups foster that kind of intimacy.

Certainly some effort is required. It's not easy to pack up the kids, drive across town, and bare our souls to others. It's not easy to give time and energy to caring for people, meeting their emotional or physical needs, loving them as Christ loved us. But no one ever said discipleship would be easy. And when you compare the benefits—friendships, spiritual growth, support, encouragement—with the costs—time commitment, child care, openness with others—the benefits do indeed outweigh the costs. Immeasurably.

■ What if there are no small groups at my church?

1. Ask for God's direction. Pray for others who would like to be involved in a small group ministry.

2. Speak with your pastor about starting a group at your church and let him direct you further.

3. Look in the New Testament for examples of small groups (the Book of Acts is a good place to start).

4. Offer to start a "curriculum pool." Review materials other churches have used in their small groups and keep a list for future reference.

5. Talk with others. If you're enthusiastic about a small group ministry, others are bound to share your enthusiasm.

■ But what do we do with the kids? They're too young to be left at home.

One of the biggest obstacles for couples who want to get involved with small groups is, *What do we do with the kids?* Here are some low-cost, essentially hassle-free (face it, there's always a *tiny* bit of hassle) ideas for child care.

► Meet at the homes of those who can't afford sitters.

► Consider using two homes—one for the meeting and another for child care.

► If your church offers child care during weekly services, inquire about meeting at the church and using its on-site child care for small group meetings.

► Bring children along and hire several responsible teenagers from your church youth group to take charge of them during your meeting. Come up with a flat fee (e.g., $5 per family) and volunteer to supply snacks on a rotational basis. Consider providing simple Sunday School curriculum so the children can benefit too.

This material is adapted from writings by Elaine Minamide of Escondido, California.

5

A Niche for the Woman Alone

■ I became a believer several years after my marriage, and I'm grateful that my husband, who doesn't attend church, is not against my attendance each week.

The problem, though, is that I don't fit in any of the Sunday School classes. Recently, the pastor asked the congregation to complete a survey. Traditionally, we've had the genders split during the Sunday School hour—men in their class, women in a separate class—but the church is planning a new mixed class for "in-betweeners"—those older than the college and career class but younger than the senior citizens' group. He said the planning committee thought the group coming out of the survey will be for singles, but that perhaps something also will be developed for the married couples in that same age group.

I looked at the form he had given us. There were boxes to check to indicate age bracket and marital status—single, married, widowed, divorced—as the basis for the new classes. But no box for someone like me. In that moment, I felt my aloneness deeply. Now what?

Too bad we can't introduce you to Karen, who found herself in the same position in a large suburban church. She wasn't comfortable in the couples' class but didn't belong with the singles' either. So, she met with the pastor and gently suggested that she teach a class for women, like herself, who sit alone Sunday after Sunday.

The pastor was surprised as she named individuals who would benefit and confessed with embarrassment that he hadn't considered that group since they quietly slipped in and out of each week's service.

The class Karen started is still going strong more than a decade later, and deep friendships have grown out of their mutual concerns. By the way, the pastor did check to see if there were any *men* in the congregation who were attending without their wives and who would like a separate class. No takers.

■ **Well, that's great for Karen, but I'm not a teacher, and I'm not going to start a class. Any other suggestions?**

We're assuming that you're praying about this—just as you would over any challenge. After you've prayed, you may want to meet with your minister. He, like Karen's pastor, may be unaware of those who would benefit from such a class, and you may get his creative juices flowing. Or perhaps another woman has already approached him about wanting to teach adults, but he isn't sure what to suggest. Remember, if you don't ask, the answer is always no.

■ **It's situations like this that make me long for the "good ol' days" when families did things together.**

Actually, situations like this have been around for quite a while. Just look at Joanna in chapter 8 of the Book of Luke. If she could speak to you, she'd say: *You're like me! You're in church without your husband. I know what that's like. It's difficult to be alone, but I served Jesus to the fullest of my abilities without my husband by my side.*

Luke 8 (GNB) begins: "The twelve disciples went with him, and so did some women who had been healed of evil spirits and diseases: Mary (who was called Magdalene), from whom seven demons had been driven out; *Joanna, whose husband Chuza was an officer in Herod's court* [emphasis ours]; and Susanna, and many other women who used their own resources to help Jesus and his disciples."

Chuza's boss, you will recall, was the one who cohabited with his sister-in-law and also murdered John the Baptist. We can only imagine what kind of personality it must have taken to serve on his staff.

Meanwhile, perhaps Joanna was sensitive to some of the "other women" who served quietly. Perhaps she sought out those with problems similar to her own. Perhaps she watched for newcomers to the group, welcoming them and helping them feel less awkward.

■ OK, so I'm a modern-day Joanna. But how do I apply that fact to my situation?

First, know that Christian fellowship is important—even when one has to overcome obstacles to find it. Joanna undoubtedly played an important role in nurturing and stimulating meaningful fellowship for the women who followed Jesus, just as you can watch for and welcome other women who worship alone. Later, after the Lord's death, Joanna was part of the group who prepared spices and lovingly took them to the tomb. While Luke 24 doesn't give details of that early morning trip, we can imagine the comfort their shared sorrow provided.

Second, the Lord is with us all the time, no matter how isolated we occasionally feel. He knows our needs, and we can feel His presence. Yet that sense of His presence doesn't excuse us from following His command to assemble with other believers (Heb. 10:25).

■ Well, your pep talk has helped some. Any other thoughts?

Just this: A woman alone can follow, listen to, learn from, and serve the Lord to the fullest of her own abilities and over the long term. She's not doomed to second-class discipleship. She is not an awkward extra. In fact, Joanna was among the first to realize the Lord had risen. Never again would she have to wonder if He was the Lord and Friend of the woman alone.

Nor do you.

This material is adapted from a Christian Herald *magazine article written by an anonymous wife.*

6

One of Those Days . . .

by Elaine Minamide

My skirmish with despair began on a Sunday, of all days. I like to think that at least one day of the week is sacred. But it wasn't meant to be.

Actually, the day started well. I spent some time with the Lord that morning, something I don't usually do on Sundays. I discovered long ago that this was one day of the week I couldn't squeeze in those ten minutes for morning devotions. Just getting my three small children ready for church was devotion enough.

This Sunday, though, was different. Somehow I found the time. I got up early. Took a shower. Made the coffee. Went over to the couch with my Bible and had a lovely time. God heard all that was on my heart, a perfect way to prepare my heart for church. Assured of God's blessing and strength for that day, I confidently strode into the rest of my morning . . . and immediately fell flat on my face.

Not more than a half hour later, my husband, Perry, and I had a devastating fight. We're talking knockdown, drag-out . . . well, let's not go into details.

When it was all over—the anger, the weeping, the forgiveness, the determination to go on—I was confronted with a terrible fact:

God, it seemed, hadn't heard a word I'd said. I'd gone to all that trouble to seek Him, to read His Word, to ask for His help, and what did I get? What is the purpose of morning devotions, anyway? Is it just a vain, empty exercise? Frankly, I began to feel that way after Sunday morning's debacle. Sundays went better, it seemed, without devotions.

Thus began my downward spiral. The rest of that day I kept my eyes downcast, refusing to even glance heavenward. The best I could do was play hymns on the piano, trying to swallow the painful lump in my throat. I was a failure, a hypocrite. Worse, I felt abandoned. I couldn't shake loose the sense that all of this—my Christian profession, my desire to live for God—was a sham. An exercise in futility. A waste of time.

The next morning I got up early, determined to persist in my devotions in spite of intensifying discouragement. Took a shower. Made the coffee. Headed to the couch with my Bible and confessed my sins, my doubts, and my hurt. I allowed my little faith to find solace in God's promised presence. Then, taking a deep breath, I prayed. I prayed for my husband. My children. Me. Finished, I got up from my knees and strode into my day, not as confident as yesterday, but assured nonetheless.

It took a little longer than Sunday. Nothing happened until after lunch, actually. There I was again—flat on my face. Enraged at my children. Reacting instead of acting. In short, I'd failed again.

Where was the patience I had asked for that morning? The wisdom to teach my children? The grace to model Christlike behavior in every circumstance?

At bedtime, I managed to ask the children's forgiveness for losing my temper. How sweet, the forgiveness of a child. They don't know any better. Just a smile, a hug, and it's done. What about God, though? Would He forgive? I went to sleep, painfully aware of a hovering emptiness.

I awoke the third day around 3 A.M. Like the watchman of the Psalms, I began to "wait for the morning." Not that I wanted to wait for the morning. I wanted to sleep. Enviously, I listened to Perry snore. Once or twice I dozed, only to be awakened by . . . something. A moth fluttering against the miniblinds. A strange man entering our bedroom (bad dream). I glanced at the clock, indicating the approach of dawn and the impending alarm.

Finally, at 5:15 A.M., I got up and took a shower, resigned to another bad day. Made the coffee. Dragged myself to the couch with my Bible and cautiously opened to the Psalms.

"Out of the depths I cry to you, O Lord." That's where I was. The depths. I kept reading. "O Lord, hear my voice. Let your ears be attentive to my cry for mercy. If you, O Lord, kept a record of sins, O Lord, who could stand? But with you there is forgiveness; therefore you are feared" (Ps. 130:1-4).

With You there is forgiveness. The words were like outstretched arms from an old friend, lifting me from despair. Yes, I'm a failure. I am short-tempered and easily upset. But God knows this, and He forgives me. In the quiet sanctuary of dawn with the God I thought had abandoned me, I was comforted.

Things went a little better that third day. When I absentmind-edly cruised into the intersection against the red light, I wasn't hit by crossing traffic. No, I hadn't asked God to protect me from my ineptitude. But He had His own way of answering prayer, and that day He answered mine.

He has not abandoned me yet.

Because of this, and for no other reason, I could get up off my knees and stride confidently into every day. Would I stumble and fall? The way things had been going, I could be relatively sure that I would. But I was equally sure of this: despite my shortcomings, despite how I perceive God's presence, despite how I feel, I know God is with me. He has not abandoned me yet.

This chapter was written by Elaine Minamide, a writer living in Escondido, California.

Every Circus Needs
a Ringmaster

· ·

■ **During a recent worship service, my husband nudged me as the pastor began the scriptural reading at Ephesians 5:22: "Wives, submit to your husbands as to the Lord."**

I fought the urge to hiss as I whispered, "How come he never preaches on Ephesians 5:21? 'Submit to one another out of reverence for Christ'?"

I'm just not the doormat type, and this business of the woman having to submit all the time makes my blood boil. My husband loves to tease me about that—thus, the nudge in church—but I'm amazed that ministers are still preaching on that subject. After all, this isn't 1810.

Submission. Amazingly, that simple, misunderstood word has caused undue tension over the centuries. Perhaps we need to take a new look at what it actually means.

Recently, a young businessman, whom we'll call Brian, sold his one-third share in a multimedia business. It had a good reputation in town and had appeared successful, so people were surprised by the sale and dared to ask what had prompted his decision.

"Equal partnership sounds good in theory, but in practice somebody has to run the show," he shrugged. "Every circus needs a ringmaster."

His simple statement represents the struggle we see too often in marriage. Joint leadership sounds good in theory, but somebody has to take final responsibility.

This issue has long caused arguments. In fact, one autumn day, after speaking in Dallas, I (Sandra Aldrich) was driving to the airport with friends. As we passed the stadium where a recent Promise Keepers event had been held, I said, "Someday I want five minutes on the platform to tell 50,000 men that even a feisty woman like me will submit to a loving man who's praying and earnestly seeking the Lord's will."

One of my friends jumped on the comment, saying that submission is a nonissue in today's world.

"Biblical submission is not a servant's duty but a protecting umbrella," she said. "Often, though, too much emphasis has been put on the woman's part and not enough on the man's responsibility to love with the love of Christ."

Then my friend snapped that if both partners are praying, there won't be a problem.

"Well, that sounds good in theory," I said, "but in reality, marriage often has its moments when even godly couples aren't going to agree. When push comes to shove, somebody has to give in. If couples can take turns making decisions, fine. But what about those times when you can't agree?"

Oh, boy. Then my friend accused me of having an *attitude*. I couldn't believe it. I'm used to having my attitude tossed back at me because I *won't* submit to every man who strolls through my office. Finally for the sake of my friendship (and my ride to the airport), I changed the subject.

Years ago, when my late husband, Don, and I publicly pledged our love to each other, I thought submission meant being a soft-spoken doormat. I knew that description would never fit me, and I was thankful that Don wasn't expecting that. He didn't seem frustrated at all that I wasn't the "doormat" type!

Over the years, Don and I moved together toward a greater understanding of what the Lord was calling us to. I learned that rather than passively sitting by and letting my husband walk over me, a wife is called to actively choose to allow her husband to take the responsibility as a servant/leader.

■ **I'm thankful my husband doesn't expect me to be the door-mat-type either. The word** *submission* **conjures images of the woman walking three paces behind her husband and murmuring, "Yes, dear" at his every comment.**

Agreed. Jay Carty, president of Yes! Ministries, discussed this topic recently. He explained the man's responsibility this way: When the couple can't agree, the husband must use his God-given responsibility as "tiebreaker." But that means he must make the decision based on what he is convinced is in his wife's best interest—not necessarily what she wants, though.

■ **Tiebreaker, huh? Wife's best interest? I like that. Maybe we ought to concentrate more on the entire Scripture of Ephesians 5:21-32 instead of taking "wives submit" and "husbands love" out of context.**

No argument there. In fact, as a youngster, I (Sandra Aldrich) attended churches where the pastors would preach for thirty minutes on the woman's duty to submit "no matter what." And their congregations—mostly women whose husbands were home sleeping off last night's drunk—absorbed his words and determined that "with God's help" they'd keep accepting the situation rather than getting help.

Those same pastors would then preach for a scant thirty seconds on the man's role—to love his wife as Christ loved the church.

I remember one preacher who leaned forward at that point and said, "That means you're willing to die for her," and that was it. No explanation of Christ's sacrifice and selflessness and what it would really mean to follow His example.

The men in the congregation seemed to relax, as though they were thinking, *Yeah, I fought in the war. I know how to protect my woman.*

Check out how one young husband today explains submission: "We men must have a willingness to lay down everything that's important as we take the role of servant/leader. The principle of loving our wives as Christ loved the church is the toolbox that shows us how to love our wives as we should, but it doesn't come cheaply. It's a daily dying to self."

A *daily* dying to self. Working as a team and looking at the big picture of what you, as a couple, have been called to.

■ **Wow. A "daily dying to self" makes the wife's role of submission easy. These are new thoughts to me. What else?**

Wise husbands know that submission works best when it's tempered with asking for the wife's confirmation of a decision. Gerald says the only way he'll move forward on any project is with Patsy's OK—but he's not "henpecked." He says he's learned the hard way that if he tries to go ahead without Patsy's confirmation then the Lord will not bless the project because it lacks unity. Often, he says, Patsy may not be able to give reasons for her disapproval. She'll just *know*.

"I'd rather she tell me exactly why something won't work, but if she can't do that, then I'd still better listen," Gerald says. "When we were first married, I borrowed money—against Patsy's wishes—to buy some business stock that was taking off. The company had secured a government contract, so I was convinced there was no place for this stuff to go but up.

"Well, then the president was indicted for fraud and the stock fell so quickly that I couldn't sell in time to keep from losing most of the investment. Then I still had to pay back the money I'd borrowed to buy the stock in the first place. It took us a long time to regroup from that mistake, but to Patsy's credit, she never once said, 'I told you so.' I'm sure I wouldn't have reacted so graciously if she had made a mistake like that. You better believe I was ready to wait for her confirmation for every major decision after that."

■ **As I'm pondering this concept, it seems that another important ingredient in the submission-love mix is a husband who leads by godly example.**

Exactly. In fact, some who have encountered me as a widow wonder what my late husband must have been like. I answer that by telling the following story of his godly example:

At one point during Don's cancer treatments, the doctors decided to do a lumbar puncture and asked me to wait outside the room.

I refused. "No. I'm going to sit right here," I said. "And when you see my head down, ignore me. I won't be passed out; I'll be praying."

They moved toward the bed without another word.

For long minutes I prayed silently as they made repeated attempts to find that spot between the vertebrate where the needle had to go. But Don's side pain from the shingles that had developed during the course of his cancer wasn't allowing him to pull his body into the proper curl position. With each of his low moans, my stomach tightened that much more. Finally, I stood up and faced the doctors.

"OK, I've had it," I said. "Now you *better* let me help. I'm through listening to you hurt him."

They glanced at each other. "All right," the resident said. "Maybe if you pulled him into a tight curl. His spine has just enough curvature to make it difficult to insert the needle properly."

I leaned down and kissed Don's perspiration-soaked cheek.

"Come on, Donnie. We'll do it this time," I said.

My right arm went around his shoulders, my left one under his knees. Bracing my legs against the bed, I pulled with all my Kentucky might.

"That's it!" the doctor said. "Now hold him just like that." For an eternity neither of us moved. With my mouth close to Don's ear, I whispered prayers: "Thank You, Lord, for being with us. Thank You for the goodness You will bring out of this."

At one point, my shoulder muscles were burning so badly that I stopped praying to take a breath. As I did, I realized that my beloved Scotsman was singing ever so softly, *What a friend we have in Jesus, all our sins and griefs to bear. What a privilege to carry everything to God in prayer.*

That's the type of man to whom it was easy to submit.

■ **I agree. But what happened to Brian, the young husband at the beginning of this account who said "every circus needs a ringmaster"?**

His comments were so intriguing that I called a major circus, headquartered in Florida, to get information about the actual duties of a ringmaster. In short order, I was connected with someone in the circus who knew a lot about a ringmasters.

"Oh, he's the pretty boy out there to announce and sing and look good," he said. "But in a large circus like ours, it's actually the performance director who is timing the acts and keeping things moving right along."

As I expressed surprise, the circus official continued. "Both the ringmaster and the performance director are equipped with whistles, so if something goes wrong with an act, either one can blow it and get the clowns out to take the audience's attention away from the problem. Both of them have equal power, but only the ringmaster is in the spotlight."

Making an analogy to the marriage relationship can be interesting: The husband may be "in the limelight" as far as being the visible head of the home, but any well-run circus, even marriage, needs both a ringmaster and a performance director. As the circus man said, they both have equal power, and either one can blow the whistle.

So, rather than arguing over the literal meaning of submission, let's concentrate on making our marriages the best they can be, based on love for the Lord, love for each other, and mutual respect.

This material is adapted from Men Read Newspapers, Not Minds. . . and Other Things I Wish I Had Known When I First Married (*Tyndale House, 1996) by Sandra P. Aldrich.*

8

There Will Be No Hangers in Heaven

. . . .

by Elaine Minamide

A lot of things in life annoy me. Things like putting on a clean shirt and ten minutes later splattering tomato soup all over it. Or finishing a letter and licking the envelope at precisely the same moment the mailman is delivering the mail and driving away. Or hearing the phone ring and running in from the backyard to answer it and the minute you pick up the receiver the caller hangs up. Gum in your child's hair; dogs barking in the middle of the night; one lone mosquito buzzing around your ear while you're trying to fall asleep.

Things like that. Nothing monumental, nothing worth really agonizing over. Just little things. Like clothes hangers. With all our advanced technology, couldn't someone at least have figured out a way to keep the tips of hangers from snagging other items of clothing when being retrieved or springing off the rod when a shirt is pulled off it? A minor irritant, granted, compared to the weightier problems of life. But an irritant nonetheless.

Most people get irritated by something. For me, it's hangers. For you, it may be that half inch of orange juice someone left in the container instead of finishing it off, or that porch light your neighbor left burning all night or somebody's car alarm ringing incessantly. We all suffer to some degree from life's irksome problems that, for all our education, talent, good looks, and wealth, we just can't seem to avoid.

The Apostle Paul calls these nuisances little troubles. "For our light and momentary troubles are achieving for us an eternal glory that far outweighs them all," he says in 2 Corinthians 4:17. Paul seems to be saying that minor problems and irritants have some sort of purpose, an eternal reward.

Assuming that's true, the question is, How do we deal with our "little troubles"? The Apostle Paul was no stranger to troubles, big or little. He tells of being perplexed, persecuted, cast down; of being afflicted, beaten, imprisoned; stoned, shipwrecked, imperiled; weary, hungry, thirsty, cold, and naked. No light afflictions, these. And yet that is exactly how he describes them.

Paul had every right to say, "For your light affliction—certainly mine has been far from light." But magnanimously, he doesn't compare. It probably made no difference to him if the worst thing the Corinthians had to endure were buzzing mosquitoes and pesky hangers. Paul simply states the facts as he sees them, yet from the perspective of one who understands eternal matters.

To him the torment of persecution, the suffering he endured, was nothing compared to what really mattered. He may just as well have been talking about car alarms when he referred to the physical torments he endured: they weighed the same in his scale of things.

The word *affliction* literally means "pressure," or, as W. E. Vine puts it, "anything which burdens the spirit." Afflictions—whether severe enough to be life-threatening or so harmless as to be practically inconsequential—have a purpose in a believer's life, according to the Bible. They are "winning for us a permanent, glorious, and solid reward out of all proportion to our pain." A heightened awareness of this purpose brings our own "light afflictions" into perspective. Yet perspective is often what many of us lack when we encounter our own light afflictions.

Sometimes, when I am at home with my children on a particularly difficult day, exhausted, beleaguered, and bewildered, I lose this perspective. These are the times, I admit, that I don't see much of heaven. I feel like a hiker who has wandered deep into a dark forest. The sun has long since disappeared under the heavy canopy of branches and leaves: the dank air oppresses, and silence weighs heavily. Though it is actually midday, the dimness belies the fact, and it becomes more and more difficult for this hiker to believe she will ever see the sun again.

That's how I feel sometimes about God in heaven. I look up, but I can't see Him; I know He's there, just like the hiker who knows the sun still shines somewhere outside the barrier of trees. But under the boughs of nuisances, frustrations, and irritations, my perspective of eternity has vanished. From my limited viewpoint, these "light afflictions" are nothing more than some sort of perverse punishment—here to trip me up, get me upset, make me angry.

Weighed down under the pressure of many troubles, it's hard for me to visualize, let alone accept, the transitory nature of troubles. I have no perspective of eternity. Besides, life is difficult. Some people refuse to accept this simple truth. They cling to a naive hope that someday life won't be difficult. When troubles continue to plague them, they become angry, even bitter—as though somehow God has it in for them. They have no eternal perspective. In the dark, dank, and chilly forest of life, they set up camp and there remain.

If they only persisted! If they would only choose to keep tramping through the forest. The sun does indeed shine; God's goodness does prevail. He waits above the gloom as we persist in our travels through the muck and mire of life on earth. There His eternal glory shines.

And when the trek is over, when we finally arrive, fatigued perhaps, and a bit mud-stained, we'll bask in the warmth and light of that glory—a glory in which there will be no more afflictions, light or heavy. No more sorrow, no more tears, no more sighing. And, without question, no more hangers.

This chapter was written by Elaine Minamide, a writer living in Escondido, California.

ALL THE TIME IN THE WORLD

While at a playground one day, Mom #1 sat down on a bench next to Mom #2.

"That's my son over there," said Mom #1, pointing to a little boy in a red sweater who was gliding down the slide.

"He's a fine-looking boy," said Mom #2. "That's my son, Todd, on the swings."

Todd, a five-year-old, continued to giggle as he got higher and higher on the swing. When he finally slowed down, he had a question.

"Mom, how much longer can we stay?"

"A little longer," said Mom #2.

The two mothers continued to make small talk over the next ten minutes. Then looking at her watch, Mom #2 called out, "Ready to go, Todd?"

"Just five more minutes, Mom," pleaded the five-year-old. "Can we stay five more minutes?"

Mom #2 nodded, and Todd continued to swing to his heart's content. Minutes passed, and Mom #2 stood and called out to her son again.

"Time to go now," she yelled out.

"Five more minutes, Mom? Can I have just five more minutes?"

"Sure, we can stay five more minutes," said Mom #2.

"My, you certainly are a patient mother," Mom #1 noted.

Mom #2 smiled. "There was a time when I wasn't so patient," she began. "You see, my older son Tommy was killed by a drunk driver while riding his bike near here. I would give anything to spend five more minutes with Tommy. Todd thinks he has five more minutes to swing. The truth is, I get five more minutes to watch him play."

9

Confessions of a Prayer Wimp

by *Mary Pierce*

I heard it again today. A radio host introduced his female guest as a "real prayer warrior." I cringed with guilt, imagining a saint who wore out countless pairs of pantyhose at the knee, whose eloquent prayers altered the course of history and inspired prodigals homeward. I felt puny and pathetic, for you see, I'm not a prayer warrior at all. I'm a prayer wimp.

Problems like the water heater exploding don't send a prayer warrior, in her ratty bathrobe, running from the house screaming, "Help, Lord! Save us!" No, a warrior never loses her cool. Instead, she prays, "Thank You, Lord, for this opportunity to wash the basement floor" as she works her mop. "Oh, and the ceiling too."

I know that if car trouble strands a warrior in the middle of nowhere with an ice-cream cake melting in her backseat, she doesn't pound her forehead on the steering wheel and shout to the cornfields, "Why me, Lord?"

No, she remains calm, even though eight giggling fourth-grade girls are waiting back at the house with an anxious birthday girl and her even more-anxious father. This warrior smiles, praying for the Good Samaritan tow-truck driver who will happen along before her cake thaws. And he'll refuse to accept her check, insisting it's his "pleasure to be of service, ma'am."

The tow truck showed up for me, too, but only after I unsuccessfully tried to dam the flow of melting ice cream with one used tissue and an old receipt I'd dislodged from the gum at the bottom of my purse. My rescuer also refused my check, demanding cash up front instead. I offered the remaining cake as partial payment, but "Happy Birth" didn't appeal to him, either.

On her knees before dawn, a warrior has the whole world prayed for before her first cup of coffee. When the alarm shatters my sleep, my mind muddles through a thick fog. Did I survive the night? Guess so. . . . Heaven will surely be cleaner than this bedroom.

When a warrior's friend calls her with a concern, the warrior says gently, "Let's pray about that, shall we?" Pity the friends of wimps like me. A phone call becomes a mutual whining session about the tough stuff of life, with a promise to pray (not out loud on the phone, of course) for each other later.

"Make time for appointments with God," the experts advise. Oh, sure! Between the kids' stuff and my countless other jobs, I'm Jonah in the whale of busyness. And those rare times when the children are at camp, or I'm sick, and I can manage those appointments, it's like spiritual teeth cleaning. All that scraping just to remove the plaque of my life. And that slick, clean feeling afterward sure doesn't last long.

While a warrior's prayers are a symphony, mine are like advertising jingles:

"Lord, I need a break today!"

"Reach out, reach out and touch me, God."

"Lord, take me away!"

A warrior's prayer times are an elegant, intimate dinner for two; mine are a fast-food run. "I'll take a new heart, a new mind, and two orders of patience, Lord. And could I please have that to go!"

Maybe I need a "Twelve Step" program in which I could stand before a mass of strangers and confess, "My name is Mary, and I am a prayer wimp." Murmurs of understanding would assure me I'm not alone. No one would throw rocks.

But thinking things over, I wonder if prayer warriors ever feel like wimps. Maybe we're all just raw recruits in God's army. What if prayer isn't about what we are or do or say, but about who God is?

I'd like to be less wimp and more warrior, but I have a feeling that doesn't happen overnight. Maybe a good first step would be to sit at God's feet awhile and say, "Lord, teach me to pray." I'll be quiet and listen. I think I'll give it a shot.

This chapter is adapted from "Confessions of a Prayer Wimp" by Mary Pierce of Eau Claire, Wisconsin.

7

....

*Moms and
Their World*

1

Moms on the Ragged Edge

■ I know I shouldn't complain. I have a good husband, three beautiful children, and I love the Lord. I should be happy, but I feel as though I'm in quicksand up to my chin. Some mornings I don't know if I can face one more pile of laundry, one more overturned glass of milk, or even one more whine of "Mommmmmy!"

On top of that, I try to prepare nourishing meals and be attentive to my husband, but life is not fun. Instead of being thankful, I'm carrying all this stress. Several of my friends are going through the same thing. What's wrong with us?

You've diagnosed the problem with the word *stress*. The demands in your life are great; indeed, you carry great responsibility being a mom.

If, as statisticians say, air traffic controllers have the most stressful jobs, mothers of young children run a close second. Granted, a few near-misses a year with planes carrying 300 passengers is serious stuff. But a mother goes through several near-misses a *day*—and with those she values most of all. Her little ones tumble down stairs, crash into mailboxes on their bikes, narrowly miss being hit by cars, step on nails, and get lost in department stores.

Children are delightful gifts of God, but they demand tremendous time, energy, and patience. More and more mothers are short on all three counts.

■ **I don't understand that, though. I'm not the first generation of women raising families. My grandmother had seven children, cooked at her sister's restaurant three mornings a week, and still managed to be calm even while canning produce and mending her family's clothing—none of which I do. She didn't have a vacuum cleaner or a washer and dryer. And thoughts of a dishwasher never entered her mind. With all of our modern conveniences, why are the pressures building?**

Part of the answer lies in the decline of the extended family. Tired mothers once had grandmas, aunts, and sisters nearby to encourage, help with the chores, and relieve them. Today's moms may be more mobile, but they're often treading unfamiliar waters alone.

You mentioned all the lessons and practices your children attend—activities that your grandmother didn't have to contend with on the scale you do. This is where our modern affluence and opportunity add to the problem. The tactical skills of a field marshal are needed to juggle soccer games, piano lessons, cheerleading practice, concerts, gymnastics, chess club, ski club, computer club. . . . Mom may be "clubbed" to death if she doesn't drown in the carpool first. Add her husband's—or her own—erratic work schedule, and you have more variables than a physics equation.

Single moms and those with abusive husbands fight even greater battles.

■ **OK, so my life is more complicated than my grandmother's. But I still think she would respond to today's stresses with more calmness than I'm mustering. Why can some women handle several children and a job outside the home, while others despair with fewer children and few outside responsibilities?**

To answer that, let's look at two women, Joyce and Bea, who both have daughters who married last June. Though the weddings were similar, each woman's reaction was unique.

Joyce was nervous but festive. Not that everything went smoothly—the wedding coordinator was bossy, the photographer was late, the cake wasn't the one her daughter ordered, and the flowers weren't quite fresh. Even when the ring bearer stood in the wrong spot and the groom forgot his vows, Joyce chuckled and enjoyed the celebration.

The wedding of Bea's daughter went a little better, but Bea was still ready to string up the photographer, the florist, and the cake decorator for what she saw as inexcusable mistakes. She cringed when the candlelighters didn't stay together, worried her husband would blow his one line ("Her mother and I"), and trembled when the best man fumbled for the ring. It may have been the happiest day in someone's life, but it was pure misery for Bea.

■ **Wait, I think I get it. If Bea is ever to gain contentment, she must change the way she thinks. Otherwise, the same perspective that ruined the wedding for her—and probably dampened her joy as a young mother—will ruin her remaining days as well.**

Exactly. To overcome stress, we must change either our situation or the way we look at it. We usually have little control over others, and we have even less control over circumstances.

So we have only one choice: adjust or accept increased anxiety. To achieve peace, we must either be in control of all of our circumstances or rely on the judgment of the One who is. Obviously, only the second option is open to us.

If we expect life to go smoothly, we continuously set ourselves up for disappointment. We are citizens of another world, and we must draw our ultimate hope from that world (Phil. 3:20-21).

We think of Lisa, a mother who was overwhelmed by the needs of her toddler and moaned to anyone who would listen. "If I'd known how hard raising children is, I'd have become a nun!" Like many others, she produced much of her own stress by unrealistic expectations of what she thought her life should be.

■ **So are you saying we need to develop some positive thinking?**

In a sense, yes. A Christian mom can be a positive thinker not because pop psychology tells her to, but because Scripture repeatedly gives her reason to be. If we believe God rules the universe and everything in our lives, we can be optimistic even when life brings a myriad of difficulties. Having biblical perspective takes us past the immediate circumstances to trust God.

Hebrews 13:8 says, "Jesus Christ is the same yesterday and today and forever"—whether a marriage splits, the church splits, or the atom splits. The truth allowed Paul and Silas to sing hymns despite being flogged and imprisoned (Acts 16:25).

Joshua and Caleb entered Canaan (Num. 13–14) and saw not only the land and the fruit but a place for their families to prosper and worship God. The other ten spies went to the same land but saw only giants—men of war they thought were bigger than God. That simple variance in perspective made a major difference in Israel's future.

■ OK, I'll work on developing a fresh spiritual outlook. What else?

Next, ask yourself a simple question: *What can I do to add brightness to my day?* For some, it will mean changing diet or adding simple exercise. Others may find they benefit by getting up thirty minutes earlier to read the Bible, pray, and reflect on the events of the day. Some need to give themselves permission to read a novel or enjoy a hobby.

Some young mothers exchange evening child care so they can rekindle their marriages. Others long to get back to church after missing numerous Sundays because of long nights over a baby's sniffles. Tapes and radio programs can help, but there's no substitute for the gentle "How are you, dear?" from another who understands.

For other women, the dramatic turnaround happens when they reach out to help others—and in doing so find their own needs met. There's nothing so exhilarating as serving Christ!

Sure, a mother needs to pace herself by refusing, without guilt, many requests that would interfere with her primary ministry to her own family. But she also needs to stretch a little at times and say yes.

Ultimately, nothing causes more stress than the victim mentality that says, "I don't have time to read the Bible, fellowship, exercise, minister, or pray." Of course, if we wait for more time to come to us, it never will. But we can ask the Lord to help us redeem every minute, even in the most demanding circumstances.

As we see God's will, His thinking becomes our own. And a mother can give no greater gift to her children—even in the challenges of today's society.

This material is adapted from writings by Randy and Nanci Alcorn of Gresham, Oregon .

2

If Mama Ain't Happy, Ain't Nobody Happy

· ·

■ It had not been a good day. I woke up late, spilled coffee grounds on the clean floor, and burned the toast. My toddler had an accident as we were walking out the door, and our new puppy did likewise on my white comforter.

That afternoon, with a PMS storm hovering on my horizon, I raced home from the grocery store to find the overnight guests had arrived early! I feverishly directed the children when the guests weren't looking.

"Jacquelyn, make the salad. Claire, run upstairs to see if the puppy pottied on the bed. Collin, don't thump Allison. Allison, quit eating the butter!"

Later that evening my third-grade daughter, Claire, slumped down on her chair to write about her day in her journal. "Mom," she said, "how do you spell 'horrible'?"

This isn't the first time the day has started off wrong for me and then gotten worse for all of us. Is it just my imagination, or is a bad attitude truly contagious?

Attitudes definitely have a way of rubbing off, and the mother's influence is incredible. Remember that old saying "If Mama ain't happy, ain't nobody happy"? Well, it's true. The mother is the thermostat in the home, regulating the temperature and atmosphere by her very presence. She's the chief operating officer, chef, chauffeur, bottle washer, and social director who plans, prepares, and performs the daily household tasks. She tries not to schedule Aunt Rose's visit when the house is being fumigated or plan little brother's birthday when older sister has the cheerleading team over.

■ **I try to model joy in my house, but I often slip into that if-Mama-ain't-happy routine. Life can be so overwhelming, and what's so joyful about the 367th load of laundry? Can you give me some hope? I never thought life would be like this.**

Author Lindsey O'Connor says that she's fought the three C's of discontent: comparisons, commercialism, and circumstances.

Lindsey believes that one of the quickest ways to breed discontentment is to compare yourself or your possessions with someone else. Comparing causes us to adopt greener-pastures thinking in which you say things like, "If only I had a family like that."

Commercialism turns our wants into needs as advertisers threaten our contentment by trying to sell us something we don't really need. Advertisements make us think, "I will be so content when I get that . . ."

■ **Lindsey has verbalized my constant "if only" thoughts—"If only I were younger, I could do that" or "If only we had a bigger house, I could entertain better." But has she ever struggled with that personally?**

Yes, she has struggled to find a sparkle of joy and fight the monster of discontent too. Years ago, she had to put her family's household goods in storage and move four hours away into a dinky corporate apartment. They left the stability of home, church, and friends soon after learning her mother had cancer.

The six-week stay became seven months. When they finally collected their possessions and actually moved, it was into an old, dark house. That and her mother's illness left her yearning for brighter days from her past.

"Lord," she prayed, "I'm not joyful. In fact, I'm miserable. I hate my circumstances, and I'm certainly not content. I want things the way they were."

She kept waiting for God to say, "OK, Lindsey. Here's your old life back" or "Here's My joy on a silver platter." But He didn't. She could do nothing but continue to heave up desperate prayers and study Philippians, the book of joy. She learned much in that familiar book from Paul, who had every reason to be discontent.

■ What did she discover?

Paul wrote, "I am not saying this because I am in need, for I have learned to be content whatever the circumstances. I know what it is to be in need, and I know what it is to have plenty. I have learned the secret of being content in any and every situation, whether well fed or hungry, whether living in plenty or in want. I can do everything through Him who gives me strength" (Phil. 4:11-13).

She latched onto one very hopeful phrase: "I have learned the secret of being content in any and every situation." After all, if Paul said he learned, then maybe she could too. He didn't say he was content with his circumstances; he said he learned to be content in them.

Here's what she learned about Paul's secret of contentment.

▶ **Renew your thought life.** Instead of moaning about his circumstances, Paul knew on what he was to dwell. Instead of focusing on what was happening to him, he looked at the bigger picture and was lifted above his circumstances. Then he found joy. Renewing our minds involves "tak[ing] captive every thought to make it obedient to Christ" (2 Cor. 10:5) and focusing on the One who is always worthy of praise.

▶ **Remember the Source of your strength.** Know who is empowering us. Our ability to harness what we think about is limited, but there is a Source who knows no limits. Remember that as believers, God is the source of our strength. Paul knew that he was not in control, but that it was Christ in him when he wrote: "I can do everything through Him who gives me strength" (Phil. 4:13).

▶ **Rest in Christ's sovereignty.** Know that God is in control of each day and of the circumstances of our life. In order to rest in God's sovereignty, we must know that His Word teaches that "the Lord is good; his love endures forever" (Jer. 33:11), and that we are to "give thanks to the Lord, for he is good" (Ps. 106:1). When we choose to believe that God is in control and that He is good, we can rest in His sovereignty.

■ **I like those three R's—renew, remember, rest—but putting them into practice is such a huge challenge. After all, how can I possibly be joyful when I feel like such a grump?**

Start with seeking Christ. We don't receive gifts from strangers, and joy is no exception. Since you liked the three R's, here are three powerful P's for becoming intimate with the Gift-Giver:

▶ **Pore over His Word.** The more we read God's Word, the better we know Him. If we read it a little, we will know Him only a little. It's here that we can begin to grasp an eternal perspective and renew our minds by learning God's thoughts. Try grabbing a few verses by listening to Bible tapes while you dry your hair, when the children sleep, or while you drive. Carry a pocket Bible in your purse for unexpected quiet moments.

▶ **Praise Him.** As we spend time in the Word and see what He has done for us, we cannot help but praise Him. The more we know God, the more we will want to praise Him, and that has a way of transforming us. It takes our focus off our situation and shifts it to the Person and presence of Jesus.

▶ **Pray.** If we want to get to know someone, we not only spend time in His presence, we talk and listen to Him. That's exactly what prayer is: two-way conversation with God. Besides daily appointments with Him, discover the importance of a lifestyle approach to praying as you work, play, drive, and rest:

"OK, kids, get in the car and put on your seat belts." *Lord, thank You that we've never had to test those seat belts.*

"Does everyone have his or her homework? Love you. Bye!" *Father, please bless their day and help Jacquelyn on her test.*

"Oh, it's a gorgeous day." *Thank You, Lord, for Your*

handiwork.

This kind of praying is connecting with the Heavenly Father in the dailiness of life. C. S. Lewis wrote, "My own plan [for praying] when hard-pressed is to seize any time and place, however unsuitable, in preference to the last waking moment."

■ So you're saying I have to make a choice to rejoice?

Yes. But sometimes even if we work on Paul's secret of contentment and practice our three powerful P's for joyful grumps, we still battle real issues in making the choice to rejoice. One of them is fatigue. Often when we blow it (such as losing our temper with our children), what is really talking may be exhaustion.

You may try to be a wonderful, fun, energetic mom with lots of patience and tenderness only to get to the end of the day with an empty emotional tank. Recognize when fatigue is reaching a toxic level and rest before you lose your cool. And if you do lose it, apologize to your children and get some sleep.

Sometimes "Mama ain't happy" because she's the victim of her own physiology, enduring the physical effects of fluctuating hormone levels. This monthly Dr. Jekyll/Mrs. Hyde routine can make even the strongest woman want to pack her bags and head to the PMS Hospice: The Escape for Hormonally Harried Women!

Become aware of your hormonal patterns (mark you calendar and adjust your schedule if possible). Remember that sometimes what's affecting Mama is simply fatigue, hormones, or emotions, and explaining it to your family can mean the difference between "ain't nobody happy" and "let's ride this one out together."

This material is adapted from Lindsey O'Connor's book If Mama Ain't Happy, Ain't Nobody Happy, *(Harvest House, 1996). Lindsey and her family live in Castle Rock, Colorado.*

3

"But the Doctor Said I Should"

. . . .

by Sandra P. Aldrich

They weren't promiscuous teenagers.
They hadn't cheated on their husbands.
They weren't selfish or antichildren.
Then why did they have abortions?

Because their white-coated, silver-haired, ever-to-be-trusted gynecologist said, "You must. You have a serious infection from this IUD, and if we don't act now, you're going to have major problems."

In the mid-'70s, as many as 5 million American women were using intrauterine devices as their major contraceptive. Of those, between 1.5 and 2.2 million were using the newly developed Dalkon Shield, Copper T, and Cu-7 IUDs, even though federal testing wasn't complete. In fact, the Copper T went on the market with the phrase "expected to receive FDA approval shortly."

The most severe complication from many of these IUDs was septic pregnancy, in which the rampant infection originating in the uterus rapidly spread to vital organs. Before widespread information was made available, 11 women died and at least 209 others were endangered. Because the septic poisoning symptoms appeared suddenly, there was often little warning. One young mother died within thirty-one hours of the fever's onset.

The FDA, Planned Parenthood, the manufacturers, and doctors were divided on what to do next. Some asked all patients using one of the three IUDs to consider having them removed. Others took a "wait and see" position, saying the Pill and pregnancy were greater threats.

Only when the patient proved to be pregnant did some doctors remove the IUD, risking a spontaneous abortion. If the IUD was dislodged and they couldn't easily remove it, they recommended a hospital abortion. Statistics on the number performed are shadowy, but several thousand women faced a life-and-death decision.

Now even into the '90s, I've met more than a few getting-on-toward-middle-age women who live in quiet agony of soul. They listen to their ministers decrying abortion, their favorite authors crusading against it with eloquence. . . and they sit quietly, their consciences twisting. Their thoughts haunt them:

Would I indeed have died if I'd gone through with that pregnancy?
Or was I conned by the medical profession?
Why did my baby have to die anyway?
Didn't I trust the Lord enough to see me through?
What would my child be like today?

Many feel they can't fight boldly against abortions because someone might step out of the shadows, announcing the supposed hypocrisy. I remember one woman sobbing against my shoulder after I presented a grief seminar at her church. "How can I tell other people not to kill their babies when I killed mine?"

Recently I gave another seminar at a women's retreat in Michigan. As I talked about ways to handle guilt, the timid-looking woman in the second row glanced up from her notebook to brush away tears. Inwardly, I said a quick prayer as I wrote the three types of guilt on the board—true, false, and misplaced.

I underlined *true guilt* then turned to the group. "This is what results when we have sinned," I said. I explained that it's our Heavenly Father's way of reminding us to correct that wrong. Thus, it's important that we immediately ask for forgiveness from Him and from those whom we have wronged. Not only does this keep communications unblemished but also protects consciences later.

But what if the person we hurt has died? How can we say, "I'm sorry," when the individual is no longer available? People often come to counselors with unresolved issues years after the death of a family member.

The woman in the second row grimaced. I hurriedly stressed the security of 1 John 1:9: "If we confess our sins, he is faithful and just and will forgive us our sins and purify us from all unrighteousness." After confessing to God, we can ask that our message be relayed through prayer. A simple, "And please tell my brother I'm sorry," helps free us from paralyzing regrets.

Another method is to write a letter we wish we could send, giving our side of the story and asking for that all-important forgiveness. Writing in itself is therapeutic.

At the Michigan seminar, I turned back to the board and underlined *false guilt*. I explained that this guilt is voiced through the I should haves—*I should have known better, I should have gotten a second opinion, I should have done more*. We've all said things like that. While we need God's forgiveness for true guilt, here we must forgive ourselves and our humanness.

That isn't saying we are blameless, but rather that we are going to make mistakes because we are imperfect and live in an imperfect world. If we refuse to forgive ourselves, we step into an emotional prison. Jesus has promised to forgive our confessed sins, so why rob ourselves of freedom by refusing to accept that?

Pointing toward *misplaced guilt* on the board, I glanced at my watch. The allotted time was almost up. I rushed to give an example of this type of guilt: We've all thought *I shouldn't have let him go to the store* when our child fell on the way. It wasn't wrong to let him go, and we wouldn't have voiced the guilt if he hadn't gotten hurt. Both false guilt and misplaced guilt can keep us from accepting forgiveness and moving forward into a productive spiritual life.

After the seminar, the woman from the second row approached as I erased the board. Almost apologetically, she tipped her head as she looked up at me.

"I had a so-called 'therapeutic' abortion years ago."

"Tell me what happened," was all I had to say before the details tumbled out and the tears started down her cheeks again. The dislodged IUD with its copper elements threatened major problems, according to her doctor. He insisted she have an abortion, and within twenty-four hours, her pregnancy was "terminated."

"Terminated!" she spat out the word. "They insisted I kill my baby and they called it 'terminated.' I wasn't given any time to think about it, there were no options, and nobody told me I'd feel worse than if I'd gone ahead and taken the risk."

She found another tissue in her coat pocket before she continued. "I even went back to my doctor several months later, asking him to explain again why it had been so important that we rush. Know what he said? He said if I couldn't handle it, I should get some professional help. All I did was ask a simple question. Even these years later this hurts. What do I do?"

My questions to her were direct: Had she talked about this with the Lord? Yes. Did she accept that medically she hadn't had a choice. No. Had she asked forgiveness from the Lord? Yes. Had she forgiven herself? No.

By then she was crying so hard there was nothing to do but put my arms around her and pray that the Lord would let her feel His presence—and His freedom. At my "amen," she nodded her thanks, gave me a quick hug, and hurried out the door.

I watched her go, marveling that her shoulders seemed straighter. Maybe she understood she no longer had to be imprisoned by what had happened years ago. Maybe she was ready to accept God's forgiveness. Maybe she was even ready to forgive herself.

Abortion is a complex matter, and in standing against its vileness, we must not jump to conclusions about people's motives. Not every woman was trying to cover up sin. Some were blatantly misled. But for all, God's gift of peace awaits.

4

Heeding Frenzy

. . . .

■ **I've heard numerous sermons on setting priorities and even more on serving others, but I'm still trying to figure out exactly how to slow down while helping others. Basically, I guess I want to get the right things right. I'd appreciate your thoughts.**

Consider this scene: It was a nut house and had been for almost two days. Servants frantically scurried about like mice sniffing out cheese. Delivery boys came and went as quickly, bringing food and flowers and wines and table settings and guest registers.

Yet for all the precise planning, chaos still prevailed. The mistresses of the manor were no better off, especially the older sister, who was quite concerned with propriety. They were about to serve dinner to the most influential man in the country. Things had better be perfect!

When their honored guest finally arrived, the younger sister immediately fell into that seemingly irresponsible behavior that ticked off her sibling: she abandoned all her preparations and went into the sitting room to chat with all their guests and listen to the words of the honored one.

After a short time, the older sister's frustration peaked. She charged into the sitting room and said to their guest, "Jesus, don't You care that my sister has left me to do the serving all alone? Tell her to help me."

Jesus responded, "Martha, Martha, you are worried and bothered by so many things; but only a few things are necessary. Mary has chosen the good part, which shall not be taken away from her."

This story was first written almost 2,000 years ago, but it has as much relevance today as it did then because it describes the tension you're feeling: the tension between *doing things right* and *doing the right things.*

You could say you have two sisters residing within you. One sister, Martha, is concerned about doing things right about propriety, appearance, timeliness, and orderliness. The other sister, Mary, is the soulful one who pushes you toward a life of impact and significance.

■ **I'm losing brain cells thinking how this applies to my life. Are you saying that it's OK to take care of myself while I'm trying to help others?**

Not only is it OK, it's necessary. Author Charlie Hedges tells the story about Sherry, a good friend of his when he was on the pastoral staff of a large Southern California church. It seemed Sherry's entire life was devoted to three primary activities: kids, work, and a "to do" list, all of which never seemed to get enough attention. The harder she worked, the more behind she got.

Somewhere along the line, however, Sherry had a revelation. She realized that if she did not somehow find a way to take care of herself, she could not possibly take care of her children. That revelation led her and other busy mothers to creatively delegate child care so that some time each month the parents could have a Saturday off to do whatever they wished. It was a great start toward the caregivers giving themselves permission to take care of themselves.

That point is so important, we want to repeat it: **It is not only OK that you find ways to serve yourself, it is *essential* for you *and* for your family.** If you don't serve you, you won't get served in the right ways—the ways that lead to restoration of your body, mind, and spirit.

Recently a sixty-year-old pastor offered reflections on the

months before and after his difficult heart surgery. Looking back on a life as a caregiver, he was forced to ask the question, "Who takes care of the caregiver?" It took more than thirty years of professional ministry to arrive at his answer: "The caregiver must take care of the caregiver. No one else will be committed to the task."

I wonder if the same isn't true for busy moms.

■ But don't my children need—and deserve—my undivided attention?

Let's begin by dispelling that popular mind-set. Parental myth says our kids deserve our undivided attention and that they are so important that there is no sacrifice too great for parents to make. It is this mind-set that makes parents feel guilty if they devote attention to themselves.

But unless you find a way to take care of yourself, there is no way you can take care of anyone else in a sustained effort. In order to take care of your family for the long haul, you must also take care of yourself in a way that is both restful and productive. Even Jesus took time out to get by Himself and pray (see Mark 1:35).

In this season of your life, you long for rest as much as anything else. You need a break from the rigors that are demanded of you day after day.

■ But what do you do when you rest?

There are times you rest simply by "vegging out." Sometimes, you need to *not think* and *not do*. But believe it or not, you rest best when you do something. Think for a moment about those rare moments when you found the time to organize your closet, clean the garage, or tend your garden. How did you feel when you were finished? You felt great because you accomplished something.

■ I can relate to that. I've found that one of the best ways to rest is doing what I love doing it—even when it might look like a flurry of productivity. I remember the night I attended my first cooking class. I learned how to prepare five new pasta

dishes. As soon as class was over, I rushed to the grocery store and purchased all the ingredients for the next night's meal. I didn't get home until much later than my normal bedtime, and yet I awoke the next morning refreshed and excited.

That's a good example of your feeling rested, even with activity in the midst of a busy schedule. You'll relate to this mother too: Rhonda felt like a taxi driver. With three kids between the ages of nine and fourteen, she logged more miles than Yellow Cab. But what was she to do? The kids had soccer, dance, and karate, and they needed rides to school and to visit friends. But Rhonda knew that if she didn't make some changes, she *and* her car would soon run out of gas.

Rhonda found restoration in creating and designing photo albums. But she required some peace, quiet, and time to do it. Understanding the importance of spending some time on herself, Rhonda set up a co-op with two other parents and arranged for regular, assigned car pooling. As a result, Rhonda got three hours to herself two days a week for an entire summer. She had identified a right thing that gave her space and sanity.

■ What are some ways to start finding this space and sanity?

Find a place to be alone with paper and pen, then consider the following:

▶ What do you really love to do? Gardening? Hiking? Reading? Socializing? Put one or two activities on a list.

▶ You possess many skills, gifts, and talents. What types of activities can you do that allow you to exercise those skills, gifts, and talents? Put one or two of these activities on your list.

▶ Write down the names of the one, two, or three friends who are the most replenishing people you know. Every time you are with these people, you come away feeling good. They know you, and you know them inside and out. Write down the names of these people.

▶ Finally, think about those things you do that help you focus your attention on God. In fact, the irony is that when we focus our attention on Him, we see even more clearly how He has focused His attention on us. Write on your list two things you do that help you focus on God.

After you've done that, you're wonderfully on your way toward taking care of the caregiver—you! Your entire family will reap the benefits.

This chapter is adapted from writings by Charlie Hedges, who is principal of a consulting company in Mission Viejo, California that specializes in management development. His book, Getting the Right Things Right, *is available in Christian bookstores.*

5

Family Heritages Matter

. . . .

■ **Yesterday, my neighbor and I got into an intense discussion about the effect of environment versus genes in the lives of our children. I agree with her that peer pressure can have an enormous effect on shaping our kids' values, but I truly believe that the family of origin has even more power. Unfortunately, I didn't have anything to back me up. Got any suggestions?**

Remember the old saying "The fruit doesn't fall far from the tree"? The family background *does* affect how the individual lives. In fact, the stories of two American families—the Edwardses and the Jukeses—demonstrate the truth of this.

The Edwardses are probably best known for producing the famous eighteenth-century preacher Jonathan Edwards. Jonathan's father was a minister, and his mother was the daughter of a clergyman. Their descendants include 14 college presidents, more than 100 college professors, more than 100 lawyers, 30 judges, and 60 physicians. The family also has given us more than 100 clergymen, missionaries, and theology professors, and about 60 authors.

Contrast the rich heritage and impact of the Edwards line to the influence of the Jukes family. It has been estimated that this clan has cost the state of New York millions of dollars over the years.

Since the eighteenth century, the Jukeses have produced 300 professional paupers, 60 thieves, and 130 convicted criminals. Sadly, this family produced at least 7 murderers.

Every family has a heritage, a model of beliefs and behavior passed from generation to generation. A heritage is the spiritual, emotional, and social legacy that children receive from their parents, for good or for bad. Fortunately, despite our circumstances, we can pass on an Edwards-style heritage to our kids.

■ **What an interesting illustration about the power of the family! But how do I give my children a solid heritage?**

Let's face it: the chief reason many of us fail to give our children a solid heritage is not a lack of desire, incompetence, or even baggage from our past, although these hurdles must be overcome. The main reason we fail to pass on a solid heritage is negligence; we just don't have a plan for doing so. The typical family reacts to the daily events of life instead of planning the heritage-passing process.

Big mistake. As a Japanese proverb says, "When you're dying of thirst, it's too late to think about digging a well." Sadly, many parents don't think about the impact of their heritage until it's too late.

A strong spiritual legacy gives children a foundation for living with confidence in the unseen realities of the spiritual life. Three elements of spiritual legacies make this clear.

First, a spiritual legacy is a process, not an event. For example, a baby dedication is only the starting point in the life of a child. A parent does not give a child a legacy in one day; he or she will do so through years of consistent and committed effort.

Second, parents model and reinforce a spiritual legacy. Spiritual realities are more caught than taught; the child observes a parent and sees the truth of the spiritual life in action. This takes place in the routine moments of life, such as dinner table conversations.

Third, a spiritual legacy prepares our children to clearly recognize the unseen realities of the spiritual life. Each of us enters this world with an intuitive awareness that life is more than what we can see. Unfortunately, because these principles are uncomfortable for many, some parents neglect this vital aspect of passing a heritage to their children.

■ **How can I know if I'm passing a strong legacy on to my kids?**

Let's look at three important facets—the spiritual, emotional, and social legacy.

1. A strong spiritual legacy:
   ► Views God as a personal, caring Being who is to be both loved and respected. Makes spiritual activities a routine aspect of life (church attendance, prayer, and Scripture reading).
   ► Talks about spiritual issues as a means of reinforcing spiritual commitments.
   ► Clarifies timeless truth and right from wrong.

A weak spiritual legacy:
   ► Represents God as an impersonal Being to be ignored or feared.
   ► Has few spiritual discussions of a constructive nature.
   ► Confuses absolutes and upholds relativism.

2. A strong emotional legacy:
   ► Provides a safe environment in which deep emotional roots can grow.
   ► Conveys trusting support.
   ► Demonstrates unconditional love.

A weak emotional legacy:
   ► Breeds insecurity and shallow emotional development.
   ► Conveys mistrust, criticism, or apathy.
   ► Communicates that the child doesn't measure up.

As they mature, children must learn to relate to family members, friends, peers, teachers, and eventually coworkers, bosses, customers, the banker, the butcher, and the baker. And for better or worse, the primary classroom of relational competence is the home, which is why it is so critical that we understand the importance of passing a solid relational legacy to our children.

To illustrate this, on August 16, 1987, Northwest Airlines Flight 255 taxied down the runway of Detroit's Metropolitan Airport, lifted fifty feet off the ground and crashed. More than 150 passengers died in the fire and tangle of debris—but four-year-old Cecilia Cichan survived.

The girl, whose parents and brother died in the crash, sustained a concussion, some broken bones and third-degree burns on her arms and hands. Crash investigators discovered that just before impact, Cecilia's mother had wrapped her body around her child to cushion the blow.

A strong emotional legacy is like that protective embrace. It creates an environment of love that sustains a child through the traumas of life. Parents cannot build a solid emotional legacy quickly; the process is more like growing a tree. It takes lots of time to develop in your child a sense of emotional wholeness.

3. A strong social legacy:
- ▶ Teaches respect for all people.
- ▶ Instills a sense of responsibility for the feelings and property of others.
- ▶ Models clear and sensitive communication skills.

A weak social legacy:
- ▶ Treats others with disrespect.
- ▶ Is dictatorial, enforcing rules for their own sake.
- ▶ Models poor communication.

■ **I'm taking notes! So how do I instill all of this into my children? I need some tools.**

With the assessment of your spiritual, emotional, and social legacies complete, you can use the "heritage toolchest" to build on your strengths and shore up your weaknesses. Your tools include a loving family atmosphere, use of "teachable" moments, a biblical worldview, and strong traditions.

Your family should give off the fragrance of love. See if your home produces the following AROMA:
- ▶ **Affection.** Demonstrate your love to your children. Hold their hands when you walk through the mall. Give them good-bye kisses when they leave and bear hugs when they return.
- ▶ **Respect.** Although parents are entitled to the respect of their children (see Eph. 6), some respect is earned by showing your love for them through hard work and fairness.
- ▶ **Order.** Make your home a safe and peaceful environment. Ensure that each family member understands the rules,

roles, and rights of the home. Be consistent.

▶ **Merriment.** Lighten up! Paint on the canvas of your mind a family in which joy and laughter are as common as eating and sleeping—and live out that vision.

▶ **Affirmation.** Tell your children, "I'm proud of you" and "I trust you"—especially when they feel down. Make every effort to encourage them in the things that matter most to them, whether it's school, sports, or extracurricular activities.

Besides a healthy aroma, use "impression points," or moments when you share your values, preferences, and concerns with your children. When the Ledbetter kids were teens, the parents, Otis and Gail, listened to a tape about sexual abstinence on a trip to Disneyland. That created an impression. They also kept a written journal of things they'd learned (much like a family book of Proverbs) to share with the children.

Moreover, see if your family's worldview lines up with Scripture. For instance, do your kids ground their self-worth in God's love for them? Do they have a healthy sense of responsibility for their actions? Can you help them explore issues of spirituality, personal priorities, and sexuality from a biblical viewpoint? If you answered no to any of these questions, ask your pastor or church librarian to help you get up to speed.

Finally, traditions that pass on your values, such as celebrating your child's spiritual birthday and telling stories about your positive family memories, are very important. Bringing out picture albums can help launch your storytelling sprees.

With these techniques in your heritage toolchest, your children will be better equipped to face the challenges that lie ahead. So make your plans, follow through—and pass on a solid heritage to your future generations.

The Edwardses would be proud.

This material is adapted from the book The Heritage *(Chariot Victor) by Kurt Bruner and J. Otis Ledbetter. Kurt is vice president of the Resource Group at Focus on the Family. He and his wife, Olivia, live in Colorado Springs, Colorado with their two sons. J. Otis Ledbetter is senior pastor of Chestnut Avenue Baptist Church in Fresno, California. Otis and his wife, Gail, have three children.*

6

Reaching Out to the Single Parent

∙ ∙

■ **Recently my husband, Frank, and I attended a get-to-know-you dessert at our church. When we first arrived, we noticed Linda, a newly single mother of two little boys. As she stirred her coffee in the foam cup, it occurred to me that she was trying not to appear alone.**

I knew that greeting her was the right thing to do, but I felt awkward. The whole evening was difficult for me after that. What should I have done?

Reaching out to others—no matter who they are—is difficult. I (Sandra Aldrich) especially know about that since I've been on both sides of the reception room.

Once I was a beloved wife who attended every social event with my husband, but then cancer all too soon thrust me into the single-parent role. Now I wonder how often I unintentionally ignored the single parents in my church simply because I wasn't sure how to respond. I've learned much in these last few years, and I feel qualified to offer this advice to couples wanting to encourage single parents:

▶ **Talk to us.** When you see us—the single parents—in church, please offer a sincere greeting. If our children are small, we are especially hungry for adult conversation. We often feel awkward in church, and your smile and greeting on Sunday morning will make a big difference.

And when you ask how we are, please hang around for the answer. If you'll take an interest in what we're doing, even for a few minutes, we won't feel so alone—and we won't be so demanding of your time. We're still interested in what's going on with the other families within the church and at our children's school. We still read the newspapers too and would love to comment on the latest political news. Ask about our hobbies or projects that fill our evenings after the children are in bed. We may have more in common than you thought.

■ **Hey, I can chat. I've been hesitant to approach single parents because I thought I had to fix everything in their lives even though my own life has plenty of areas needing repair. . . . OK, what other advice do you have?**

► **Talk to our children.** When my family and I attended a small church in New York, one of the couples invited my son, Jay, over for a Sunday lunch and afternoon of working on the car. Jay was delighted to do "guy" things with the husband.

► **Pray for the single parents.** We may appear strong, but the load of single parenting and career juggling is heavy. If we're new to this role, then we're struggling with unfamiliar territory and need all the encouragement we can get.

If we're already friends, we'd welcome your praying with us for a few minutes each week—perhaps before Sunday School. We love praying with our children, but we miss hearing an adult voice take our concerns to the Father. But if we haven't developed that closeness yet, please pray for us—and our children—in your own quiet time. If the Lord gives you specific direction, please listen. He knows our needs—whether it's for help with grocery money or for someone to take our sons to a church event.

■ **I appreciate that suggestion since I'm prone to wait for someone to voice a need before I act. What else?**

▶ **Provide emotional safety.** Those of us who are hurting the most can't take one more rejection, so we'll put up emotional walls. It takes a strong person to help us ease them down. One way to help is by making us feel emotionally safe by not judging us; we're doing the best we can. We didn't want our lives to turn out this way. We didn't plan on being single again, and we weren't trained for this role.

We're also a little afraid of you, especially that you'll blame our children's normal misbehavior on their growing up in a single-parent household. We read the newspaper reports that present the frightening statistics about kids from single-parent homes having more discipline problems than others. More trouble with the law. More time in jail. Rather than condemning us, please remind us that the statistics are just that—statistics—and that our children don't have to fit them. We're frightened. Please help us not to be.

▶ **Be a sounding board.** One of the greatest things we need is someone to bounce ideas off of—whether we're wondering about normal behavior for our children, buying a used car, or maintaining our home. If we're struggling with what is usual behavior for an eleven-year-old, it helps if you'll share a similar experience in your own family. And if we're facing home repairs, we may need someone to interpret the jargon. Many times we need an interpreter for statements such as "Your car's got a cracked head gasket" or "That roof has a four-inch pitch."

Wives, please allow us to ask your husband for occasional advice without thinking that we're "after" him. We need only his advice.

■ **Oh, dear. It's almost as though you've been reading my mind on that point. Any last suggestions?**

▶ **Offer practical help.** Some churches have auto clinic days in which single moms can bring their cars for tune-ups, oil changes, or winterizing. Other churches keep a file of handyman teams who are available to trim bushes or caulk around the windows.

Sometimes our needs are a bit more bizarre. One young mother was having trouble potty training her two-year-old son, Drew. She didn't have any male relatives close by to give the little guy an example of how to tackle this latest milestone. One evening, as she purchased toddler diapers, she ran into her neighbor, Liz. With some embarrassment, she stammered her frustration that her son just wasn't catching on.

Liz, bless her, didn't shrug and flippantly say that the child would figure it out before he got to college. But then she had a practical suggestion: Bring Drew to her house each evening for the next week so her husband could give the little fellow a lesson. It worked!

► **Share events.** The only "normal" family the children of single parents may see is yours. What a wonderful ministry you can have just by inviting us to join you for a family night. Invite us into your home just as you would any other family. And please accept when we invite your family over.

► **Offer occasional encouragement.** When you see a single parent doing something right, please let us know. Some days are so bad that we can't see anything but our mistakes, and your words will make a profound difference.

Truly, you can be a blessing by reaching out to those around you—especially single parents.

This material is adapted from Sandra P. Aldrich's book From One Single Mother to Another *(Regal/Gospel Light).*

WHAT YOU CAN DO

If you are a single parent, keep these few strategies in mind:

▶ **Express emotions with peers, not with kids.** If your children are your main source of emotional support, go to a church counselor or single-parent recovery group instead. Don't choose an opposite-sex adult going through the same situation to support you. Stick with a support group or Christian counselor.

▶ **Listen to your children's feelings.** Often a single parent may work overtime to avoid his or her own feelings and won't even try to understand the child's feelings. The solution: A regular time for kids to talk about how they feel. Use drive time, bedtime, or a weekly fast-food outing for the listening session. Try to sum up what you've heard them say to their satisfaction. Remember, this is a time to understand your children—not fix them.

▶ **Keep your word.** Children often won't trust other people—including their parents—to do what they say they will do. To rebuild their trust, keep your promises and be on time. A predictable parent can help turn around a child's loneliness and mistrust of adults.

▶ **Take time for touch.** Hugging, rocking, hand stroking, and other affectionate habits will help restore broken trust. Even teens can enjoy back rubs in the privacy of home. Don't be shy!

Pray for your child. Be spontaneous. Pray out loud as you walk, make lunch, or drive with your children. Be planned. Write down each month what you are praying for them and how God answers your requests. Strive to be consistent.

▶ **Set realistic expectations.** Since you don't have a partner to share the parenting load, cut yourself some slack. Don't try to do everything—just the important things.

▶ **Nurture yourself.** Destructive patterns often surface after crisis periods, so instead of eating too much or abusing alcohol, find ways to recharge yourself. Take walks, window-shop, or play your favorite sport. Swap child care with other singles for these special times.

▶ **Remember when.** In dealing with children, recall what you liked—or didn't like—about how your mom and dad treated you. Parenting is difficult. But when you "do unto your kids that which you liked done unto you," the load lightens.

▶ **Settle with your ex.** In the case of a divorce, clearing the air with your former mate can help you and your children avoid destructive patterns. Two or three self-counseling sessions between cooperative ex-spouses can help children adjust to the split and bring a sense of closure to the marriage.

"What You Can Do" is adapted from writings by Dave Carder, assistant pastor for counseling ministries at First Evangelical Free Church of Fullerton, California. Mr. Carder has personally counseled hundreds of single parents.

7

Developing Strong Values

. . . .

■ **Over the years, I've heard politicians and the news media talk about family values. Well, with three kids ten and under, I'm interested in family values for my family. What can I as a mom do to raise children who are responsible, respectful, compassionate, and honest? How can I instill strong values in my kids?**

The good news is you are the best person to build a solid moral foundation in your children because you are the parent who is with your children the most. The best place to start is the home, which is another plus for mothers. Besides, developing values in your children is some of the most important mothering work of all.

Some experts suggest that children with strong values aren't as vulnerable to peer pressure, develop the confidence to make a positive difference in the world around them, are less likely to abuse drugs or alcohol, are more likely to practice abstinence, and are better prepared for the challenges of life. And although many schools around the country are beginning to use values curriculums, they are no substitute for moms and dads teaching values at home.

What your children learn from you about being honest, thankful, and kind has a much longer and more powerful influence than what they learn about values in school. Your consistent example can reinforce these values on a daily basis. And when you practice, discuss, and read about these values as part of your everyday routines of living together, you'll be fostering your child's growth in morals and character.

■ **What are some core values that I need to be sure I impart?**

The first step in passing values to your children is to identify the core or central values you want them to understand as they grow up. A good place to look when you're considering these "most important values" is the Bible. Absolutes are given in the Ten Commandments, and Galatians 5:22 lists the fruits of the Spirit as love, joy, peace, patience, kindness, goodness, gentleness, faithfulness, and self-control. Another good place to refer to is the Book of Proverbs, which is full of descriptions of good and bad character traits.

Values such as respect for others, kindness, honesty, service, responsibility, work ethic and stewardship, perseverance, and determination are usually considered universal values. However, faith should top the list of values that your children will need most as they enter the twenty-first century. Faith is what gives children a sense of worth and purpose and helps them thrive no matter what difficulties they face.

After some reflection and reading some of the above biblical resources, write down eight to ten of the most important values you want to help your children integrate into their lives. Then jot them down beside your list of values in a family notebook, titling them "My Own Family's Values." From time to time, get your list out, jot down new ideas, and check to see how you're doing.

■ **How can I make sure I keep up my end of the bargain? I can still hear my mother telling me, "Actions speak louder than words."**

They still do. Did you know that because children learn best by imitation that your role modeling is the most persuasive, positive tool you have to impart values? For example, if you want your son to stay on the soccer team even though it's lost every game of the season, then let him see you persevering on a difficult project at home or at work. Then when you say, "I know your soccer team's had a rough season, but that's no reason to miss practice or games. Hang in there!" it will have much more impact.

Values are transferred as we nurture our children day by day. For example, loving and caring for others is a vital value, but kids learn it first by being loved and cared for.

Developing values is a lot like building muscles—it takes daily training and regular workouts. Let's say you want to build perseverance in your children. Here are some long-term activities that develop not only perseverance, but also patience and a bit of determination:

1. Gardening (such as growing pumpkins, tomatoes, or watermelons from seeds) is a great activity for perseverance-building.

2. Collecting stamps, coins, rocks and minerals, or building a collection of any kind over time.

3. Adopting an elderly person in a nursing home whom you and your children faithfully visit each week, even when you don't "feel" like it or have a busy schedule. This not only develops perseverance but also a great sense of compassion.

4. Decrease your family's television watching. Many TV shows encourage quick fixes, gloss over difficult problems, and develop short attention spans in children. Instead, encourage projects your children can do with you, such as woodworking or crafts, making a book, writing, working a 1,000-piece puzzle, or sending out a family newsletter to extended family members.

Whatever character or values you're trying to pass on, giving your children opportunities to do things alongside you has a dramatic impact. For instance, getting your kids involved in community service or a ministry such as Project Angel Tree, a Christmas ministry to prisoners' children, is very worthwhile. Your daughter could help you select and sort the gifts for the prisoners' children. They can go with you when you deliver the presents to the church or to one of the parents.

Remember, character is caught as much as it is taught, so look for opportunities to let your kids be involved with you on all kinds of ministry, church, service, and household projects.

■ **What are some ways to impart values to my children that don't take so much effort? I work part time, but I'm always home when the kids are home from school.**

Reading, everyday conversation, and storytelling are great ways for moms to instill those values. When these are happening as you go about your normal everyday activities, the values are reinforced in a pleasant, fun way.

You can tell stories, which give children a sense of who they are and what values your family holds dear, even back a generation or two. For instance:

▶ Share about times your grandfather kept farming despite crop failures and obstacles.

▶ Tell a story about a time you kept trying at a job or task when you were tempted to throw in the towel.

▶ If you're a home-schooling family, your children could do some interviewing and write family history stories as part of their English and social studies assignments.

Reading books is another good avenue. Read aloud about people who persevered despite difficulties and even tragedy—such as Florence Nightingale, Joni Eareckson Tada, missionary Amy Carmichael, former major league baseball player Dave Dravecky, and scientists such as Thomas Edison (who tried and failed hundreds of times before making his world-changing discoveries).

Those are the people who should be our heroes, not just sports stars and movie stars who make millions and appear on the cover of *People* magazine. Then there are a host of biblical people who have much to teach us, such as Noah, Joseph, Paul, and many others, including those listed in the "Hall of Faith" in Hebrews 11.

Besides people in history, current news may offer portraits of perseverance. Look in newspapers and magazines to find appropriate stories.

Books such as William Bennett's *The Book of Virtues* and William Kilpatrick's *Books That Build Character* are wonderful resources. Classics such as Conrad's *Lord Jim* and Dostoevsky's *Crime and Punishment* show the consequences of good and bad behavior and offer an opportunity for your child's mental and moral development.

In addition, quotes and wise sayings that relate to the values you are trying to teach your children are good to collect and post on the refrigerator to provide "food for thought." Family conversation, whether at the dinner table or in the car while traveling, provides many opportunities for sharing values. When you give money to a man holding a sign on the corner that says, "Please help," but your husband says, "I think if the man put his efforts into finding a job, his family would be better provided for," then a lively discussion might occur during which you and your husband disagree respectfully but talk about moral issues and virtues.

Experts agree that young people who learn to talk about moral and values issues at home will be much better prepared to tackle the difficult decisions they will face in adulthood.

TIPS TO DEVELOP YOUR CHILD'S VALUES

► When your children start collecting things, help them organize them instead of letting them turn into clutter. Collectibles can be stored in shoe boxes, egg cartons, clear plastic bins, albums, and notebooks.

► When you visit grandparents or other elderly relatives, ask them if they have special memorabilia or family treasures. Inquire if they can show them to your children and tell the stories behind an old clock, a wedding ring, a photograph, a medal, or a trophy.

► At dinner every night, ask each family member to write a small note about a blessing he or she received that day. Place the notes in a "Thankful Basket" in the center of the table and once a week, read the notes aloud to remind everyone of the many good things that happened in the last few days.

► Be aware of the values in the stories and books you read to your child. Think about these questions: Does the author portray the characters in the story with qualities you hope to develop in your children's lives? What values does the hero live by? After reading, talk about the story and the character qualities.

Many children don't try new things because they fear failure. Explain that no one can win all the time. Then together read about people who failed initially but persevered and made outstanding contributions, such as Jonas Salk, Pearl Buck, Winston Churchill, Harry Truman, and Dwight Eisenhower.

■ **Something I've noticed is that I can go for days without remembering to do anything about teaching values. What can I do to keep this on the tip of my tongue?**

Don't forget to give a regular dose of encouragement whenever you see your children's progress in developing character and values. Be sure to focus on their efforts and little steps of growth (the doughnut), not just the finished product or what they haven't done properly (the hole). Kids are works in progress and rarely act perfectly all the time. When your children do show perseverance, say something about it in a nurturing way: "You could have just quit when that puzzle got difficult, but you kept at it. I really admire your perseverance!"

You don't have to profusely praise everything they do, but give

WHAT'S BEING TAUGHT AT SCHOOL?

While you are working on moral development at home, it is important to know what values are being taught in the classroom so that mixed messages aren't being given to your child. This is especially true since values are being taught as part of the curriculum in many schools.

Besides the overt teaching of morals, many values and beliefs are subtly transferred in the teaching of science, social studies, literature, and other subjects. Find out what they are, first by observing classes before you enroll your children in a school, and then by knowing teachers, reading textbooks, and considering these questions as you have opportunities to observe.

► What character qualities is the teacher praising?

► What kind of person is the teacher, coach, and other adults who work with your child? Is this the kind of person you want your child to emulate?

► As you read textbooks, consider the weight a book assigns to certain issues. Does it seem lopsided in its presentation of a subject? Does the author seem to have an agenda? If so, what? A textbook author's treatment of history or science can impact your child's view of the world.

► Overall, is what your children are learning in school in line with or in conflict with what you're trying to teach them? If you are willing to take the time and effort, even omissions in schoolbooks (such as downplaying the role of motherhood or a biology book that omits creationism) can provide opportunities for you to discuss issues and read other resources with your child.

them little booster shots of encouragement. "You gave your friend the biggest piece of cake even though it's your favorite kind," you might point out. "Now that's what I call kindness."

Or you could comment, "I really appreciate the way you helped your younger sister clean up her mess. You were showing a real servant's spirit."

There's another principle at work here, and it's called the "1 Percent/50 Percent Principle."

■ How does that work?

Be encouraged that as you talk, play, learn, read, and share your own beliefs and experiences with your children, you will be giving them one of the greatest gifts of all—a strong foundation of values. This is the way that principle works. If you see only 1 percent growth in a particular value in one week, in a year you'll see 50 percent growth, and 100 percent in two years!

In this way, you'll be equipping your child for a lifetime of fruitfulness that will yield a harvest of virtue for generations to come. Now that's what any mother can call real "family values."

This chapter is adapted from writings by Cheri Fuller, author of 365 Ways to Build Values in Your Child *(NavPress).*

8

Moms and Their Work

1

From Business Suits to Sweat Suits

■ My mother married right out of college, and I was born less than two years from their wedding date. When it came to married life, however, I didn't follow the same path. After graduating from college, I moved to Washington, D.C., where I worked in my local congressman's office. My job was to monitor legislation on Capitol Hill.

A half-dozen years passed before I met Steve, who had a similar position with another big-state congressman. When I married at age thirty, it barely interrupted my exciting career on the Hill. But four years later, with my body clock ticking, a yearning for having a child overwhelmed me, and I stopped using birth control.

I became pregnant a year later, but that was nothing compared with how my life changed with the onslaught of labor pains and the realization that Steve and I had become two very proud, if slightly dazed, parents.

About two weeks after the delivery, I felt like I was dumped on the slippery banks of what I dubbed "The Quagmire"—a seemingly giant, muddy pool of change, choices, and challenges. *What do I do now?* I asked myself. *Do I quit my career*

and become a stay-at-home mother?
I'm teetering. Please tell me what to do.

If this book convinces only one mother that she'll never regret leaving a career to stay home and raise children, then *The Christian Mom's Answer Book* will be a success. Being a mom can be the best career you have.

But there's no one-size-fits-all answer to young moms facing The Quagmire. Only you and your husband intimately know your financial or family situation, and thus we do not have all the facts to advise you on what you should or should not do. But we can inform you that very few mothers regret leaving a career to stay home and be there for the children.

You and your husband will need to ask yourselves tough questions and give honest answers. What do the financial numbers tell you after deducting for taxes, child-care costs, business attire, transportation, and other expenses?

The decision of whether to bid adieu to working full time outside the home is a decision that will have to be made between God, your husband, and yourself. That decision will not be able to be made until you are ready to make it—and not a minute earlier. Most likely, you will have to take baby steps along the way, just like your infant son.

Here's some advice: If you possibly can, wait until after the baby's arrival to make a life-changing decision. You've never had a baby before, and you can't anticipate the intensity of the change.

■ **My emotions tell me to stay home, but my husband says the numbers have to work. How can we resolve this?**

He says the "numbers have to work." They rarely do. No family ever has too *much* money coming in, so it's a matter of choices. The difference is you'll probably have to drive a ten-year-old car and continue living in a small home. Can you do that for your children?

■ **But what about giving up all that expensive education? Aren't I throwing away everything I learned?**

Not if you plan to teach your children what you've learned over the years. Laura Fares Farley-Marino of Hamilton, New Jersey says that when she graduated from high school, her brother was in medical school, and her education would have been a financial burden on the family. Her godfather asked her dad why he was sending Laura to college when she would probably just marry and have a family.

This is how her father replied. He said, "Educate a man, and you educate an individual. Educate a woman, and you educate a family."

You're not throwing away an education, you're educating the next generation. You're not leaving your job, you're being promoted to another. Look at the situation as a career move, with a good percentage of the fledgling corporation's success resting on your shoulders. The balance sheet will get a little low without the second income, but it will be clear that the decision is right.

Others have gone before you. Once, a young opera singer scarified a budding career in her early twenties with the birth of her first child. Two more children followed. All along, she gave that decision up before God, asking for His grace to raise her children and be a good wife. Years later, after her children were well into their school years, the Lord resurrected her career.

■ **My worry is that staying home days on end and having one-way conversations with a baby can make one a little loony tunes. Any suggestions?**

You'll find that cultivating friendships with other stay-at-home moms will be vital to your sanity. A women's Bible study, whether through your church or through an organization such as Bible Study Fellowship, will provide spiritual and moral support. Use daily walks, library visits, and even car rides to break up the day. Who knows? Maybe you'll even discover your neighborhood and your neighbors.

■ **My professional friends can't relate to my decision to leave the law firm. I'm sure they were shaking their heads in disgust and amazement after I visited the office with Shana.**

That's OK. If you remain open, these relationships may be renewed under different circumstances. Besides, there's a good chance that someday those women are going to bear children. Then they will remember your example.

Besides, it's not like you have to give up all sense of your corporate identity. You can transfer any professional habits, such as keeping a day planner to help you keep schedules, lists, and records of projects accomplished in your home life. Doing so will give you a sense of achievement.

■ What do I do when The Quagmire threatens to overwhelm me?

After pouring the energy once reserved for your job into cleaning house, give yourself a treat sometimes. Understand that everyone needs a break sometime, even if it means reading a good book during nap time.

Through it all, realize that the decision to be a stay-at-home mom will not be an easy one. Some days will be like looking into an abyss, but you'll learn that we mothers are all replaceable except in one area—the life of your child.

You have only one opportunity to mold your children's lives. This should be one roll-call vote you don't want to miss.

This material is adapted from writings by Elizabeth Kepley Law, who left a position as director of government relations with the Family Research Council in Washington, D.C., following the birth of her first child, Elizabeth. Christine Dubois lives with her family in the Seattle area.

ROMANCING THE MOM

by Christine Dubois

I'm meeting an old lover today.

No, it's not a man who sets my pulse racing. It's an office. The office I left two years ago to stay home with my son.

Teresa, my old department manager, asked me to drop by to discuss a consulting project I could do out of my home. I clutch my briefcase tighter as I step off the atrium elevator onto the third floor. It's abuzz with action. Sales reps pound out memos, managers huddle in private conference rooms, secretaries in tailored business suits juggle blinking phone lines.

continued next page

Instantly, I'm caught up in the romance of it all. I feel again the sweet, heady intoxication of being at the center of the action, the thrill of being successful and important.

Teresa has a private office now. A photo of her six-month-old daughter—who spends the day with her grandmother—sits on her desk. As we chat, a woman rushes in with bad news from the printer. The press broke down. Can the job arrive on Tuesday?

Teresa pulls out a notebook. "Only if we can have it by 2:30," she says flatly. The woman rushes off again.

After the meeting, I walk down the hall to find my old cubicle. It's still there. Someone else's name is on it now.

Back home, I've traded my business clothes for jeans and a rumpled sweatshirt. Here there are no promotions, no end-of-the-year bonuses, no executive washrooms.

And I wonder: *Have I thrown away my chance for success?*

A voice at my knees interrupts my thoughts.

"Hug, Mama," Lucas says, wrapping his chubby arms around my legs. I lean down and squeeze him back. Suddenly the office seems as illusory as the false fronts of a Hollywood ghost town.

Here on the front lines of the Mommy Wars, it's not hard to see where society has marshaled its heavy artillery. Money and prestige reward those who make the politically correct choice. Yet the politically correct choice isn't always the right choice, for us or for our children. The bottom line is that there's more to life than the bottom line.

Sure, there are mothers who *have* to work, especially single moms, but for some married couples, the smell of those twice-a-month paychecks dulls the senses and makes us incapable of listening to our best selves. "Give me an office with my name on the door, and I'll gladly sell my soul and throw in my firstborn as well."

For many women, the rewards of success are all the more seductive because they weren't available just a generation ago. We're eager to escape from lives of domestic drudgery and do something "important."

But, let's face it, a private e-mail address is hardly a lasting contribution to world peace. Much of what happens in corporate offices is simple busywork—glamorous busywork to be sure, but busywork just the same. I could go back to my job and feel I hadn't missed a beat. For all the STATs and ASAPs, nothing's really changed.

I remember cleaning out my files after I resigned, tossing stacks of URGENT,

continued next page

CONFIDENTIAL, and TOP PRIORITY correspondence into the recycling bin. One weighty file was devoted to the Communications Strategic Planning Task Force. Six months of meetings, memos, and resolutions. Then the vice president who chaired the task force was laid off, and the whole project died. All I had to show for it was a file I couldn't bear to throw out.

On the other hand, six months of rocking, nursing, and nurturing produces lasting and noticeable results. In six months, an infant sits up. Another six months, and he's beginning to walk. Suddenly, he's not a baby anymore.

My son is a different person than he was two years ago. And so am I. I've witnessed the everyday miracle of human development, been part of the wonder of discovering Lucas. I've fed and dressed, worried and laughed, comforted and cared. But most important of all, I was there.

After two years away from the office, I still feel the lure of e-mail and business suits. But I can honestly say I'd rather talk to Lucas than meet with VIPs, rather read *Humpty Dumpty* than study top-secret memos, rather eat peanut butter and jelly than dine well during "power lunches."

So, if you see my old lover, tell him this is good-bye. He wasn't really my type anyway.

2

Ways for Moms to Make Money at Home

. . . .

■ When my three children were small, my husband and I agreed it was important for me to stay home and care for the kids. Losing my income, however, stretched the family's budget to the limit. I dreamed of having enough money to buy fabric to make the children's clothes.

The answer came when a friend asked me to make a bridesmaid's dress. After that successful venture, I began doing alterations and sewing for other friends. At first, I worked fifteen hours a week sewing clothes, but as business increased, so did my hours. I earned enough money to purchase a new sewing machine and start a college savings account for my children.

Today, my children are grown and on their own, but the second income helps my husband and I take mission trips to construct churches in Mexico and Alaska. We can also afford to visit a daughter living in California. For us, having a home-based business has been great, and I highly recommend it to today's moms.

Home-based businesses are a growing trend. An estimated 26 million people—10 percent of the U.S. population—now work at least part time in their home. No doubt some are white-collar professionals who, thanks to the growing availability of personal computers, fax machines, and modems, can work out of a spare bedroom.

But millions more are women who jumped off the career track to become mothers and raise a family. While some mothers start a home business as a creative outlet, many more moms work at home to bolster the family's income. A stay-at-home job bringing in a couple hundred dollars a month can often be the difference for young families struggling to make ends meet.

■ Do you really think I can clear several hundred dollars a month? If I could, that would sure help keep food on the table.

You should know at the outset, however, that a home business may not make much money when you're just beginning. At first, any profits will have to pay off materials and equipment. But as your home business grows, you should be able to earn enough money to pay for special family outings, unexpected medical bills, the children's education—or put more food on the table.

■ What can I do to get started?

First, assess your strengths and skills. If you haven't already decided what to do, ask: *What do I enjoy most? What are my hobbies and interests?* Be sure to consider volunteer work, as well as jobs you've held and skills you've acquired along the way.

Barbara Brabec, author of *Homemade Money* and the newsletter *National Home Business Report*, says, "One passionate interest could be turned into a business." For example, Cathy Bolton Adkinson's love of cooking led her to build a thriving home business that began with baking and selling chocolate chip cookies. That grew into cookie bouquets, cookie pizzas, her patented "cookie fries," and, ultimately, a gourmet bakery and cafe in Stillwater, Oklahoma.

Posy Lough, a Kentucky mom, grew up in a family that had money for gifts only if they made them. For Posy, this led to a home business that produces historic counted cross-stitch kits for museums, educational crafts, toys for children, and Advent and Lent calendars for families.

■ What other questions should I be asking myself?

Before beginning a home business, you also need a clear understanding of yourself:
► Are you a self-starter?
► Do you enjoy working independently?
► Can you set up and follow your own schedules and deadlines?
► Are you organized and resourceful?
► How much money can you invest in this endeavor? Are your spouse and family supportive?

"Having the support of your family is important," says Cathy Adkinson. "My husband has iced cakes at 4 in the morning, babysat, and typed menus. It wouldn't have worked if he wasn't supportive. You can't have your spouse feeling bitter or resentful."

■ How important is researching my home-based business before jumping in?

You'd better learn all you can. Successful home workers say that after defining their business interest, they went to the library and read about the field. It's also important to study the basics of running a small business. Be sure to read trade journals and magazines in your area of interest.

After Amy Webster had the idea for a line of greeting cards, "Blessed Are These," she spent three years learning the graphics business and how to draw children. She and her husband, Glen, went to home-business seminars and checked out library books. They read all they could.

All that research paid off: The following year, her cards were displayed in eighty stores in the Southwest. A children's Scripture art book and calendar followed, and other new products are in the works.

■ Are there certain zoning rules I have to follow?

You will have to investigate your local zoning laws, and chapters of the U.S. Small Business Administration can provide information, a free business start-up kit, and counseling services. Check also with the extension services of local universities. Many offer practical seminars on how to develop a business plan and keep tax records.

It's also important to check out the competition. Ask yourself: Does anyone need my product or service? Where are my customers? How will I reach them? Can I make any money?

"Be courageous and ask questions," says Amy Webster. "Ask a million of them, and learn from the answers. If you don't ask the questions, you won't find the open doors."

■ **I've read those tiny advertisements in the back of women's magazines: "Envelope stuffing. Make big bucks at home." Are they legit?**

Don't be a sucker for get-rich-quick schemes. That come-on you saw in the magazine usually asks you to send $15 "for more information," and what you get back is a letter detailing how you can set up a phony business like theirs. The U.S. Postal Service has clamped down on thousands of these fly-by-night operators. Remember: if it sounds too good to be true, it usually is.

■ **How do I guard from getting overextended financially?**

By starting small. Sometimes in our enthusiasm of starting something new, we go out on a financial limb. Keep your expenses low. If you're going to sell cosmetics out of your home, for instance, begin with a small inventory. Keep supplies to a minimum, and scan the classified ads for second-hand office equipment.

You can save on advertising by sending out your own press releases, making brochures or flyers to put on community bulletin boards, spreading the word through friends and relatives with business cards; sending postcards to prospective customers, and finding other creative ways to let people know about your products or service.

Like most home business operators, Sherry Eden didn't have any money to advertise her gift basket business, "A Basket Case." So she started telling everyone she knew about her new venture. Sherry and her partner also sent invitations to "basket open houses" just before the holidays and the spring wedding season.

Soon, friends told friends, and the world was beating a path to Sherry's door. "Word-of-mouth has been our greatest advertising, and generating that interest has cost us very little," she says. One guest, a bakery owner, ordered fifty baskets, leading to a big account with a major corporation.

■ **My businesman-deluxe husband tells me I should "network" with others in home-based business. What does that mean?**

Because those of us who have home businesses can feel isolated, it's vital to network—stay in touch—with others for moral support. We need to share problems, ideas, and encouragement. One way to do that is through newsletters, such as those listed in the resource box. You can also join small business and entrepreneur groups in your community.

■ **To make this home-based business thing work in our home, I can do work only while the kids are at school. That's not much time. How can I manage it to my advantage?**

You have to make hay while the sun shines, and when the kids are in school, you need to take advantage of every moment. Make "To Do" lists,

IDEAS FOR HOME BUSINESSES

Family day care

Teaching cooking, music, or art (classes or one at a time)

Word processing and desktop publishing

Editing newsletters, freelance writing, or technical writing for local businesses

Handcrafted toys, dolls, bears

Pottery, needlework, wreaths, ornaments, woodcrafts

Designing and producing jewelry, bows, headbands, T-shirts, and sweatshirts

Custom sewing, alterations, monogramming

Opening a bed-and-breakfast inn

Beauty consultant

Food: catering, specialty cookies, wedding and birthday cakes

Gift baskets

Gardening: fresh and dried herb products

Bookkeeping and accounting

Income tax preparation

Designing or refinishing furniture

Marketing: selling clothes or other products through sample sales or parties

Freelance graphic artist

but be flexible when your frozen pipes burst or a child is sick. An answering machine can help avoid interruptions during working hours. Try to find your own niche at home where your materials or papers can be left at a moment's notice. If you have a spare room, that's great, but even a card table set up in your bedroom will work. Finally, try to schedule your errands together so you're not constantly running in and out.

■ I'm a mom with preschoolers. Is working out of my home going to work?

It will be difficult to set aside time—any amount of time—to work on a home business. Your first priority is to your children. Perhaps you could work an hour or two while they nap or during a three-hour block one evening a week. You could trade baby-sitting with a friend, or utilize the library story hour to do research, make lists, or outline plans.

On the other hand, Judy Dungan, a mother of three living in the Washington, D.C. area, manages a congressman's fund raising, bill paying, and bookkeeping from her basement office, which also houses the children's playroom.

"I worked there when my two- and three-year-olds napped. I appreciated being home with them, and now they are entertaining each other more so I can work while they play beside me," she says.

Some of the blessings of a home business include being there for first steps, impromptu trips to the park, and hearing the "hot off the press" news when your children get home from school.

■ But how do we handle business and still spend time with our families?

One seasoned home business mom advises, "Don't bite off more than you can chew!" That's especially true if you have toddlers or preschoolers. Remember: children don't stay little forever. As they grow, so will your time for the business.

Some moms find creative ways to involve their children in work. You can fill a desk drawer in your office with crayons, paper, scissors, and paste so the kids can work alongside you on their own projects.

"One of the benefits of my home business has been the tremendous bond with our son, David," said Cathy Adkinson. "From the time he was two, he went on deliveries with me and made his own dough creations while I worked in the kitchen. David has really grown up with the business. As a result, he has great language skills and is fun to be with."

Kyser Lough earns money by helping Mom stamp and stuff envelopes in the "Posy Collection" mail-order business. As a preschooler, he went along on business errands. "We talked, sang, and learned in the car. We took side trips, got a balloon, and went to the park," says Posy. "I loved being available for him, and I still had an enjoyable outlet that provided extra money."

■ **I know that working out of my home will save money on transportation, restaurant lunches, wardrobe, and child care. But what are the unique difficulties and challenges of having a home-based business?**

One of them is burnout. You'll wear many hats—designer, production worker, secretary, bookkeeper, file clerk, and even custodian. When you add taking care of children, it's a recipe for exhaustion.

"The number-one thing that can kill the business is burnout," says Amy Webster. "As home business people, we get weary. The business is three years down the road and doesn't seem to be any further along. We burn the midnight oil or get up at 5 A.M., working on a new idea."

It helps to remember to be obedient to the Lord's leading, and keep your relationship to Him *first*. Listen to Him and do what He tells you, for it's one step at a time in a home business. If you're doing what God asks you, He'll strengthen you to do it, without sacrificing your family in the process.

This material is adapted from writings by Cheri Fuller of Oklahoma City, Oklahoma.

3

Is This the Year to Get Organized?

Editor's note: Richard Foster has written such best-sellers as Celebration of Discipline *and* Freedom of Simplicity. *If you're thinking that you need to shape up, bear down, or get tough with yourself, take another look at what discipline really means.*

■ **You're known for your books about the disciplined life. Have you ever made a New Year's resolution?**

Richard Foster: No! And notice how the very question reflects a popular but distorted image of discipline. Discipline is not a specific act, like going on a diet or curbing your TV time. Discipline is a style of life.

I define it this way for mothers: the disciplined mom is the mom who does what needs to be done when it needs to be done. You see, the disciplined mom is the person who lives life appropriately.

The French writer Jean-Pierre Caussade said, "The soul, light as a feather, fluid as water, innocent as a child, responds to the initiatives of divine grace like a floating balloon." Now that describes a disciplined person.

There's a time for work and a time for play. The disciplined mom works when work is called for and plays when play is called for. If you work when it's appropriate to play, you've lost it. That's not discipline, that's rigidity.

■ **But most people would say the disciplined person is the one who works all the time. That happens to moms a lot.**

Richard Foster: And I say that shows a basic lack of discipline. The glutton has the same problem as the extreme ascetic or anorexic: neither one is doing what needs to be done when it needs to be done.

■ **Should mothers be asking themselves "What needs to be done?"**

Richard Foster: Absolutely. You must always ask that. How can you live "light as a feather . . . responding to the initiatives of divine grace"? In other words, how can you build into your life the habits that allow you to respond to God as you should?

To be disciplined, you need to be free from certain habit structures while taking on certain other habit structures. That's why Paul said in Philippians to give our attention, our focus, and our lives to "whatsoever things are true . . . honorable . . . just . . . pure . . . lovely . . . gracious." Those are the things that transform us.

■ **Do you think our generation is less or more disciplined than our grandparents? They worked awfully hard, but these days a lot of mothers are getting up at 5 A.M. to make school lunches and start the laundry. What's the trend?**

Richard Foster: I don't think the situation is significantly different, except for this: there are more opportunities to be a workaholic.

■ **What do you mean?**

Richard Foster: In the past, mothers were locked into certain foundations just to survive. Doing the laundry used to take a full day. You went down to the river and scrubbed for hours.

Today's convenience items allow you mobility, flexibility, and freedom. You and your husband don't have to work all the time, unless you and your family choose an economic level that requires two jobs. You face more choices.

We need to help parents be free from such burdens. This passion to get ahead drives some mothers and fathers mercilessly. Climb, push, and shove are not fruits of the Spirit! Overworking is not a sign of discipline. It's a sign of gluttony—a gluttony for money, for prestige, for accumulation, for looking good in the eyes of others.

Christians, you know, have an almost insatiable desire to please. It connects with Christian teaching about loving our neighbor and so on, but it can turn into a desperate need for approval.

Some mothers think rigidity is a sign of discipline, when many times it signifies a lack of discipline. Rigidity is the first sign that discipline has gone to seed. Christians are particularly tempted to this excess because of our love of legalism. We love to define the parameters of what makes a person right with God.

■ **What is the difference between being disciplined and being legalistic?**

Richard Foster: Legalism says, "This is the way it always must be done." Discipline says, "I'm going to learn to respond to the initiatives of divine grace like a floating balloon."

Legalism says, "I must read my Bible every morning." Now that's a good thing to do—but there may be times when it's not a disciplined thing to do. Perhaps on some mornings we should learn to love our neighbor.

Conversely, there may be times when we should come before the Scriptures for a whole day, learning to grow with God.

■ **What about the mother who says, "Richard, what do you mean 'initiatives of divine grace'? I don't know what you're talking about. I don't sense any divine orders to respond to."**

Richard Foster: Jesus said, "I am the Good Shepherd . . . My sheep know My voice." Spiritual discipline means learning to be responsive to Christ's teaching. You see, Jesus Christ really is alive; He rose from the dead, and He's here to teach us Himself if we'll learn to listen.

Sometimes I feel led to say no to conference speaking in order to say yes to my family. Out of about 300 speaking invitations a year, my family and I have felt, as we've listened to God and talked about it to each other, that I should accept approximately 8. That is an act of discipline. It means saying no in order to say yes.

■ **What do you think of Vince Lombardi's phrase "No pain, no gain"? Does discipline always hurt?**

Richard Foster: No. Many times discipline is joy, it's freedom. But when it comes in conflict with aspects of our lives that need to be redeemed, yes, there's pain.

As we give ourselves to certain disciplines that bring us directly in contact with our flesh, we find out the flesh needs to be controlled. St. Francis of Assisi called the human body "Brother Ass." His point was that we need to ride the donkey rather than letting the donkey ride us. Whenever the donkey rides us—yes, it hurts!

■ **Let's take an obvious example: fasting. How many do it joyously?**

Richard Foster: The central idea of fasting is to deny yourself an otherwise normal function for the sake of intense spiritual activity. If our concentration is on the denial, the physical process of going without food—"I'm so hungry!"—yes, fasting will be a burden.

But if we focus on the fact that God has called us to concentrate on Him and His way, then it's a joy. We enter the presence of God in a special dimension. We are feasting as we fast, feasting on God and His Word. The Word of God is life to us; it is substance to us. In fasting we are sustained by "every word that proceeds out of the mouth of God."

That doesn't mean there is no pain. The first times I tried to fast, prayer was not easier for me—it was harder. I was caught up with the physical part and wasn't able to focus.

In time I learned that if God is calling me to a fast, I'm to enter His presence in a special way. He will be my Teacher, my Comforter, my Rebuker—whatever I need. That's a signal for joy in my life: God wants to be very close to me.

■ What parts of your life are the toughest to discipline?

Richard Foster: One of them is learning to pray, especially learning to listen to God. Kierkegaard once said he first thought prayer was talking, but as he became more and more quiet, he realized prayer was listening.

That continues to be hard for me. I went on a thirty-six-hour retreat once for the purpose of praying. When I got there, I began reading the Book of 1 Samuel. Then I went on to 2 Samuel. I wrote some things in my journal. Then I went for a walk . . . I did everything but pray!

It wasn't till the next morning, in a worship service with other people at the retreat center, that God showed me I was afraid to pray. I was afraid to be exposed to God.

After that, I went jogging and used the time to be open to God, to listen to Him. When I came back, I sat down in a little garden area and had a couple of hours of the most beautiful worship. Things finally seemed to open up—but it had taken me a whole day.

Another area of struggle is to be responsive to the needs of my wife, Carolynn, and to our two sons. Rather than setting up rules that will forever settle this or that, I'm trying to listen to God about how to live faithfully as a husband and father.

When I was a pastor, it was easy to allow the ministry of caring for people to take up all my energies. I would come home so exhausted that I had nothing left for my wife. In time I realized that was sin, an affront to the covenant of marriage. I had to repent of religious work in order to be faithful and disciplined to my marriage vows.

■ How does God speak to you?

Richard Foster: Well, there are many ways, of course. Certainly coming before the Scripture is one. Many of the old writers talk about "praying the Scriptures," allowing the Bible's words to become a form of prayer. I've been experimenting with that.

Of course, the Psalms are very easy to pray, but many other passages can also sink down into our spirits and become our cry to God. In addition, I may ask God to teach me through the Christian community. If I'm facing some concern or decision, I might seek out trusted friends to whom the Word of God can come. Sometimes this occurs through simple listening or counsel; at other times they may employ one of the spiritual gifts, such as a specific word of knowledge or prophecy.

There are also times of simply being open to God myself, listening, receiving strong mental impressions or a sense that such-and-such is right. The heart sort of jumps as if to say yes, and then I will often test that impression with others.

I remember one of the first times I ever acted on an impression of the Holy Spirit. I had a notion I should call someone. I even jotted it on a little note pad. Finally I dialed the number and said, "Rod, I didn't call to ask you to do anything; I just wanted to say hi."

From the other end of the line came this deep sigh. "Oh, I'm so glad you called," he said. Then he shared a huge need he was trying to carry by himself.

Well, when that kind of thing happens, you know you aren't crazy after all.

Now when I got that impression, I could have said, "Oh, but I'm supposed to be studying my Bible now. I can't go call somebody." That would not have been discipline but rather rigidity.

One time at a conference, I was meditating between sessions, and it seemed as though God was giving me great ideas for a sermon. I was furiously writing them down; it was wonderful. Then right in the middle, the whole flow of ideas stopped—and into my mind came the name of a book on raising children that Carolynn wanted me to read.

I had sloughed it off: "No, I'm not interested." Now it seemed God was dealing with me. Are you going to read that book?

Only when I resolved to read it did the sermon ideas resume. When I got home, I casually said to Carolynn, "Where's that book you've been wanting me to read?"

She didn't say much, but a couple of hours later she came up and gave me a hug. You see, the disciplined act was to deal with the problem rather than keep worrying about sermon preparation.

■ **Did the book turn out to be worthwhile?**

Richard Foster: Yes, it was very helpful. And this meant humbling myself, admitting I didn't already know everything in that book.

■ **Are some people more naturally inclined to discipline than others? What about the folks who say, "Well, I'm just a free spirit, and that's part of my charm"?**

Richard Foster: Discipline does not come naturally to any of us since the Fall. Structured persons have real temptations toward rigidity; they have to work at being responsive. Free-flowing people have just as much difficulty the other way. Both struggle knowing what to do when.

■ **What's the opposite of discipline?**

Richard Foster: There are two opposites, if that's possible. One is rigidity. The other, of course, is anarchy, the total lack of structure. Both of these end up failing to do what needs to be done when it needs to be done.

Discipline, on the other hand, is being responsive to God in my life, which allows for structure when it's needed and the freedom to let go of structure when that's needed.

■ **What if there is too much that needs to be done? All moms feel that way sometimes.**

Richard Foster: One of the acts of discipline is saying no. That's a problem today because of the pervasive gluttony of activity in our society. Most of us could cut 20 percent of what we do without reducing our output one iota. No is not a bad word, especially for moms.

■ **In other words, you're saying it all doesn't need to be done?**

Richard Foster: That's right. Our calling is not to solve every problem in the world. It isn't to help every person in the world. It isn't even to pray for every person in the world. Remember this: not everything we tackle is something God wants accomplished.

This material is adapted from an interview by Dean Merrill.

9

Moms and
Tough Times

When Mom Is Really Sick

■ **For months, my best friend—a mother of three—endured test after test, trying to uncover the reason for her miserable health. Then her doctor breezed into her hospital room and matter-of-factly told her that she had lupus—an incurable disease that causes the body's immune system to attack its own tissue.**

I tried to help out as best I could, but her grandmother moved in and took over her role of homemaker and mom. The only responsibility my best friend could continue was reading a daily Bible story to her children. I feel awful, and I know she feels guilty that she can't be a mom to her children. What are some ways I can assist her in her hour of need?

A mother is not only the heart of the home but its hub. When she's ill, life around the house ceases to roll smoothly. But family and friends can help an incapacitated mother in numerous ways. Here are a few:

▶ **Pray for your friend and her family.** Pray for healing, yes, but also pray that God will be glorified in the situation. Our Great Physician knows her illness and the outcome of it. If you study the Old Testament accounts of how God worked in the lives of the ancient believers, you will see the mercy, faithfulness, and power that God revealed through mighty miracles.

► **Avoid platitudes.** "I understand just what you're going through" isn't encouraging when your sick friend knows you don't even suffer from monthly cramps.

"We'll be praying for you" is more reassuring. But it's even better to pray with her right at the time. Nothing will comfort your friend more than being able to hold your hand and pray together about her burden.

► **Express heartfelt concern.** What should you say? "I'm sorry you're going through this" is a genuine statement. "Can I do something?" is always welcome.

Don't say, "Call if you need something." (She won't.) Instead, call to ask how you can help.

■ Do you mean as in bringing meals?

Yes. Delivering a home-cooked dinner is one of the best things you can do. However, check to see if the sick mom or anyone in the family is on a special diet. Hearty casseroles and big salads are always a big hit.

Call and arrange to bring dinner over before you cook, however, since someone else may be preparing something hot for the family. When you do drop by with the food, be interested in the person's illness—or at least act as though you are! If your sick friend wants to talk about it, be a good listener. While a person is engulfed in a serious illness, her mind doesn't have room to squeeze in much else. She needs to express her fears, anxieties, and hope—just as Job did.

■ Another friend and I visited a sick mom, and all my friend could talk about was the great trip she and her family took to Disney World. I could tell it wasn't the right thing for a bedridden mom to hear about.

It wasn't. That's why you should be sensitive by avoiding dramatic monologues of all the exciting things you and your family are doing. Hearing about the latest vacation—from start to finish—can be discouraging to a mom who's sick in bed with her life on hold. Encourage your sick friend with these words: "Just rest and concentrate on getting well. The world will take care of itself while you recuperate."

When you phone or visit, keep it "short and sweet." Most sick people don't have the strength for long visits or phone conversations, but frequent brief communications, even notes, show you are still thinking of her. The isolation of an illness can be overwhelming, so do visit. Just remember to phone before you drop by.

■ I'm never sure if I should bring along a gift. Is that appropriate?

Do you know something your friend would especially like? Perhaps a certain perfume or a bouquet of flowers? What are her reading or music preferences? Gifts chosen with her in mind will make her smile.

The best gift of all might be providing tapes of your church services. Since your friend is unable to attend worship services, this thoughtful gift can keep her connected during her convalescence. Listening to the routine announcements, songs of praise, and the pastor's sermon will brighten any gloomy week.

■ Should I bring my children when I visit?

You better leave them behind. Perhaps you could trade babysitting with another friend and alternate your visits. Better yet, offer to watch your friend's children. As dear as children are, they are difficult for even a *healthy* mom to keep up with. Children continue to be their usual challenges when Mom is sick. Sometimes, their antics even escalate. When Mom is not feeling well, life often dwindles to the necessities. Your friend's children will enjoy being included in fun activities and projects.

Also offer to carpool her children. Remember that life continues for the sick mom's family. They still have to be driven to Little League games, Bible clubs, and after-school lessons. Groceries still need to be purchased and errands run. Your help will be a great encouragement to the whole family.

But don't forget that your sick friend may need rides to the doctor's office or to the hospital. With her husband trying to maintain his work schedule, being a chauffeur can be a tremendous help.

■ **A bunch of ladies at the church were talking about helping this one particular mom who had a dirty house. It didn't sound like a fun thing to do, but we offered to clean her home.**

The old bromide "Cleanliness is next to godliness" goes out the kitchen window when a mom becomes sick. Having lower standards probably depresses the family as well. Clean and vacuum for your friend, but don't comment on the mess—to her or anyone else. It's embarrassing when the friend who scrubs the refrigerator spreads a vicious rumor that she's growing her own penicillin to save money.

Other ideas are to help financially. With a long-term illness, bills pile up—even with good insurance. This is one way the church can help, but any kind of assistance will be appreciated. Even a bag of groceries shows you care.

Many friends give aid at the onset of a disease but forget as time goes on. The sick person is left alone to cope with prolonged disability. If you think you're tired of your friend's lengthy illness, imagine how she feels.

In closing, don't be overwhelmed by this "To Do" list. Choose one thing you can do without jeopardizing your own family. If each friend helps in some way, it won't be a burden on any one person.

So, when a sick mom calls and says, "I was just at the doctor's, and he says I have . . . " you can answer with, "Don't worry about a thing. I'll be right over. I know just what to do."

This material is adapted from writings by Cynthia Culp Allen of Corning, California.

2

I Can't Raise Kids Alone

. . . .

■ I'll never forget the day I sat in the counselor's reception room, waiting my turn to pour out my hurt and anger at having to cope with an impending divorce, all because my husband no longer wanted to be married. I struggled to hold myself together, but tears kept leaking out. The pain was so great I didn't think I could bear it.

All of a sudden the realization hit me with the shock of a physical blow. After the divorce I would be a single parent! I couldn't do it! My sons were only four and six years old. What did I know about raising sons alone? I had never been a little boy!

I panicked. How was I going to support all three of us on my meager salary? How was I going to teach them all they had to know? Was I wise enough to cope?

Countless questions like those blur in the heads of single parents everywhere. You're sure that you can't do it.

But you can.

Life as a single mom is sure to be one of laughter and tears, highs and lows, fun and fears. Sometimes all of these emotions will occur in just one day. You will feel you are on an emotional rollercoaster ride full of unexpected turns and twists. One day your son may win a swim meet, and the next he could be suspended from school for misbehavior. You'll feel as if you are a total failure!

■ **There have been tough times financially since I became a single mother last year. Making ends meet has taken an extraordinary effort and long hours of overtime. There have been tough times emotionally when we found ourselves at the family counselor's office, struggling to hold together as a family. There were nights when I paced the floor both angry and scared because my fifteen-year-old had broken his curfew. There were hours when I sat up late devising new ways to challenge the boys to do better in school or in real-life situations. So where is the hope?**

You have to take it in the little moments of joy that come your way: special holidays; close, cuddly times, just the boys and you; unexpected moments of honesty and shared feelings; flashes of maturity, hinting of what your children are becoming.

You will never survive some of your experiences with your sanity intact if you don't have the Lord's help. You will need a strong, unshakable faith in God and His miraculous power. Know that God loves you enough not only to send His Son to save you, but also to care about your daily walk, struggles, and triumphs. Whenever you cry out to God for help and wisdom, claim James 1:5 (RSV) as your personal promise: "If any of you lacks wisdom, let him ask of God."

The best you can do is teach, train, set a good example, provide role models, and then turn your children over to God. After all, they are His children too, and He cares about how they grow up. So you must learn to trust in His power, not only when yours begins to wane, but also when you are feeling strong.

You can make it! You can do it! And you can even enjoy it!

■ **I've found that there are many different responses to being a single parent. I never feel the same way all the time, often experiencing several conflicting emotions at the same time. Can you sort this out for me?**

There are four basic responses to single motherhood. See if you find yourself in one of them:

Type 1: "I Can't Do Anything!"

You feel this way whenever you have tried your best and everything seems to be going wrong. Like when you try to put together a bike for Christmas (why don't they come assembled?) and the pedal screw got stripped because you twisted it the wrong way. Or when the budget won't stretch far enough to cover things the boys really want. Sure, you'll feel inadequate, but these times will become fewer and further between as you gain confidence that you are doing the best you know how.

A mother experiencing this response may feel helpless, discouraged, and depressed; she may give up easily, appear dependent or weak; not enjoy family times; sleep a lot; be nonassertive; not have a strong supportive group of friends; blame others; or have very few house rules for the children.

The basic beliefs behind this feeling may be

▶ I am not a capable person.
▶ I have been abandoned, so I am worthless.
▶ Life is unfair, so why try?
▶ I cannot cope.
▶ I am a failure.
▶ I have no control over my life.

When the mother is feeling this way, her children tend to respond accordingly. They experience a loss of self-esteem and display their inadequacies; they have little self-control. They learn to be manipulative and play on the guilt of the mother. They become experts at taking advantage of the parent.

Type 2: "I'll Do It or Die!"

Most of the time during a single mom's early years, this will be her basic approach. She is convinced that she has to do it all. Who else is there to do it? So she gets up early to pack lunches, clean house, do chores, and iron clothes.

Many single moms do this early in the morning, get everything ready for breakfasts, leaving little love notes, then get into work early so they can work overtime for extra money and keep her evenings free to be with her children.

But that takes planning and energy—energy you will begin to run out of as you meet yourself coming and going. Sure, you'll be home in the evenings, but you will be too tired to be much company. You need to set realistic expectations for yourself and for the children so your lives can settle into a more livable routine.

Some women respond to the challenge of single parenting by showing their determination to conquer any obstacle. They are compelled to work, work, work, and feel guilty if they sit down to relax.

These moms tend to be assertive and perhaps a bit aggressive, particularly if their schedules are interrupted. They set absolute rules for their children, and when the children fail to follow the rules or live up to their pace, these moms may become critical and angry.

Women who behave as described usually believe the following:
- I must be a good parent.
- I can/must do everything by myself.
- I dare not fail.
- I must maintain control of everyone and everything.
- No one must suspect I sometimes get scared and feel like giving up.
- If even one thing goes wrong, it is a disaster.

Children typically respond to this do-it-or-die approach by letting their mothers do all the work. They learn that if they procrastinate long enough, do the job poorly or too slowly, Mom will step in and quickly handle the task herself. Also, the children sometimes feel pushed, rushed, resentful, rebellious, or insecure because "supermom" is a hard act to follow.

Type 3: "I'm Surviving!"

Single moms all fall into this approach from time to time. It's tough to keep everything going in the household, but then that's when the refrigerator quits, the plumbing clogs, or the car won't start. The worst months are September through December. Getting the boys back to school, handling birthdays, Thanksgiving, and Christmas will deplete the budget and your energies and patience. Every New Year's you'll resolve to take it easy next year. But the following fall things will be very nearly the same!

Single moms in the survival mode may feel overwhelmed sometimes and OK at other times. They may appear courageous or frazzled or both. But they have learned to acknowledge their inabilities to meet everyone's expectations all the time, so they try to meet the needs they can. They find that no is frequently their first answer, but too often they can be talked into a yes. They change the house rules too frequently, based on the situations, their feelings, and their energy levels. Sometimes they encourage and affirm the children, but sometimes they yell at them or criticize and blame them.

A survival-oriented parent is often operating on these beliefs:

▶ I think there's hope, if I can just hang in there.
▶ I take just one day at a time, because I can't face any more than that!
▶ Just when I think that things are on an even keel, I can expect them to fall apart.
▶ Things will settle down someday, I hope.
▶ Surely one day I will be repaid for surviving and have peace and quiet and the whole house to myself.

The children will probably respond by testing Mom's limits frequently to see what the rules are today, taking advantage of her rough days to get their own way, and being confused about what is acceptable and what isn't. On the upside, they will also learn flexibility!

Type 4: "I'm Doing OK!"

This last approach to being a single mom is the one that makes the most sense but is not always the easiest to adopt. You'll have to constantly check yourself to ensure that you are looking at parenting in the appropriate light.

First, remind yourself that children are a gift from God (Ps. 127:3) and that they are people, not your possessions. Make a list of ways you are attempting to train up your children in the ways they should go, per Proverbs 22:6. When you feel inadequate, check your list. If you are doing everything on the list and can't think of anything else to do, then you can be assured that you are doing your best.

Next, make a list of the ways God has promised to help children without fathers and women without husbands. You will find so many promises that you cannot list them all here.

The third thing you need to learn to do is compare your feelings and experiences with those of friends who are in a similar situation to yours. Their feedback will help you maintain a proper perspective of the daily ups and downs of parenting alone.

The single mom with a positive self-image and a high level of self-esteem will probably feel good about her parenting role and will accept the fact that there will be times when things are out of control. She has learned when to say no to the demands of others, to be fairly assertive, and to prioritize expectations and goals. She makes time for herself, in addition to family times, and accepts the limitations of her time, energy, and abilities. She is reasonably even-tempered (with some highs and lows), has fairly consistent family rules, and usually encourages and affirms her children.

The I'm-doing-OK mom believes:

► Nobody's perfect.
► I'm doing the best I know how.
► This too shall pass.
► In the final analysis, the children will make their own choices.
► I am an important person, as well as a parent.

Her children tend to respond by growing toward maturity (at their own rates, of course), accepting themselves, and testing the limits whenever possible. And she knows that some of them will grow up and succeed in life, while others may not.

Life is a series of peak-and-valley experiences. The good times don't last forever, but neither do the bad. As long as we remember that one setback doesn't mean we have lost everything, we can keep on keeping on. The struggles and the wear and tear are worth it when every so often, just when you need it most, your son or daughter gives you a quick hug and says, "You're the best mom in the whole world!"

This material is adapted from writings by Bobbie Reed, Ph.D., a single mom of two sons living in San Diego, California.

HELPFUL PROMISES FROM SCRIPTURE

Here are some Bible verses that are especially helpful during tough parenting times:

When You Are Unhappy and Upset
Psalm 51:12—God gives joy.
Isaiah 26:3—God will give you peace.

continued next page

John 15:9-11—Christ wants your joy to be full.

John 15:11—Christ's joy will remain in you.

Philippians 4:6-9—You can have peace.

When You Need Help

Deuteronomy 10:18—God promises to provide justice, food, and raiment to the fatherless.

Deuteronomy 14:29—God promises sufficient food for the fatherless.

Psalm 10:14—God promises to help the fatherless.

Psalm 40:17—God knows you and will help you.

Psalm 46:1—God is a very present help in trouble.

Psalm 68:5—God promises to be a father to the fatherless.

When You Feel Your Efforts Are in Vain

Psalm 30:5—Your weeping won't last forever.

Proverbs 22:6—If you train your children in the way they should go, even if you don't see signs now, they will not depart from it when they grow up.

When You Can't Take It Any More

Psalm 18:32—God girds you with strength.

Ephesians 3:16-20—God will strengthen your inner self.

Philippians 4:7—God will keep your heart and mind.

When You Don't Feel Smart Enough

Proverbs 2:6-7—God stores up wisdom for you.

Proverbs 3:5-6—God will direct your path.

When You Have Your Own Needs

Isaiah 54:5—God tells Israel that He is her husband (a promise I claimed when I felt I needed a man to turn to—a spouse to help me with the parenting task).

Matthew 21:22—God will answer your prayers.

Philippians 4:19—God will supply your needs.

When You Have Failed

Joshua 1:8-9—You can be successful if you make the right choices.

Psalm 37:4-5—If you trust Him, He will work things out.

Colossians 1:13-14; 2:13—God will forgive you.

Ephesians 1:6—You are accepted in Christ.

3

The Time I Was Attacked on the Beach

. . . .

■ **I'm a young mom in my mid-30s who worries constantly about my personal safety—and the safety of my two-year-old son, Josh. We live in an area where it's not really a good idea to go out at night. I've taken to deadbolting my front door whenever I'm home. My husband assures me that I'll be safe when he's at work, but I'm not so sure. Am I being paranoid?**

A lot depends on the neighborhood you're living in, and only you and your husband can be the best judge of how many safety precautions to take. There are two sides of the coin at work here: One side says that you can never take too many precautions when it comes to the safety of you and your loved ones. The other side says you can't go around living as if you expect to get mugged or assaulted in the next moment.

If you feel better having that deadbolt on during the day, by all means, deadbolt your front door. Perhaps if you want to go for a stroll with Josh you should ask a friend and her child to join you. Safety loves numbers. Unfortunately, too many streets in urban areas are unsafe at night. Be cautious.

■ **How should I react if I *do* get assaulted? Should I resist?**

No one size fits every situation. Here's how one woman handled an assault:

Deanna McClary was in her forties when she was strolling down the beach near her home in Pawleys Island. On a beautiful spring morning, she decided she wanted a workout. One of her favorite ways to exercise was to walk in water up to midthigh, pushing against the force of the sea. That got the leg muscles burning.

Deanna, an attractive woman who once won the Mother/Daughter USA beauty pageant with her daughter Tara, slipped on a blue one-piece bathing suit before leaving the house. The suit was made out of stretchy material that tied behind her back. For some reason, instead of tying it in a bow as she had done countless times, Deanna double-knotted it that morning. She threw on an old polyester shift for a beach covering and set out for the beach.

When she got to the water, she saw a few people near a hotel, but no one else on the beach. *Just the way I like it*, she thought. She took off her cover-up and rolled it up, carrying it in one hand. She walked a couple of miles down the beach, then moved into the shallow water and headed back up the beach as briskly as possible.

She pushed slowly against the water, feeling it push against her leg muscles. About a hundred yards up the beach, she saw a man walking toward her. He was huge, shirtless, and tanned. He had long pants rolled up to midcalf. Usually, Deanna enjoyed greeting strangers, but something about this man made her feel uneasy. As he drew nearer, she could see that his black hair was cut in a blunt, bowl-cut style. He was walking on the sand heading one way; Deanna was in the water heading the other. As they passed, she pretended to be studying the horizon and whistling lowly to cover the fact that she had not said anything.

■ **This sounds creepy! I've had weird experiences like that, and my first impulse was to run. Is that what Deanna did?**

Deanna felt a small voice telling her, *Run! Get out of the water!* But she ignored that impulse because she didn't want the man to think she was scared. She didn't want to offend him. Why should she be running away from him all of the sudden?

■ **I've asked myself the same questions when I've been followed by a strange male. What did she do next?**

Deanna decided to keep moving and just casually look back to
see if he was still heading down the beach. He wasn't. He was in
the water behind her. When he noticed Deanna looking, he sat
down, almost like a child playing in the water.

■ **How did that creepy guy get from the beach to the water
without Deanna seeing or hearing him?**

That can happen, even if you are the most careful of human
beings. Deanna stepped up her pace and whistled more to appear
unafraid. Just as she was about to sneak a peek to see if she had dis-
tanced herself from the sitting giant, he lunged for her and grabbed
her thighs from behind, leaving ten black-and-blue marks where
his fingers dug in.

Deanna froze in fear. Then he reached up with one hand,
grabbed the back of her suit, and pulled it to her ankles.

■ **Did he then try to rape her?**

Deanna figured that was next, but when the attacker yanked her
suit down like that, exposing her backside, that was the worst mistake he could have made. The material in Deanna's suit stretched
almost to the breaking point and strained at her neck. She reached
for her neck so the suit would not give away and then reached back
and pulled the suit back up, not screaming, not panicking. Then
she spoke to him in a deliberate, firm, yet controlled voice.

"Leave me alone! Do you understand? Leave me alone!"

He tried to pull the suit down again, but Deanna had a vise grip
on the material and wouldn't let him. He splashed around to the
front and grabbed at her suit, pulling as hard as he could. The dou-
bled knot wouldn't budge, but it strained against Deanna's neck.

■ **It sounds as if all he wanted to do was strip her just to get a
big charge.**

Deanna thought so, but she also thought this guy was insane. "Get away from me right now!" she yelled. "Leave me alone! Get away from me now!"

Deanna stared defiantly at him and held tightly to her suit. He gave up, probably because he found her uniquely stubborn and probably unsure what she might do next. So he charged out of the water and ran up the beach.

■ **So the incident was over. I thank God that nothing happened to Deanna.**

But listen to what happened next. Deanna chased after the guy! You read it correctly. She chased that man up the beach like a mad dog, screaming at him. "I'm going to get you for this! You're going to be sorry!"

■ **Isn't that what you're not supposed to do?**

Right. If you're ever attacked, you want to run the other way, of course. But this attack happened in broad daylight on a public beach. Deanna was not in a dark alley. She ran after him, but she shouldn't have.

Meanwhile, that man was big and slow, and Deanna had the advantage of anger and adrenaline. She gained on him as she zigged and zagged. He stared back at her with amazement as he started running faster.

"I'll get you!" she screamed.

Fortunately for Deanna, the man sprinted away.

"You are a very sick person!" she yelled at the running man. "Do you know that? You're sick! In God's eyes, you need help! Come back here and give me an apology now! I mean it. You owe me an apology for what you tried to do to me!"

He waved disgustedly at Deanna, then turned and ran into the trees and out of sight into a new housing development. Deanna ran down the beach to a hotel, screaming for help.

She ran into the hotel and pleaded with the front-desk people to call the police. When she told her story, the police officer announced that anyone with knowledge of such an incident or the attacker should meet him downstairs. Ten women showed up, all victims or friends of victims.

■ You mean all these people had been attacked?

A few had, but they hadn't reported it. Looking back at the incident, Deanna says it's very important for women to report attacks, especially sexual assaults. *Because this guy was still free to run around and attack unsuspecting people like herself! How was she supposed to know there was a nut running around?*

■ What about retaliation? That's why I wouldn't report a crime. I would be scared he'd come find me again.

You'd have every right to be scared if you found yourself in that situation. From a spiritual perspective, you have a mighty God who can and promises to protect you. Why does He allow acts of violence to happen?

That is an answer we will not discover until we meet Him, but until then, we have to count on His promises to provide protection and sustenance to our lives. Not reporting an assault because you "don't want to get involved," however, is a disservice to others because the police need our cooperation if they are going to catch the "bad guys."

■ What happened to Deanna? Did they ever catch this bad guy?

Deanna became a woman on a mission after the assault. She wanted to see that man brought to justice! She used her righteous anger to warn others, describe what the man looked like, and ask if anyone had seen him. Amazingly, a woman and her young daughter saw the man coming after them on the beach a few days later, and based on Deanna's description of him, fled for help.

Deanna's husband, Clebe, had an idea on how to catch him. He staked out the beach for a few days and nights, deciding that the man wasn't a resident. Since most assaults seemed to happen around midday, he was probably a worker from a new housing development who stalked the beaches during his break.

Construction workers often broke from 11 A.M. to 3 P.M. to beat the heat.

The police interviewed a bunch of workers and found one that matched Deanna's description. He denied everything and threatened to sue the McClarys for false arrest. The police asked Deanna to identify him in a lineup.

Deanna said she would try. To make sure he didn't take revenge on her, she took along five women friends. As soon as she saw the suspect, she *knew*. As soon as he saw her, he confessed. He had been denying everything all along, but when their eyes met, he broke down.

He had seen the truth.

This material is adapted from Commitment to Love *by Deanna McClary with Jerry B. Jenkins. Used by permission.*

4

When Your Worst Fear Comes True

∙ ∙

■ **We live in a sleepy town of 2,000 in northeastern Arizona, a place where my husband and I have always felt confident we could raise our five children in peace and safety. One afternoon my neighbor, Dianne, learned that her three-year-old daughter, Tiffany, had been touched in her "private area" by a twelve-year-old baby-sitter, Wesley. In horror, Dianne raced Tiffany down to the police station, where her little girl was subjected to vaginal exams by trained medical personnel, who confirmed the rape. What will happen next in this tragic situation?**

Normally, Tiffany will immediately see a counselor to begin the process of working through the trauma. As for Dianne, it will be very hard for her to get over what that boy had done to her innocent little girl. Resentment will dominate her, and she will blame Wesley—and rightly so—for the hurt he's caused their family.

Don't be surprised if it takes a while for your friend to feel God's grace amidst such devastating turmoil. It's times like these that the words of Romans 8:28—"And we know that in all things God works for the good of those who love Him"—often ring hollow. Her daughter's life has been victimized. At this point, she isn't ready to forgive Wesley. Sooner or later, however, Dianne will need to trust

God to use the worst in her life to glorify Himself and benefit others.

■ **What would cause a twelve-year-boy to molest and then rape a precious toddler?**

Pornography.

At a vulnerable age and a crucial time in Wesley's life, the youth was probably introduced to hard-core pornographic materials. It was only a matter of time before Wesley acted out what he had seen.

Wesley's story is sadly repeated in dozens of cities each year. Despite the proof that harmful pornography was the fuse, our nation's lawmakers don't have the backbone to eliminate child pornography and illegal hard-core porn from the open market, and our court system will not enforce what antiporn laws there are on the books.

■ **What steps can I take to prevent someone from molesting my precious child?**

To provide your children with some extra protection against victimization, here are some suggestions:

► Establish open communication with your children on every subject, even uncomfortable ones like sex and anatomy.

► Be a concerned friend to your children, listening to them and taking them seriously.

► Teach your children to say no. Sometimes "good kids" haven't been taught to set boundaries or follow their instincts. They want to be polite.

► Tell your children that if something feels wrong to them, it's OK to make a scene—hit, kick, bite, scream, or run. You want them to avoid danger by doing whatever is necessary.

► Give your children a lesson on right and wrong touching. Tell them no one has the right to touch them in a way that makes them feel uncomfortable, no matter who it is. Major video stores offer free community service videos that teach "appropriate touching."

► Proper words are, "No one is allowed to touch your private areas." Don't say, "Never let someone touch you" because this puts the responsibility on the child, where it doesn't belong.

▶ No matter who they are with, don't leave your children unattended for long; check in on them at various intervals. Molestations by friends or relatives are more common than by strangers. Abuse can occur in a matter of minutes, and usually a child won't cry out or even tell you afterward.

▶ Work on having a solid family and home. Give your children the affection, attention, and recognition they crave. A pedophile often targets needy kids in problem situations.

This material is adapted from writings by Cynthia Culp Allen of Corning, California.

CHILD MOLESTATION: WHAT TO LOOK FOR

In Dianne's case, a mother's worst fear became reality: child sexual abuse. The thought is so repulsive most parents won't even consider it.

But, according to some studies, anywhere from 25 percent to 66 percent of girls and 25 percent to 50 percent of boys will be sexually molested by age 18. As Dianne discovered, the tragedy of child sexual abuse can happen to any family.

There are, however, certain tipoffs in your child's behavior that would indicate a need to get further information, or check it out with a counselor:

▶ Sexually "acting out" with dolls or toys, drawing naked bodies, speaking or acting seductively, or making acts of sexual aggression

▶ Behavioral changes at home and school, such as withdrawal or rebelliousness, a feeling that "something is not quite right"

▶ Sleep disturbances and increased nightmares

▶ Bed-wetting

▶ Clinging—fear of being left alone

▶ Depression

▶ Lack of appetite

▶ Psychosomatic illnesses

CHILD MOLESTATION: WHAT TO DO

If you discover that your child has been victimized, here are some important actions to take:

1. Listen calmly without reaction. Reassure your child as he or she talks.

2. Write down exactly what your child says and include dates. Record any unusual behavior that might confirm the incident. Quote your child word-for-word.

3. Go to the authorities. School officials, police, or your family doctor are trained in this area.

4. Assure your child that neither the abuse nor its outcome is his or her fault.

5. Respond to your child's fears; don't disregard them.

6. Permit him or her to talk, but don't force it. Sometimes a child will refuse or deny earlier statements due to confused, painful feelings.

7. Realize that your child may not have negative feelings about the abuse, and may perceive it as affection.

8. Offer therapy, but don't insist on it until the child is ready and feels comfortable with the counselor. If possible, choose a Christian counselor who will honor your family's values.

5

The Death of a Child

. . . .

■ **Some dear friends from church recently lost an infant son to SIDS—sudden infant death syndrome. What can I say to my grieving friends?**

The loss of a child, whether by death or when an adoption goes haywire, is one of the most devastating tragedies a couple can endure. They need the comfort that a Christian family can provide.

The first thing to do is not avoid your friends. The most painful event in their lives has just taken place, and they need your concern and prayers.

■ **How then should I express my concern?**

"I'm sorry," "I care," or any words sensitive to their pain will be just right. Statements such as "It must have been God's will" (no matter how theologically sound) are not helpful.

But most of all, express concern by being a good listener. Grieving parents need to talk about their loss. Don't hesitate to ask gentle questions. They may want to get out the photo album and remember him or her. Be attentive in that situation. Some parents, however, feel they can't tell the story one more time. In that case, your presence is enough.

Don't be afraid to touch. A despondent person needs a physical expression of sympathy. Often, a hug says what you can't.

■ What are some things I can do to assist in practical ways?

Preparing meals, running errands, and baby-sitting other children—especially the latter—are appreciated when a person is involved in any crisis.

If you can help financially, offer to do so. All too often, medical insurance doesn't cover everything, and for those who were trying to adopt, that process requires great amounts of money—money that is seldom returned when the adoption falls through.

■ How long do parents usually grieve?

For those of us not closely involved in the crisis, our lives resume quickly. But the grieving parents continue to feel the loss for months and even years. For the year following the tragedy, mark your calendar with the child's birthday and the anniversary of the loss. On those days, send a thoughtful card or perhaps make a phone call. These acts will mean much to your friends, especially as it gives them a chance to talk about their child again.

This material is adapted from writings by Cynthia Culp Allen of Corning, California.

6

What Makes Alcoholics Stop

....

Two decades ago, Jim Broome's drinking problem had cost him one marriage and was about to cost him another. A newspaper distribution manager, he'd been drinking since high school and had "committed every sin there was."

He and his second wife, Mary Lou, enjoyed bar-hopping, but before long, she too was contemplating a divorce. Then came the emotional crash that saved Jim Broome's life—and their marriage.

Today, he is a real estate appraiser, a member of Ward Presbyterian Church in suburban Detroit—and sober for twenty-five years. He is the founder, along with Bill Keaton, of Alcoholics for Christ, a nondenominational support group with numerous chapters around the Detroit area and others springing up elsewhere. The following interview reveals his nononsense approach that breaks through the alcoholic's denial to introduce the power of Christ.

■ **Just what is an addiction?**

Broome: It's exactly what Romans 7:19-20 describes: "For what I do is not the good I want to do; no, the evil I do not want to do— this I keep on doing. Now if I do what I do not want to do, it is no longer I who do it, but it is the sin living in me that does it."

For years, those two verses summed up my total existence. I didn't want to be an irresponsible husband and father, but neither could I control what was happening.

Control is the key word. If we're struggling to control something, we've already lost the battle. We can't control the thing that already has us controlled.

■ That's hard to see, isn't it?

Broome: Definitely. But I've discovered that if you want a problem to grow, just try to keep it hidden. Psalm 32:3 states the point dramatically: "When I kept silent, my bones wasted away through my groaning all day long."

I remember trying to hide my addiction by saying I drank just to be sociable. But everything I did had to have alcohol in it someplace. I chose restaurants, friends, social gatherings, and even outings with my children based on whether alcohol would be available.

■ Is alcoholism a sin or a disease?

Broome: It's both. The Bible makes it clear that drunkenness is a sin. We choose to sin at the beginning. But as we become controlled by addiction, we find ourselves dealing with a disease.

The alcoholic is the greatest con man in the world. He'll do anything to keep his lifestyle, even pretending to get help. His attitude will be "I have a disease; feel sorry for me."

I say "he," but obviously there are plenty of women who are substance abusers as well. It's just easier for me to refer to alcoholics as men, since I'm talking from my own experience.

Psychologists have very little success with alcoholics because the problem is more than mental or emotional. It's a spiritual problem compounded by physical addiction. Many psychologists like to try to figure out why a person drinks, but what good does that do? It just gives the alcoholics more excuses, more ways to place the blame on someone else.

■ **What turned you around?**

Broome: It wasn't until I almost died from overdrinking that I whispered the most profound prayer anyone can utter—"God, help me." It was at that point I began to climb out of the pit I had dug for myself.

I had suffered terribly. The sad part is, it was all unnecessary. But I had chosen to fool myself into thinking I could handle my liquor until I was trapped by it.

After having almost died and finally crying to God for His help, I checked into a hospital treatment center and began one of the most terrifying battles of my life.

■ **What made it terrifying?**

Broome: The alcoholic has a pattern of handling all of life's challenges with booze. If he has an argument with his wife, he goes to the bar. If he makes a great sale, he gets drunk to celebrate. But when the booze is taken away, he has to learn a new way to behave—and that's frightening. How is he going to face his problems without his crutch?

The first argument Mary Lou and I had after I became sober was an eye-opener. I went storming out of the house, jumped into my car, and squealed the tires around the corner. All of a sudden, it hit me: where was I going to go?

I couldn't go to the bar now that I was finally sober. And I couldn't keep driving around all night. I had to go back home and talk it out like an adult. I never could have come to that point while I was still fighting for control of the booze.

■ **Then how does an alcoholic ever get started toward help in the first place?**

Broome: The first of the twelve steps of Alcoholics Anonymous (AA) has it exactly right: we must admit we are powerless. Once we've admitted that our actions and even our thoughts are obsessed by the substance, then we realize we must totally abstain from it and replace it with something greater than we are.

In AA, that replacement is called a "Higher Power" or "God as you understand Him." That concept wasn't big enough to fill the terrible void in my life. I had to find out who that Higher Power was. My search led me to Jesus Christ. But I never would have become free if I had continued to deny I had a problem.

Denial is the biggest hurdle both for alcoholics (or substance abusers) and their families. Until they get to the point where they can say, "Yes, there's a problem," they won't try to get help. They'll just keep trying to hide from their neighbors and from themselves. And the problem never goes away—it just keeps growing. Families, out of pride or a false sense of love, become enablers.

■ What is an enabler?

Broome: Someone who helps the person continue his lifestyle. An alcoholic can't function unless he has enablers. Alcoholics have a knack for picking out caring people to marry. The wife is usually one who's prone to guilt, too, thinking if she were a better cook, housekeeper, lover, whatever, he wouldn't drink.

One of the first things families need to know is "You didn't *cause* the alcoholism, you can't *control* it, and you can't *cure* it." That is profoundly simple—but also hard to sell sometimes. It can be difficult to undo years of enabling.

Families need to be reminded they aren't God; they aren't going to change anybody. And God is a gentleman; He won't force His way into someone's life. He waits to be invited. The trouble is, families keep looking for a miracle, not realizing they're the ones keeping the miracle from happening. People don't change because of words; they change because life becomes too unbearable the way it is.

This is called "hitting bottom." Knowledge about alcoholism isn't the important thing; the *application* of that knowledge is what counts. The family member who refuses to apply that knowledge is most often the alcoholic's wife. She cleans up after him. If he's hung over from the night before, she'll call the office for him, because she's terrified he'll lose his job.

■ What should she do instead?

Broome: Nothing. She needs to show the kind of love God shows us—tough love. He lets us fall on our faces when we are determined to go our destructive way. Families must do that too.

I don't mean to heap more guilt on spouses because they're already carrying enough. But I've had family members tell me repeatedly that it wasn't until they stopped covering up for the alcoholic that he hit bottom and sought help.

Most families don't want to face the truth. Often some of the young men in our group will tell their mothers, "I'm an alcoholic," and the immediate response will be "No, you're not! You just have a little problem with alcohol, that's all."

One of the classic stories of denial is about a man who had died, and his wife and daughter were receiving visitors at the funeral home. A neighbor came up and said, "I'm so sorry. What was the cause of death?"

"Well," answered the wife, "cirrhosis of the liver."

"How terrible!" the neighbor replied. "Why didn't he go to AA for help?"

"Oh," the wife said quickly, "he wasn't that bad."

Jesus once remarked, "There is nothing concealed that will not be disclosed, or hidden that will not be made known. . . . What you have whispered in the ear in the inner rooms will be proclaimed from the roofs" (Luke 12:2-3). As long as I tried to keep my problem a secret, it grew and came close to destroying me.

Too many times the alcoholic is stereotyped as some type of wino. If drinking is causing problems in your life—whether at work or within your family—now is a good time to face it. Remember, no one drinks because he has problems; he has problems because he drinks. It never gets better by itself.

■ But isn't it difficult to tell someone he needs help?

Broome: Of course it is. But until you say that, and put teeth into your words by refusing to help him keep the problem hidden, there's no hope. Look, we all need help in one area or another. The church isn't a place for good people; it's a place for sinners. It's a spiritual hospital. Too often people walk around looking pious and not applying the Word to their lives. We don't get saved until we say, "I'm a sinner." And we don't stop drinking until we say, "I need help."

I don't believe in the anonymity that some groups strictly enforce. For me, honesty was a great relief after all those years of being afraid of the label *alcoholic*. Right at the beginning, I told my extended family and coworkers I'd joined AA. People reacted just the opposite of what I expected—everyone was encouraging. Instead of ridicule, I found support and even admiration.

Within six months, people were coming to me for advice. I discovered everybody has problems. I had a problem too, and I was doing something about it. People saw strength in that, not the weakness I had expected. And what a wonderful feeling not to have to hide anymore.

■ **How does alcoholism affect the family?**

Broome: The family usually carries horrible guilt over the whole mess, because the alcoholic blames everyone else for this drinking—the stress of work, some big disappointment, his childhood, even the children's normal daily noise. Everything becomes a reason, an excuse to drink.

The unfortunate part is that the alcoholic becomes the leader of the family, because everything revolves around whether or not he's drinking. Think about that—the *sick* one becomes the leader! Everyone else is controlled by his actions; they in turn become sick.

Children of the alcoholic will follow the strongest person in the family, who is usually the problem drinker. Young women often marry alcoholics or a dominating men because they don't know what normal family life is. Most of them, after putting up with so much garbage during the important growing-up years, have such a low opinion of themselves that they think they don't deserve any better. The idea of a family being a team and working things out together is foreign to them.

■ **What is the most important thing an alcoholic can do?**

Broome: You're finally going to get a short, and easy, answer. The most important thing is to invite Jesus Christ into your life and ask Him to control it instead of the alcohol. Alcohol is a controller that will progressively destroy you and severely damage all those you love.

The first step begins with the prayer I whispered those years ago: "God, help me." It only gets brighter from there.

This material is adapted from an interview with Jim Broome by Sandra P. Aldrich.

7

Do Real Christians Get Depressed?

. . . .

■ **For several months, even though I've been careful to keep a cheerful public face, I've been battling deep depression. I'm not talking about just feeling a little "bummed," but the deep emotional hole where I feel abandoned even by God.**

In fact, I wonder if I've lost my faith. I can't talk to any of my church friends; they never appear to have any struggles in that area. What's happening to me?

First, let us reassure you that depression is far more common in Christian circles than you think. In fact, some of those "perfect" women may be looking at *you*, thinking you have it all together. Life does not have to be lived behind the grinning mask, though. There is hope. But first, let's take a look at the three main types of depression, which require at least three different kinds of treatment.

O. Quentin Hyder, M.D., has written about the depression he struggled through while in medical school. Things were tough: not enough money, his girlfriend had rejected him, he was living in a strange city, too busy to make new friends, badly out of physical shape, wasn't sure where his career was headed. And on top of that, he wasn't sure God still loved him or had an intelligent plan for his life. In short, he was *depressed.*

He says he should have gone for help but decided to grit it out instead. Somehow, he'd come out of this. Well, he did, but with more personal pain than was necessary. Looking back, he realizes that God had two reasons for letting him wallow through this. First, it greatly deepened his prayer life and Bible study. Although he'd become a Christian several years before, he had never drawn so close to Jesus as he did during this difficult time. His prayers about the depression where simple: "OK, Lord, what's this all about? Where are You trying to lead me? What am I learning here?"

Second, he found out firsthand what depression feels like. That was good information for becoming a psychiatrist later on. When patients came to him depressed or anxious—as often happened—he could look them in the eye and truthfully say, "I really know how you feel. I've been through this pain myself."

His depression was the kind doctors call *reactive*—caused by an outside loss, failure, or disappointment. His problem didn't stem from a chemical imbalance in his brain, the serious kind of depression that can lead to total withdrawal or even suicide. He was simply responding to external problems.

■ **OK, that sounds familiar. He was still functioning, as I am, but just not excited about anything. Wasn't he embarrassed about being a depressed *Christian?***

He says the fact that he was a Christian didn't shield him from a rough combination of events but that God used his suffering to teach patience, endurance, humility, and greater dependence on Him. Remember, God "causes his sun to rise on the evil and the good, and sends rain on the righteous and the unrighteous" (Matt. 5:45). Sometimes we later see the purpose of the "rain," but other times we don't.

Here's where our faith is tested. We're called to believe that *nothing* happens to God's people outside of His very best plans. He even can use our rebellious sin and its consequences for our own good or someone else's.

When a believer is depressed over a loss, failure, or disappointment, it's good to remember that the cause of this grief was not only foreseen by God from eternity past but is actually being used by God for the person's ultimate good. Therefore, reactive depression is a time to change the changeable, accept the unchangeable, and remember that God does not inflict pain beyond what we can bear. God's love will never run out—and to acknowledge this can in itself lighten our burden and elevate our low mood.

You don't need a professional counselor or psychiatrist during this temporary affliction. And caring, mature Christian friends can help put things back into the proper perspective.

■ **Well, that's encouraging. I was feeling like the only one on the planet—well, at least the only one in my church—who has ever gone through something like this. So, what is another kind of depression?**

The second type, *neurotic depression,* is a little more complicated from reactive depression. Here the blue feeling is a symptom of a whole lifestyle, a way of looking at the world's problems as overwhelming, unfair, insurmountable, too much to handle. This is usually learned early in life, and often from one's parents. Neurotic moms and dads produce neurotic children.

Neurotic Christians are especially hard to help, because they often mix self-pity and a tendency to blame others with some bad theology. They say their problems stem from being persecuted for their faith, or from the fact that God "hates" them.

■ **Can an unbelieving therapist be helpful here?**

Not usually. It takes understanding and insight to discern between what's neurotic and what's genuinely spiritual. Some non-Christian therapists will even *blame* the religious beliefs for aggravating the depression. Mercifully, however, others do see that personal faith can be a source of strength to the person, and they will encourage this even though they don't understand it or agree with it.

Far better, however, to be in the hands of a counselor with spiritual understanding and a personal relationship with God. This individual can help the person sort out the neurotic feelings and behavior, then guide her toward necessary changes. Reality therapy, which emphasizes dealing responsibly with situations and relationships, is especially useful.

The counselor can also employ the wonderful power of *forgiveness*. As the client verbalizes the early memories of hurt, parents and others can be forgiven. Finally the neurotic Christian has to forgive himself for shortcomings in many areas of life, repenting and confessing before a holy God the sins that have led, directly or indirectly, to the present pain. Then comes the joy of a reestablished relationship with Jesus, which can do much to lift the clouds.

■ **"Lift the clouds," huh? I like that. This information is encouraging. What's the third type of depression?**

This depression is the most serious—a hereditary medical condition of biochemical imbalance. While it's not "catching" like the flu, it's still a very real disease.

Actually, *endogenous depression*, as it's termed, is triggered in a variety of ways:

▶ Hypothyroidism—too little thyroid hormone production. We have known this to be a culprit for more than 100 years.

▶ Hypoglycemia—low blood sugar.

▶ Diabetes mellitus; also, its opposite, a tumor on the pancreas that leads to too much insulin production.

▶ Other endocrine imbalances from the pituitary or adrenal glands

▶ Viral and other infections

▶ Fatigue

▶ Toxicity

▶ Insomnia

▶ Premenstrual syndrome

▶ Electrolyte disturbances in the blood (sodium, potassium, and other elements getting out of balance), which can cause manic-depressive illness.

▶ Imbalance in the biogenic amines. This is the basic cause of most endogenous depression. Nerve cells in the brain don't actually touch each other. They link up via small sacs called *synapses*, where a fluid contains millions of molecules of hormones and electrolytes. These are called *neurotransmitters*, because they relay messages from one cell to the next.

The most common neurotransmitters are the biogenic amines. They come in several varieties, three of which have a lot to do with psychiatric disorders. Without enough norepinephrine (what most people call *adrenaline)* and without enough serotonin, the person gets depressed. Without enough dopamine, the person often turns schizophrenic.

■ **I'll never remember all those big medical terms, but I'm impressed that medical science knows so much about this type of depression. What do doctors do about it?**

Up until the 1960s, the only mood elevators we had were the amphetamines (Dexedrine, for example) and the illegal drugs of marijuana, cocaine, or heroin. All of these caused addiction.

"Down" drugs—sleeping pills, tranquilizers, alcohol—would temporarily relieve depression, but they also tended to destroy the patient over the long term. Today, medicine has found ways to lift mood with new antidepressants that increase the biogenic amines without causing addiction.

Doctors are aware that many people are skittish about such treatment. But the fact is that a medical illness needs a medical solution. Some well-meaning Christians have decided that all such medications are evil and have even talked believers into throwing out their pills. Even Christian doctors find this unfortunate, saying that in our generation especially, God has revealed to scientists great knowledge about healing drugs.

Most Christian physicians use them carefully, believing they are gifts from a loving God to help relieve suffering in the human race He loves so much. The patient must be restored to health by the best medical means available. The psychotically depressed person must get back in touch with reality. Once that has been accomplished, follow-up counseling can begin, preferably by a fellow Christian who has had professional training.

■ **Curing this last type sounds like a long road.**

It is. Most people do not "snap out" of depression. The road to recovery can take a long time. Both the counselor and the sufferer must be patient. New physical and mental activities can do a lot to take the person's mind off himself and lift his mood. The truth of the matter is that Christians are not above depression—any of the three kinds.

But we have spiritual and scriptural resources to lift us up. If we believe there's a God who cares, you have reason for hope. With Job, who suffered grievously from reactive depression, we can say, "Though he slay me, yet will I hope in him. . . . Indeed, this will turn out for my deliverance. . . . I know that my Redeemer lives" (Job 13:15-16; 19:25).

Since the Fall, God never intended that this life would be invariably happy. But He *did* promise to go with His people through all their sufferings and eventually to bring them into His heavenly presence.

This material is adapted from writings by Dr. O. Quentin Hyder, when he was a psychiatrist with the Christian Mental Health Center in New York City.

SCRIPTURES FOR THE DEPRESSED

Here are some of the Bible's best words for those suffering from depression:
► "The Lord has heard my weeping. The Lord has heard my cry for mercy; the Lord accepts my prayer" (Ps. 6:8-9).
► "When you pass through the waters, I will be with you; and when you pass through the rivers, they will not sweep over you. When you walk through the fire, you will not be burned; the flames will not set you ablaze. For I am the Lord, your God, the Holy One of Israel, your Savior; . . . Do not be afraid, for I am with you" (Isa. 43:2-3, 5).
► "Do not let your hearts be troubled. Trust in God; trust also in me [Jesus]. . . . I will ask the Father, and He will give you another Counselor to be with you forever—the Spirit of truth. . . . Peace I leave with you; my peace I give you. . . . I have told you this so that my joy may be in you and that your joy may be complete" (John 14:1, 16, 27; 15:11).
► "And we know that in all things God works for the good of those who love Him, who have been called according to His purpose. . . . May the God of hope fill you with all joy and peace as you trust in him, so that you may overflow with hope by the power of the Holy Spirit" (Rom. 8:28; 15:13).
► "God is faithful; he will not let you be tempted beyond what you can bear. But when you are tempted, he will also provide a way out so that you can stand up under it" (1 Cor. 10:13).

8

Innocent Victims

■ My sister often asks me how she can help her little son get through his parents' divorce. Two years ago, she and her husband ended their marriage. Their son, Jared, suffered through their bitter quarrels and inability to avert the disaster that lay ahead. Neither of them had the Lord to help them, and two non-Christian counselors recommended separation because of "irreconcilable differences." Jared became the innocent victim.

A year after the divorce, my sister's ex-husband moved to Oregon, 1,500 miles away. She told me that five-year-old Jared cried in her arms, "Why did Daddy leave?"

She took him to a counselor. During the counseling session, he turned all the sandbox figures face-down in the sand as the counselor urged him to talk about the divorce. He drew a picture of his family with his father and mother on one side, the pets in the center, and himself on the far edge. He was dressed in black and had a confused look on his face. When the counselor tried to talk to him, Jared hung his head over the end of the couch upside down and giggled. He was a hurt little boy who was crying for help.

Jared's healing will take a lot of time, but how good that he has you loving him and praying for him. In her book *Helping Children Cope with Separation and Loss* (The Harvard Common Press), Claudia Jewett Jarratt says healing from major loss takes a minimum of two years, but usually between three and five. How much time Jared's healing takes will largely depend on your sister's healing and her willingness to let go of anger. Here are some of the ways you and your sister can help this little guy:

Be on your knees. Prayer is the greatest tool we have in helping children heal. Pray in private for the pains you see your sister and her child go through. Pray out loud, letting them see you verbalize their needs to God. Pray consistently. Encourage your sister to teach Jared how to pray, or if she's not comfortable with her own prayers yet, ask if you may teach him. Explain to her that prayer allows children to express their sad feelings and give them to Someone who can make a difference.

Be willing to listen. Parents should lay aside their own hurts while listening to the pains of their children. Jared "talked" about his pain through the pictures he drew and the figures he placed in the sand. Your sister—and you, too—can listen and help him put into words the pain he expressed through his actions. "You're really sad, aren't you? When do you feel that way the most?"

A parent can pick up a young child and hold him or her. With older children, we can encourage conversation by listening, validating, affirming, and giving feedback. We should guard against interrupting, putting words in their mouth, or trying to talk them out of their pain.

The biggest roadblock to attentive listening is our fear of the child's pain. It can make us unable to hear what he is saying. Look him in the eyes. Touch him. Let him know that you really hear.

When Jared says he misses his father, that's your sister's clue that it's time to listen. She may feel threatened that he misses his dad. Through practice, however, she can quiet those inner voices and listen to the pain her son expresses. She can say, "I'm sure you miss him. I'm sorry."

Quiet tears fall from a little boy filled with the pain of a divorce that tore his parents apart. These tears say, "I am powerless. I miss my daddy. Why can't you make it OK?"

■ **Jared often throws temper tantrums, which keeps my sister intimidated and off-balance. I confess his tantrums intimidate and even irritate me too. Why does he give into those rages?**

Right now, he's acting out of control because he's feeling out of control. As your sister gains greater emotional strength, she will be able to help him set boundaries and find appropriate ways to express his feelings. Undoubtedly, because your sister is trying to compensate for his loss and because her own feelings are out of control, she is unable to provide the boundaries he needs.

As she deals with her pain, she will be able to help him with his. Many parents find that a counselor can assist them in shedding the anger and help the children to do the same. After all, anger can hold all of us in bondage and create bitterness.

Truth will also help. When author Martha Goudey-Price's son was eight years old, she took him to an eight-week divorce-recovery group sponsored by a local church. The children attended classes upstairs while the parents met downstairs. Each week leaders led the children through a series of games and exercises to help them understand their feelings about the divorce. One exercise involved making "rose-colored glasses."

The children made cardboard frames and pink-plastic lenses. Then they talked with the children about "seeing life through rose-colored glasses," especially their desire to see their parents back together again. In fact, their parents weren't going to reconcile, and the leaders helped the children come to terms with that.

The pain that Martha's son was feeling didn't go away, but he felt free from false expectations and crushed dreams. Upstairs, the parents learned how to reinforce the message that was being taught to their children. Each session opened the door to more truth, understanding, and healing.

BOOKS TO CHECK OUT

▶ *If My Parents Are Getting Divorced, Why Am I the One Who Hurts?* by Jeenie Gordon (Zondervan Publishing House)
▶ *Helping Children Survive Divorce* by Archibald Hart (Word)
▶ *Kids Caught in the Middle* by Gary Sprague (Thomas Nelson)

■ **Do you know what really hurts in all of this? To see how my sister's actions and hurtful words added more pain to Jared's life. One of these days, she's going to have to face that. What suggestions do you have for that time?**

This is where that all-important word—repentance—will have to come into play. When Martha's son was eleven, she realized she had never asked his forgiveness for the stupid, hurtful things she had done. One day they sat down, and she shared those areas where she needed to ask his forgiveness. She had already asked his forgiveness for the divorce. But there were also times that she had yelled at him or lost control, so she asked for his forgiveness for those things. A huge weight lifted from her shoulders when she asked, "Will you forgive me?" She did not say, "If I hurt you, I'm sorry" because she knew she had hurt him.

That took courage, but her son respected her for doing it. After she had asked forgiveness for the big stuff and acknowledged, "Yes, I did that to you," it became easier to ask forgiveness for the day-to-day things, such as misplaced anger, an insensitive remark, or impatience with his behavior.

As a result, it has become easier for her son to ask for forgiveness for his own shortcomings. He is growing into an adult who is able to acknowledge his own unwholeness and seek healing and forgiveness in his life in spite of what he has been through. Martha and her son have survived and grown through their ordeal, and, we trust, your sister and her son will too.

This material is adapted from writings by Martha Goudey-Price, who lives in Washington with her now teenaged son, Jared.

9

Dreaming: The Business of Hope

. . . .

■ **My life is not turning out the way I planned. My husband is not abusive and our children are healthy, but all of my youthful goals have been set aside.**

Some days I feel as though I'm just going through the motions. I'm not depressed; it's just that I've been hit with reality and don't dare hope for anything better. I see all these smiling people around me and wonder what dreams they're holding. Then I wonder what I did to lose mine.

We want to encourage you that it is possible to regain your dreams. But first we have to admit that losing a dream is part of the human condition for many of us.

For instance, Susan's world crashed the day her husband, Bryan, left her and their preschool children. She found herself in culture shock as a woman alone in a two-parent world. She started working full time and juggling carpool, day care, and a learning curve at her job. Her new life left her with little energy to spend on herself.

"My dreaming days stopped the day Bryan walked out the door," she says. "I'm too busy trying to survive to envision better things."

Caroline loved being at home with her children, but then her husband was "downsized," and she had to take a position at the local department store. Margie was looking forward to traveling with her husband, Clarence, throughout their "golden years." But when their thirty-four-year-old daughter and son-in-law were killed in a car accident, Margie and Clarence were thrust back into a parenting role when their four grandchildren came to live with them.

■ **OK, so my life isn't that tragic. But comparing myself to others who have bigger problems doesn't make my pain go away.**

Of course not. Our purpose in presenting those examples wasn't to disregard your disappointment but merely to remind all of us that pain, truly, is often part of the human condition. But we also want to encourage you that nightmares can be turned back into dreams.

In fact, dreaming is one of the most powerful abilities God has conferred on all of us. We're not talking about dreams in the night or supernatural visions. We mean a God-given idea, plan, goal, or vision about a better future that He places in our minds.

It's about seeing with our mind's eye the possibilities that something good can happen in the future, even when the world is dominated by malignant misery. It's about believing that God is at work enlightening the hearts of men and women so caught in darkness that they seem beyond hope of redemption. It's about believing great things will continue to happen, even in the midst of calamity, because God is great and good.

Dreaming is the business of hope.

Dreaming is about seeing reality through God's eyes, unlimited by how someone else defines what is and isn't possible. It is about letting our imaginations run wild, beyond our own finite perceptions and limited abilities, and seeing the immeasurable possibilities defined by God's power.

Dreaming looks into the future and sees the world as God meant it to be. We long for an ideal world because that is what we were created to live in. Dreaming puts color, texture, and details on the picture in our minds of the hope we have in Christ. He will personally recapture and redeem His fallen creation, and "He will wipe every tear from their eyes. There will be no more death or mourning or crying or pain, for the old order of things has passed away" (Rev. 21:4).

■ **OK, OK. But why should *I* dream in the midst of all my day-to-day problems?**

Because dreams are absolutely essential for us personally, for our families, for society, as well as for the kingdom of God. And it is serious business for people who want God's best for their lives. Every great step the human race has taken began with a dream.

William Wilberforce dreamed of a day when every person in the British Empire would be free before he made a single impassioned plea in Parliament to abolish slavery.

The Apostle Paul dreamed of evangelizing Europe before he set one foot in Greece.

As a young girl, Jane Addams saw poor children and dreamed of helping them. She founded Hull House in Chicago, a home for the homeless. She continued her work on behalf of people everywhere and in 1931 won the Nobel Peace Prize.

These once-impossible endeavors sprouted from the seeds of dreams, and in the process, the dreamers learned that when we engage in what God has called us to do, every part of our spiritual lives comes alive. There's a reason to grow. We have a compelling reason to pray, to stay in close contact with our Leader and Guide when we walk unfamiliar, threatening paths.

There's a strong drive for fellowship, allies, and friends close at hand because what God calls us to, we can't do alone. There's an undeniable need for worship, a clear vision of who God is and His commitment to meet our every need as we walk with Him into the future. In short, dreaming draws us closer to our Creator as we cooperate with Him in the pursuit.

■ **Well, maybe I can agree that dreaming is a splendid idea for the sake of others as well as the individual. But is dreaming really something anyone can do?**

Grand dreams about new businesses, inventions, discoveries, missions, and ministries are waiting to be conceived by ordinary people who have an extraordinary God, a God who equips us to dream those dreams. Because God is infinite, all of the good ideas cannot possibly be exhausted. In fact, God has grand designs for you to dream, no matter your giftedness (or seeming lack of it), your marital status, or your history.

■ **Sadly, I don't feel the freedom to dream. I'm not capable of accomplishing anything.**

Some of us are living so fast and furiously today that we miss God's messages about tomorrow. Some believe that great things are done only by great men or women, and they don't feel a part of that elite group. For others, dreaming stopped in the second grade when they were reprimanded for gazing out the window and thinking wonderful thoughts.

Anyone can dream, and any dream can be a dream from God. When we talk about God's work, we tend to think of Bible heroes or other historic figures who did "big" things. In reality, our dreams, and what we do with them, affect all parts of our lives. A dream doesn't have to be about an invention, a miracle, a cure for cancer, an end to war. Sometimes the "smallest" of dreams are the most profound. Children, spouses, families, friends, financial security, one's relationship with God—all these can be the subjects for our dreams.

■ **You're getting my hopes up. If—and notice the if—if I decide to risk dreaming again, how do I discover what dreams are sent specifically from God? How do I know what He is calling me to do? In other words, how do I pinpoint my dreams?**

God has given us an internal compass, and that compass is passion. Passion is given to guide us to God's will for our lives. Passion is the God-given ability to feel so deeply about something that it causes us to move toward the object of desire. This passion stems from an urge given by God: a burden, an emotional response to a need or opportunity He wants us to move toward. It's not a feeling that we experience and then lose easily. It's persistent and powerful. We can't ignore it.

The question is, how do we get in touch with this passion? First, we need to pay attention. God is at work both within our hearts and behind the scenes, orchestrating events and directing people providentially to bring us to the place He wants us to be. He is weaving a beautiful tapestry of events to lead us along supernatural-ly, and He never drops a stitch.

There is no such thing as a coincidence. What is God doing in your life right now? Whether you recognize it or not, He is preparing you for something down the road. Bear in mind that:

1. Passions come naturally. God speaks to most of us through the everyday events of our lives. If we're really listen-ing, God will have only to whisper, and we'll get the point. If we're waiting for burning bushes and dramatic signs to reveal God's will to us, we'll likely miss His voice as we encounter the needs and opportunities that exist in the world around us.

2. Passions come emo-tionally. It's not something we work up, but something God plants in a receptive heart. Significantly, the size of our tears will determine the size of

> **TOOLS FOR GETTING STARTED**
>
> To help determine your passions, ask yourself these questions.
> ► What do I weep about? When I lie awake at night, what do I think about when I'm staring at the ceiling? What do I pound the table about?
> ► What kind of issues, needs, oppor-tunities, activities, and ideas really motivate me and seem to give me energy?
> ► If I could meet any need in the world, have every resource I need, and knew I could not fail, what would I attempt to do? What need would I attempt to meet? What opportunity would I want to seize? What idea would I want to see come to fruition?
> ► What things deeply concern me? What are the greatest opportunities in each of the following areas: my family life? my workplace? my church? my country? my community?

our work. What are we praying for? What is our passion? What do we cry over? What do we desire more than anything else?

3. Passions come fearfully. Often people discern God's will by the "peace" they feel surrounding the decision. The fact is that peace does not always accompany God's will. When our security is threatened, when what we are asked to do by God is something that is bigger than anything else that we've ever imagined, fear will often result. This is not sin, or the sign of a sinful dream, but our human response to risk.

■ **I have to take a deep breath here because I feel as though you're inviting me to play in spiritual "traffic." Is there something I can do to determine my God-given passion?**

Actually, there are several actions you can take.

▶ **Be faithful right where you are.** Where you are is God's purpose for you today until He tells you to move. When you are faithful in small things, God can make you faithful in larger things as well. If you feel anxious, remember that in His timing God will bring you the information you need about where He wants you to go.

▶ **Focus on needs and opportunities.** When World Vision puts the picture of a starving child on the TV screen, look at it. If you hole up in a cocoon, you put yourself in a position where it is hard to hear God's voice. You need to allow yourself to feel others' pain. That pain, though uncomfortable, may lead you to the door of your dream by showing you where there is a hunger you can meet.

▶ **Be available.** It doesn't take a person with awesome skills or even spiritual maturity to be used by God. What it takes is a person who is willing to be used, who says, "Lord, I am available to You. Use me as You want."

The late Dick Halverson, when he was chaplain of the U.S. Senate, said it well: "It doesn't take a big person to be used by God . . . but it does take all there is of him! You don't need a five-foot water pipe to irrigate a garden. You can do it with a quarter-inch hose, assuming an adequate source."

Depend on that source in your life. Dreams are a gift from the God who loves you. Explore your passions and begin to wonder, *What amazing thing is waiting to be birthed in me?*

This material was adapted from the book Daring to Dream *by Bill and Kathy Peel, who live in Nashville, Tennessee.*

10

Hope Beyond Suffering

· ·

■ **I'll spare you the details, but because of a series of life's blows, I'm having trouble finding a reason to go on. So how do I keep putting one foot in front of the other, day after day, when I'm feeling so much pain?**

Life hurts right now, and your dreams have faded. And while words can't erase your pain, perhaps the following thoughts from pastor and author Charles Swindoll will offer some hope:

We don't look alike. We don't act alike. We don't dress alike. We have different tastes in the food we eat, the books we read, the cars we drive, and the music we enjoy. You like opera; I like country. We have dissimilar backgrounds, goals, and motivations. We work at different jobs, and we enjoy different hobbies. You like rock climbing; I like Harleys. Our weights and heights vary. So does the color of our skin.

But there is one thing we all have in common: we all know what it means to hurt.

Suffering is a universal language. Tears are the same for married or unmarried or divorced; for Jews or Muslims or Christians; for white or black or brown; for children or adults or the elderly. Each one of us knows the sting of pain and heartache, disease and disaster, trials and sufferings.

Joseph Parker, a great preacher of yesteryear, once said to a group of aspiring young ministers, "Preach to the suffering, and you will never lack a congregation. There is a broken heart in every pew."

Truly, suffering is the common thread in all our garments.

■ **Pardon me, but hearing "everybody hurts" doesn't help me get through all the chaos in my life right now. Got any other ideas?**

In fact, we do, says Chuck Swindoll, whose writings make up the basis of much of this chapter. When the Apostle Peter wrote his first epistle to fellow believers scattered throughout much of Asia Minor, he focused on the one subject that drew all of them together: suffering. These people were being singed by the same flames of persecution that would take the apostle's life in just a few years. Their circumstances were bleak. Yet Peter didn't try to pump them up with positive thinking. Instead, he gently reached his hand to their chins and lifted their faces skyward—beyond their circumstances to their celestial calling (1 Peter 1:1-2).

The men and women Peter wrote to knew what it was like to be away from home, not by choice but by force. Persecuted for their faith, they had been pushed out into a world that was not only unfamiliar but hostile. Peter wanted to encourage his fellow believers to put pain in perspective and find hope beyond their suffering.

The good news Peter gives us is that we are "chosen by God." We aren't just thrown on this earth like dice tossed across a table. We are sovereignly and lovingly placed here for a purpose. God has given us a purpose for our existence, a reason to go on, even though that existence includes tough times.

■ **I'm still listening. So *how* am I supposed to rejoice through hard times?**

Peter's first letter presents six reasons why we as believers can rejoice through hard times and experience hope beyond suffering.

1. We have a living hope. We don't have to concern ourselves over what happens on this temporary planet when we know that it is all leading us to our eternal destination. Peter calls that our "living hope," and he reminds us that it is based on the resurrection of

Jesus Christ (1 Peter 1:3). If God brought His Son through the most painful trials and back from the pit of death itself, certainly He can bring us through whatever we face, no matter how deep that pit might seem at the time.

2. We have a permanent inheritance. We also can rejoice through suffering because we have a permanent inheritance—a secure home in heaven (1 Peter 1:3-4). Our place there is reserved under the safekeeping, constant, omnipotent surveillance of Almighty God. Nothing can destroy it, defile it, diminish it, or displace it. The Living God will ultimately welcome you home to your reserved inheritance. Your name is on the door. That's a reason to rejoice!

3. We have a divine protection. Under heaven's lock and key, we are protected by the most efficient security system available—the power of God (1 Peter 1:5). There is no way we will be lost in the process of suffering. No disorder, no disease, not even death itself can weaken or threaten God's ultimate protection over our lives. No matter what the calamity, no matter what the disappointment or depth of pain, no matter what kind of destruction occurs in our bodies at the time of death, our souls are divinely protected.

Two words will help you cope when you run low on hope: *accept* and *trust*.

Accept the mystery of hardship, suffering, misfortune, or mistreatment. Then deliberately trust God to protect you by His power from this moment to the dawning of eternity.

■ **So you're saying that even though we can't choose whether we will go through difficult times, we can still choose how we will go through them? Hmmm. Is that right?**

Correct, which leads us to Chuck Swindoll's last three points:

4. We have a developing faith. Peter's epistle (1 Peter 1:6-7) reveals three significant things about trials:

- ► First, trials are often necessary, proving the genuineness of our faith and at the same time teaching us humility. Trials reveal our own helplessness. They put us on our faces before God. They make us realistic. Or, as someone has said, "Pain plants the flag of reality in the fortress of a rebel heart."
- ► Second, trials are distressing, teaching us compassion so that

we never make light of another's test or cruelly force others to smile while enduring hardship. Feel what that person is feeling. Walk quietly and compassionately in his or her shoes.

▶ Third, trials come in various forms. The word "various" comes from an interesting Greek word, *poikolos*, which means "variegated" or "many colored." We also get the term "polka dot" from it. Trials come in a variety of forms and colors. They are different, just as we are different. Something that would hardly affect you might knock the slats out from under me—and vice versa. But God offers special grace to match every shade of sorrow.

This variety of trials is like different temperature settings on God's furnace. The settings are adjusted to burn off our dross, to temper us, or soften us according to what meets our highest need. It is in God's refining fire that the authenticity of our faith is revealed. And the purpose of these fiery ordeals is that we may come forth as purified gold, a shining likeness of the Lord Jesus Christ Himself.

5. We have an unseen Savior. You don't have to see someone to love that person. The blind mother who has never seen her children still loves them. You don't have to see someone to believe in him or her. Believers today have never seen a physical manifestation of the Savior. We have not visibly seen Him walking among us, but we love Him nevertheless. In times of trial we sense He is there, and that causes us to "greatly rejoice" with inexpressible joy.

6. We have a guaranteed deliverance. How can we rejoice through our pain? How can we have hope beyond our suffering? Because we have a living hope, we have a permanent inheritance, we have divine protection, we have a developing faith, we have an unseen Savior, and we have a guaranteed deliverance (1 Peter 1:9).

But when it comes to spiritual delivery, we never have to worry. God guarantees deliverance of our souls, which includes not only a deliverance from our present sin but the glorification of our physical bodies as well. Rejoice! You're going to get there—guaranteed.

■ **So you're saying that when we are suffering, only Christ's perspective can replace our resentment with rejoicing. And**

our whole perspective changes when we catch a glimpse of the purpose of Christ in it all. Take that away, and it's nothing more than a bitter, terrible experience. Right?

Exactly. Nancy and Ed Huizinga in Grand Rapids, Michigan know all about this. In December 1995, while they were at church rehearsing for the annual Christmas Festival of Lights program, their home burned to the ground.

But that wasn't their only tragedy that year. Just three months earlier, Nancy's longtime friend, a widow with two children, had died of cancer. Nancy and Ed had taken her two children, Jeff and Katie, into their home as part of their family, something they had promised the widowed mother they would do. So when Nancy and Ed's house was destroyed, it wasn't just their home that was lost; it was the home of two teenagers who had already lost their mother and father.

As circumstances unfolded, irony went to work. The tragedy that forced the Huizingas from their home allowed Jeff and Katie to move back to theirs. Since their home had not yet been sold following their mother's death, they and the Huizinga family moved in there the night after the fire.

On the following Saturday, neighbors organized a party to sift through the ashes. Somehow a piece of paper had survived. On it were these words: "Contentment: Realizing that God has already provided everything we need for our present happiness."

To Nancy and Ed, this was like hearing God speak from a burning bush. It was the assurance they needed that He was there, and He was not silent.

Nancy's biggest frustration now was dealing with insurance companies and assessing their material losses. Many possessions, of course, were irreplaceable, such as photographs and things handed down from parents and grandparents. But her highest priority was Jeff and Katie, along with her own two children, Joel and Holly. The loss was hardest on them, she says.

"They didn't have the history of God's faithfulness that Ed and I had. We've had years to make deposits in our 'faith account,' but they hadn't. We've learned that if you fail to stock up on faith when you don't need it, you won't have any when you do. This has been our opportunity to use what we've been learning."

While the world might view this as a senseless tragedy, deserving of resentment, Nancy and Ed saw God reveal Himself to them and refine them through this fire as He poured out a full measure of grace and peace.

Suffering comes in many forms and degrees, but His grace is always there to carry us beyond it.

Charles R. Swindoll has pastored for thirty years, and in 1993 was named president of Dallas Theological Seminary. This material is adapted from his book Hope Again *(1996, Word Publishers, Nashville, Tennessee. All rights reserved.)*

Epilogue

We (Sandra Aldrich and Mike Yorkey) know this book has been a long read, but thanks for joining us. In closing, we'd like to share one last story that is one of our favorites. In a sense, author Patsy Lovell captures what parenting is all about. We hope you agree.

Hold Fast!

by Patsy G. Lovell

When our second daughter, Kathleen, was thirteen, she was as lively as any young teenager could be. One night, she excitedly asked permission to buy a leather miniskirt, one like all the other girls in her class were wearing.

As she described the benefits, I could tell she was expecting a negative response. Nonetheless, she acted surprised when I said no.

Kathleen then launched into great detail about how she would be the only one in the class without a leather miniskirt. I reminded her that my answer was no and explained my reasons.

"Well, I think you're wrong!" she retorted.

"Wrong or right, I've made the decision. The answer is no."

Kathleen stomped off, but quickly turned on her heels. "I just want to explain why this is so important to me."

I nodded.

"If I don't have this miniskirt, I'll be left out, and all my friends won't like me."

"The answer is no," I quietly repeated.

She puffed up like a balloon and played her final card. "I thought you loved me," she wailed.

"I do. But the answer is still no."

With that, she "whumped"—a noise made only by an angry junior high kid trying to get her way. She ran upstairs and slammed her bedroom door.

Even though I had won the battle, I felt I was losing the war. I went to the living room and sat down. My husband was working late; I was the only parent "on duty." Then one of those unexplainable things happened: An inner voice said to me, *Hold fast!*

It dawned on me that Kathleen and I were not locked in a battle over a miniskirt but rather a battle of *wills.* A mother versus her thirteen-year-old daughter. *Hold fast* meant I needed to prevail even though I couldn't stop my hands from shaking or my stomach from churning.

The whumping noise from Kathleen's bedroom started once more, and sure enough, she appeared on the stairwell. This time, she was breathing fire.

"I thought you taught us that we have rights!" she screamed.

"You do have rights. The answer is still no."

She wound up again, but I cut her off. "Kathleen, I have made my decision. I will not change my mind, and if you say another word about this, you will be severely punished. Now go to bed!"

She still had a few words left, but she held them in check. She loped off to bed, still seething.

I sat on the couch, shaking and upset. None of the children had ever pushed me so far. I leafed through a book, too wound up to go to bed. Just when I thought our skirmishes were over, the sound of whumping came again. Kathleen came down the stairs.

"Well," she announced, "I'm just going to tell you one more time. . . ."

I met her at the bottom step, planted my hands on my hips and looked her in the eyes. "Do not answer," I said. "Do not say yes or no. Do not say anything. Do not say 'Yes, ma'am' or 'No, ma'am.' Turn around and go to bed. And do not make a single sound!"

She slowly turned and trudged upstairs without a word. I dropped onto the couch, thoroughly exhausted.

For several minutes I stared into space and wondered what my blood pressure count was. Then I heard her door open. Kathleen, her nose and eyes red from crying, walked down the stairs in pajamas. Curlers were in her hair. She held out her hands to me.

"Oh, Mom, I'm sorry."

We hugged as she said through her tears, "I was so scared!"

"Scared of what?"

"I was scared that you were going to let me win!" she sniffed.

You were scared that I was going to let you win? I was perplexed for a moment. Then I realized that my daughter had wanted me to win!

I had held fast, and she was convinced I had done what a mother needed to do. Her simple words gave me the reassurance I needed.

Children love their parents, but they cannot handle being equal with them. Deep down, they do not see themselves as grown up. In fact, they will, if they can get away with it, bring a parent down to their level, so that all the family seems like a group of kids.

Deep down, teens know they need guidance and leadership. Parents, it's up to us to give it to them.

Remember: *hold fast!*

Patsy Lovell is a middle school teacher in Hazel Green, Alabama.